THE NINETEENTH-CENTURY AMERICAN SHORT STORY

THE NINETEENTH-CENTURY AMERICAN SHORT STORY

edited by
A. Robert Lee

VISION
and
BARNES & NOBLE

Vision Press Limited
Fulham Wharf
Townmead Road
London SW6 2SB

and

Barnes & Noble Books
81 Adams Drive
Totowa, NJ 07512

ISBN (UK) 0 85478 096 3
ISBN (US) 0 389 20593 1

Printed and bound in Great Britain by
Unwin Brothers Ltd.,
Old Woking, Surrey.
Phototypeset by Galleon Photosetting,
Ipswich, Suffolk.
MCMLXXXV

Contents

		page
	Introduction by *A. Robert Lee*	7
1	Poe's Tales: The Art of the Impossible by *Michael Wood*	13
2	Washington Irving and the Land of Was by *Howell Daniels*	40
3	Authorship and Authoritarianism in Hawthorne's Tales by *David Timms*	57
4	Voices Off and On: Melville's Piazza and Other Stories by *A. Robert Lee*	76
5	Reporting Reality: Mark Twain's Short Stories by *Andrew Hook*	103
6	Stephen Crane: Interpreting the Interpreter by *Harold Beaver*	120
7	'Our Bedfellow Death': The Short Stories of Ambrose Bierce by *Herbie Butterfield*	134
8	Kate Chopin: Short Fiction and the Arts of Subversion by *Judie Newman*	150
9	'The Infected Air' and 'The Guilt of Interference': Henry James's Short Stories by *Eric Mottram*	164
	Notes on Contributors	191
	Index	193

Introduction

by A. ROBERT LEE

Of all the literary *kinds* of writing to emerge from nineteenth-century America—Emerson's esay-sermons, Whitman's *Leaves of Grass* as archetype of the American Long Poem, the 'romance' narratives of Hawthorne and Melville, Thoreau's *Walden* as the diary of his singular 'experiment in living', the tensile, dash-laden poems of Emily Dickinson, even the burlesquerie and arch black humour of the frontier—none has more steadily caught the reading imagination than the short story. Singly, or in cycles and collections, the story (Twain thought there was a difference between it and 'the tale') plays into a tradition if not uniquely then most markedly American and which through moderns like Faulkner, Fitzgerald and Hemingway has continued unabated into our own era. The names to which this new volume of essays gives attention, therefore, in turn Poe, Irving, Hawthorne, Melville, Twain, Crane, Bierce, Chopin and James, rightly can assume founding status at home though in no way at the expense of an appeal which goes well beyond national borders.

Why the short story should have made so striking a bow in nineteenth-century America as against, say, nineteenth-century England, is not readily determined. Certainly there were magazines with a subscription readership eager for copy. One has only to think of Poe and the *Southern Literary Messenger*, Hawthorne and the *Democratic Review*, Melville and *Harper's* or *Putnam's*, or James and others and the *Atlantic Monthly*. Certainly, too, for the story-writers themselves, often as uncertain of their royalties as they were of their copyright, magazine publication meant the prospect of a quicker turnaround and payment. No doubt, in addition, to a society manifestly about the endeavour of settlement and nation-

7

building, the story seemed just about appropriate to the available reading time. It may even have been, given the diet of Victorian three-decker novels from both sides of the Atlantic (the form in which *Moby-Dick* was first published), that story-length fiction simply offered the welcome contrast of brevity. All of these factors have their place, but they go only so far.

More theoretical discussion of the story form suggests that it has flourished best when written from, or about, the margins of a society. English-language stories, to be sure, have proliferated from writers situated at the edge—by class or sexual style in the instance of England, by the operations of colonialism or Empire (Ireland, Africa, India, especially), or by expatriation as shown in the careers of Joyce, Conrad, James and Naipaul. In the case of America, one can begin with the often repeated observation that writers by their very vocation in a culture given to business—be it the business of nationhood, the business *à la Crèvecoeur* of becoming 'a new man', or to invoke President Coolidge 'the business of business'—self-appointedly lie to the further sides of the nation's life. Similarly, for all that American public rhetoric has stressed oneness its more honest inclination has been towards an ethos of self, elevated at no small and frequent cost to those failing to meet the standard into a near cultist worship of 'self-reliance'.

Historically, the reasons for marginality in America are not too difficult to invoke. In the first instance the New World might have beckoned as utopian dream, a 'fresh, green breast' in Fitzgerald's words from *The Great Gatsby*, but it also by its very size and space could threaten and diminish its settlers. The succeeding frontier belief in individualism, as much as it could create industrial and prairie empires could also lead to a world of loners, outlaws, dissenters, nay-sayers and cynics. Then, too, the bruising jostle of an eclectic immigrant citizenry all in pursuit of pride of place inescapably bred resentments as much as success, the ache of exclusion as well as inclusion. At another level, only latterly have women begun to win their recognition in having shaped and in continuing to shape America, too readily denied access to executive power and too readily thought the lesser partner be it as mother, homemaker,

8

or companion in the assumed male enterprise of nation-making. Is this why, from Harriet Beecher Stowe through Kate Chopin to contemporaries like Flannery O'Connor, Katherine Anne Porter, Carson McCullers, Jean Stafford, Zora Neale Hurston and Alice Walker, women have contributed so powerfully to the story tradition in America? Similarly, both the old and the young or adolescent have long featured as subject-matter in American short and (to be accurate given Stowe's Little Women, Huckleberry Finn and Holden Caulfield) long fiction.

Of late, furthermore, however persistent has been the W.A.S.P. cultural hegemony in America, story-writers from other ethnic and regional backgrounds have found voice—Jewish, Black, Indian, Hispanic, Southern and Western (whose late nineteenth-century and turn-of-the-century exponents include Mark Twain, Jack London and Bret Harte). And, from the Puritan foundation on through the westering nineteenth century into industrialized and suburban modern America, there has been the perception of the country as quite simply, for all its ready 'democratic' opportunity, a lonely place. For despite the prospectus of a *United* States, America has been as often ununited, whether by Civil War, slavery, race, wealth or region, and whether in small-town or city, a society as much of outposts and margins as of consensus. That experience, to be met with in Irving's legendary Knickerbocker fables, Hawthorne's New England stories, or Melville's Piazza fiction in the nineteenth century, or in Sherwood Anderson's small-town portraits in *Winesburg, Ohio* (1919) or Richard Wright's 'underground' stories in *Uncle Tom's Children* (1938) and *Eight Men* (post-1961), or in contemporary short fiction by J. D. Salinger, Bernard Malamud and James Alan McPherson, to give three representative names, has been a recurring feature of the American short story.

As a specific nineteenth-century phenomenon, the American short story raises still other issues. Is it to be differentiated from the novella, of which there is an abundance, from Melville's *Israel Potter* (1855) and *Billy Budd, Sailor* (1888–91), to Stephen Crane's *The Red Badge of Courage* (1895) and Henry James's *Daisy Miller* (1878) and *What Maisie Knew* (1897)? Is the view that the short story speaks essentially from a single point of view, and with a single 'cast' or locale, born out in the American case? Where, and how, do terms like 'fable', 'tale', 'sketch', '*conte*', best apply? What theories from the story-writers themselves afford usable terms of discussion—Poe's famous contention in his review of Hawthorne's *Twice-Told Tales* in *Graham's Magazine* for April–May 1842, about the desirability of 'a certain unique or single effect', or Twain's distinctions between witty, comic and humorous story-telling in 'How To Tell A Story'? And, more than any other American story-writer, is not Poe to be credited on the basis of the Dupin narratives with his own genre, or sub-genre, that of the detective story? Is not, too, the American short story more than any other and in keeping with American writing at large deeply taken up with and shaped by an interest in myth? Irving, especially, offers the example in stories like 'Rip Van Winkle' and 'The Legend of Sleepy Hollow' of European folk sources actually under transformation into indigenous form. What effect, finally, does it have to read these stories in the context of a collection—one of diversity in unity, or of recognizing an enclosing voice or tone, or a reading-experience somewhat altered and enlarged because it draws upon the cross-play of motif or setting? Think of Hawthorne's New England domain, or Crane's Bowery, or Bierce's Civil War backdrops, or Chopin's Louisiana Cajun world. These, and related concerns, serve as touchstones and points of departure for the contributions to *The Nineteenth-century American Short Story*, some dealt with head-on, others more implicitly.

Michael Wood opens the account with a fresh look at Poe, the author of the so-called Gothic, Ratiocinative and Detective stories as a model of self-reflexivity, signalling his own tactics even as he takes inventive care to conceal them. In this Poe points the way towards Borges and Beckett, for good or ill the classic American artist of the self-conscious. Howell Daniels then examines Washington Irving's short fiction, especially its use of dream, somnambulance and self-displacement as Irving's way of at once telling a story and acknowledging his own part in its creation.

David Timms's focus in considering Hawthorne's stories also falls upon the complication of authorial rôle, the New Englander's sense of his own ambiguity as narrator and the 'negotiation' in story-form put out to the reader. Melville's Piazza and other 1850s short stories I approach through his adeptness as a story-telling voice, the energy and vibrancy of tales which on first view paradoxically depict depletion and costly ruling illusions. Andrew Hook raises the question of what in actual fact constitutes Twain's shorter work, uncollected in his own lifetime and much of it close to the border territory of sketch and episode. He tackles, too, the complex issue of the 'vernacular' in Twain, his creation of an idiom made over from oral into written delivery.

In his account of Stephen Crane, Harold Beaver proposes a 'coded', self-aware Crane—a writer who in the very form of his short stories undermines the naturalism/realism with which he is customarily associated. Herbie Butterfield offers a view of Ambrose Bierce as more diverse, more meticulous and deliberated, in his short-stories than the sobriquet 'Bitter Bierce' has traditionally tended to suggest. Similarly, in her critique of Kate Chopin, Judie Newman argues for a writer wholly analytical of inherited female stereotype but without resort to the crudification of her art into mere sexual politics or programme. Eric Mottram's approach to James's short fiction explores the complex of themes having to do with renunciation, entrapment, the psychology of powerlessness and unenacted desire, and the peculiarly Jamesian vocabulary in which these themes are given expression.

No one approach governs the essays in this collection. But they each do recognize an essential Americanness to the nineteenth-century story tradition—without losing sight of story-telling wholly individual and possessed of its own identifying style and timbre. Nor does it go unrecognized that all these landmark American authors wrote other than short stories, that their stories represent but one dimension in otherwise more far-ranging careers. Nonetheless, they are bound both to the national literature and to each other as having bequeathed a unique short-story legacy, a spectacular American historical genre. In this respect, if no other, the present volume offers a reassessment, a new set of critical orientations.

1

Poe's Tales: The Art of the Impossible

by MICHAEL WOOD

> But I was sorely put out by the absence of all else—of the body to my imagined instrument—of the text for my context.
>
> —'The Gold-Bug'

1

Following in the worried tracks of Allen Tate and T. S. Eliot, Harold Bloom remarked recently that he could think of 'no other American writer . . . at once so inescapable and so dubious' as Poe.[1] In this view Poe's importance is not denied, but the flashiness and thinness of much of his work are felt to be an embarrassment. The immense admiration for Poe of major French writers from Baudelaire to Valéry is awkward too: taken as a puzzle when it is not taken as a joke. Other critics have thought, of course, that Poe is not inescapable at all, but merely an author we read when we are young and then grow out of; and I would argue that most of Poe's poetry is not even dubious, it is just terrible. What are we to do with lines like 'At midnight, in the months of June,/ I stand beneath the mystic moon.'?[2] Still, the question of Poe remains.

We do grow out of him; but then we grow into him again. At least that has been my experience. His virtues as a writer are hidden, but they are hidden, like the purloined letter, on the surface. If we cannot find them, it is because they are not where we choose to look. What is hidden, Jacques Lacan said, is what is not in its place, and Poe's virtues are placed where criticism has no habit of seeking.[3] We cannot make him seem deep, or academically serious. We cannot convert him, by some sleight of hand, into Henry James—although people do keep trying, with dispiriting results. But we don't have to give him up for all that.

> The variety and ardour of his curiosity [Eliot wrote of Poe] delight and dazzle; yet in the end the eccentricity and lack of coherence of his interests tire. . . . There is just that lacking which gives dignity to the mature man: a consistent view of life. . . . He appears to yield himself completely to the idea of the moment: the effect is, that all of his ideas seem to be *entertained* rather than believed.[4]

We must quarrel with much of this. Are we tired by Poe's eccentricity and lack of coherence or by his uneven performances? Are we tired at all, or are we baffled, made edgy? Does a consistent view of life always lend dignity to a man? Cannot we think of consistent views which are undignified and childish, even evil? Is maturity itself all that ponderous critics crack it up to be? Does not it often mean only a dreary abandonment of desire? All I shall suggest here is that Eliot, as he so often does, has stumbled into a brilliant insight while facing the other way. Poe does entertain his ideas rather than believe them. That is his great gift, his open secret. It is his entertaining them which lends them their air of daring hypothesis, their eerie mobility, and which keeps us guessing even when we think we know the answers. Their scaffolding looks flimsy because it is about to be taken down and erected elsewhere.

Poe's styles, pursuing such ideas, become a matter of impersonation, a trying on of masks. Allen Tate spoke of a 'glutinous prose' which made Poe hard to read in any quantity, and certainly Poe could write stickily enough.[5] But he also wrote: ' "Listen to *me*," said the Demon, as he placed his hand upon my head'[6]; and:

> Of course I shall not pretend to consider it any matter for wonder, that the extraordinary case of M Valdemar has excited

14

discussion. It would have been a miracle had it not—especially under the circumstances.[7]

and: 'And shud ye be wantin to diskiver who is the pink of purliteness quite, and the laider of the hot tun in the houl city o' London—why it's jist mesilf'[8]; and:

> In the meantime let us survey this image. What is it? Oh, it is the god Ashimah in proper person. You perceive, however, that he is neither a lamb, nor a goat, not a satyr . . . Put on your spectacles and tell me what it is. What is it?
> 'Bless me! it is an ape!'
> True—a baboon; but by no means the less a deity.[9]

There is much that is borrowed here—from the moral fable, from the learned or legal report, from the Irish joke, from Carlyle—but then much is borrowed in the later parts of *Ulysses*, and in the prose of Nabokov. Poe, as his 'How to Write a Blackwood Article' makes clear, was an expert parodist ('then there is the tone laconic, or curt, which has lately come much into use. It consists in short sentences. Somehow thus. Can't be too brief. Can't be too snappish. Always a full stop. And never a paragraph'), and may have been a parodist more often than we think.[10] I do not mean he is always spoofing the genres he adopts. His outright spoofs invariably make it quite clear that that is what they are. I mean a parody may not be very different from the real thing when the real thing is only being entertained.

James W. Gargano and James M. Cox have valuably pointed us in this direction by insisting on the element of performance and posturing in Poe's narrators and heroes.[11] Poe mimes their dilemmas rather than expresses his own, and Roderick Usher and Ligeia, Cox says, 'are the decadent artists who haunt the narrator; they are his madness, his disease. . . .' They are Poe's madness and disease too, since he returned to their types so often; and to hide him entirely behind his narrators, as Gargano tends to do, is to shift the problem but not to solve it. But this perspective allows us to see Poe the artist at work, entertaining his ideas, putting on his make-up, testing his accent. The styles which now seem rather hard to take—the carefully vague, as in 'I cannot, for my soul, remember how, when, or even precisely where, I first became acquainted with the lady Ligeia'; the arch-and-beautiful, as in 'the lulling melody that had been softer than the wind-harp of Aeolus and more divine than all save the voice of Eleonora'; and the long-winded lugubrious which I do not need to exemplify—can be seen as masks which have worn thin.[12] What the *wearing* of the masks is about remains to be seen. This is not a biographical question.

Poe's ideas, like his styles, come together not because they add up to a doctrine or a coherence but because they constantly qualify and comment on each other. Their shifting relations, the effects created by their revolving or alternating entertainment, are, I suggest, the source of Poe's peculiar power, the one we grow into. It may be that in assessing Poe's importance we shall need at some stage to revise or complicate our notion of importance itself. Poe's detective Auguste Dupin is very clear about this. 'There is such a thing as being too profound', he remarks. 'Truth is not always in a well. In fact, as regards the more important knowledge, I do believe that she is invariably superficial.'[13] Dupin is not simply teasing. He is questioning the confidence with which we claim to know what matters and where to find it. Dupin would have given Eliot a hard time over his concepts of coherence and dignity and maturity. For a later version of the argument we may want to contrast Lévi-Strauss's appetite for geology, psychoanalysis and Marxism, which he sees as sciences of buried and centralized meaning, with Lacan's insistence that 'man is inhabited by the signifier', which is a way of saying either that there are no buried depths or that we have no means of knowing how deep the surfaces go.[14]

I want to look at Poe's tales in this flickering light, to watch him entertain some of his ideas, and to see how they work in fiction, where they are no longer quite the abstract entities I have so far been juggling with. An 'idea' in a story is not the same as an idea in a debate. There are three chief sets of such working ideas in Poe, I think, and they cluster round the concepts of death, detection and perversity. I have not separated, in what follows, Poe's comic or burlesque tales from his solemn ones, because I believe we need to know what it means that he should be able to say similar things in such different registers; that he could see being buried alive, for example, both as a gag and a nightmare. Odd changes take place in a nightmare once you have seen its potential as a gag. Still less have I wanted to split the writer, as Julian Symons does, into a Visionary Poe and a Logical Poe.[15] There is only one Poe, and he is the most logical of visionaries. But he has many voices and stances, and his agility in getting about among them is very much part of my subject.

2

'Death triumphed in that strange voice', Mallarmé wrote in a famous sonnet on Poe.[16] He meant that in death Poe found the enduring identity which eluded him in life, and that is precisely the sense of the sonnet's much-quoted first line: *Tel qu'en Lui-même enfin l'éternité le change*. But the poem is also coloured by a delicate, riddling irony—here is an eternity which changes a man, a man changed into himself—and Mallarmé does not *say* that Poe triumphed in death. He says that death triumphed in Poe. He had been listening, I suspect, to the voice of M. Valdemar, and wanted to suggest, lightly, that Poe was death's messenger and agent, that he conquered it by specializing in it.

Death was in the air when Poe was writing. Gothic novels are full of crypts and tombs and ghosts, and the early nineteenth century, E. H. Davidson tells us, 'shuddered to its heart's content' as it indulged its 'delight in fictive death'.[17] The fear of being buried alive, David Galloway notes, was 'commonplace': 'charnel houses were equipped with alarm systems so that the "dead" could signal for help, and luxury coffins were fitted with ventilators and speaking tubes.'[18] We may guess then, correctly, that Poe followed a fashion—he was out to make a living, after all, and why not from death?—and at times he does seem simply to do what others do, only better. The end of 'The Facts in the Case of M. Valdemar', for instance, is both brilliant and crude in its calculated shock.[19] M. Valdemar has been mesmerized just before his death, and has died while in an induced trance. The trance keeps him rigid for seven months, and still possessed of some sort of sleeping consciousness. His tongue vibrates when questions are put to him, but he does not breathe, and his blood does not flow. At last the mesmerist and M. Valdemar's physicians decide to wake him, with predictably messy results:

> his whole frame at once—within the space of a single minute, or even less, shrunk—crumbled—absolutely *rotted* away beneath my hands. Upon the bed, before that whole company, there lay a nearly liquid mass of loathsome—of detestable putridity.

Death is disgust, or rather the terror of death is hidden in disgust at the dead body. This is a good horror movie, but it is not more than that. The voice of M. Valdemar, however, is a different matter, and Mallarmé was right to listen to it.

When M. Valdemar is first put into the mesmeric trance he is asked a series of simple questions. 'M. Valdemar, are you asleep?' 'Do you still feel pain in the breast, M. Valdemar?' He answers with some difficulty, his lips moving sluggishly. 'Yes—asleep now. Do not wake me.' 'No pain—I am dying.' A little later, when M. Valdemar is very close indeed to death, the mesmerist repeats his question: 'M. Valdemar, do you still sleep?' Then M. Valdemar dies; but courteous *in extremis* and beyond, or perhaps merely obedient as the mesmerized are supposed to be, he struggles to answer the question. 'Yes;—no; I *have been* sleeping—and now—now—*I am dead*.' We are still in the realm of the horror movie, and may be on the borders of the ridiculous. Or we would be, were it not for Poe's uncanny description of M. Valdemar's voice; 'a voice,' his narrator says, 'such as it would be madness in me to attempt describing.' He has a go all the same:

> I might say, for example, that the sound was harsh, and broken and hollow; but the hideous whole is indescribable. . . . There were two particulars, nevertheless, which I thought then, and still think, might fairly be stated as characteristic of the intonation—as well adapted to convey some idea of its unearthly peculiarity. In the first place, the voice seemed to reach our ears—at least mine—from a vast distance, or from some deep cavern within the earth. In the second place, it impressed me (I fear, indeed, that it will be impossible to make myself comprehended) as gelatinous or glutinous matters impress the sense of touch.

The voice is buried and decomposing, and because the effect is applied to what cannot be altered or moved in this way, it is no longer simply an effect of horror. Death itself seems to talk, and that is horrible enough; but *that* death should talk is more of a transgression or a trespass than a shock, and it muddles the resurrection, which requires a new state of existence after death, but not that death should have a murky life of its own.

'What is a ghost?' Stephen Dedalus asks, and answers himself, 'One who has faded into impalpability through death, through absence, through change of manners'.[20] That is how we make ghosts of the living, and how we gradually lose our dead. But the other kind of ghost is the dead person who cannot die, a reminder of restless, unsettled accounts, and this is precisely how the dead make themselves felt in Poe. It is one of the ideas he repeatedly entertains, and it is hard to see how he could do more than entertain it, since as a belief it is either nonsense or unbearable.

In 'Metzengerstein', one of Poe's earliest stories, a horse descends from a tapestry to haunt and destroy a distant descendant of his master's enemy. In another story, a manuscript reaches civilization in a bottle, the text of a man who is now either dead or a member of a company of ghosts or both. In yet another, the heart of a dead man continues to beat and informs on his murderer—or at least the murderer thinks he hears the heartbeat, and this perhaps tells us something about these hauntings. They seem to beset only those who are anxious or doubtful about conclusions, nervous grandchildren of Macbeth, always afraid that a thing is never done when 'tis done. In 'The Black Cat' a live animal is walled up with a corpse, and howls until the crime is discovered, so that the dead can luridly testify against the living: 'The corpse, already greatly decayed and clotted with gore, stood erect before the eyes of the spectators.'[21] How can the killer have been so careless? Did he not see the cat? Did he not want to bury the dead? He did, but he could not bury the crime in his mind, and so mimed and betrayed his unfinished mental business by his actions. Premature burial, a terror if you are to be buried, can be a sort of wish if you are the gravedigger, an eager dream of banished complication. It is worth recalling that the words 'no more' and 'nevermore' have a weird charm in Poe's poems, express a regret which in its perfect finality is tantamount to a reward.[22]

The idea of death leaking back into life is present in a quite different kind of Poe story. Here the heroes are not haunted, and they have not died. But they have escaped a death so certain that their current life seems a miracle, and they have the spectral, reprieved look of revenants. In 'The Premature Burial', a man thinks he is buried alive, but is not; in 'Loss of Breath', after a series of macabre accidents which includes a hanging that does not come off, another man *is* buried alive, and yet resurfaces to tell the joky tale. In 'King Pest', a pair of drunken sailors meet up with the unruly spirits of the plague itself, and get off scot-free. It is true that the plague spirits may be a gang of actors who have set up their quarters in a stricken part of town where no one else will step. The man who descends into the maelstrom returns with white hair and nerves unstrung—'the six hours of deadly terror which I . . . endured', he says, 'have broken me up body and soul'[23]—and the narrator of 'The Pit and the Pendulum' survives seemingly ineluctable death at least three times. He misses a yawning pit in the dark, escapes a swishing, descending scythe by allowing rats to eat his bonds, and is rescued by the occupying French army as the red-hot walls of his chamber have all but closed in on him. 'The Man That Was Used Up', a very funny story which anticipates much gruesome modern humour, introduces Brigadier General John A. B. C. Smith, a fine figure of a man who turns out to be, when not assembled for public display, 'an odd looking bundle' on the floor. He has only one leg, one arm, one eye, no teeth, no hair, no palate and not much tongue. It is literally a case of a man not being a hero to his valet, whose 'manipulations', the narrator says, 'made . . . a very striking difference in the appearance of the personal man', since they quickly fitted him out with all he is lacking, including artificial limbs, a wig, and a voice machine.[24]

Brooding or light, the tales in this group toy with an uncertainty or inefficiency in death. They are cheerful on the whole, even when they are threatening, like 'The Pit and the Pendulum', and in this they contrast with the tales of the previous group. Plainly we are looking at alternative faces of a single idea. How we feel about death's possible lack of finality will depend on how we feel about our lives. If they have been riotous or happy, we shall be pleased to see them continue. We shall be less pleased to keep the books open on our crimes. 'Now and then, alas,' Poe writes in 'The Man of the Crowd', 'the conscience of man takes up a burthen so heavy in horror that it can be thrown down only into the grave.'[25] Not even there, in Poe's favourite darker fantasies. We may therefore want to wonder whether life itself may not be a crime for many of Poe's characters, and this is very much what is implied in a cluster of his most famous stories.

The most familiar, the most haunting ghost in Poe, with the exception of M. Valdemar's otherworldly voice, is the insufficiently loved woman, the figure Harry Levin calls 'the posthumous heroine'.[26] The ingredients of this recurring situation are themselves haunting. A man is blessed by the company of an exceptional wife, both beautiful and learned. His response to her is too pure or too lukewarm. He is either frightened of his blessing, or does not know it is a blessing until it is gone. Or perhaps he does not *want* a blessing? This would be in keeping with the perverseness I shall discuss a little later. At all events, 'the fires were not of Eros', the narrator of 'Morella' says. 'I never spoke of passion nor thought of love.'[27] The narrator of 'Ligeia' is 'busily occupied' with his studies during the early years of his marriage, and while he is delighted to have his wife's intellectual help, has no idea, until she dies, how much she loved him, and loved life:

> the outwardly calm, the ever-placid Ligeia, was the most violently a prey to the tumultuous vultures of stern passion. . . . But upon this subject I cannot bear to dilate. Let me say only, that in Ligeia's more than womanly abandonment to a love, alas! all unmerited, all unworthily bestowed, I at length recognized the principle of her longing with so wildly earnest a desire for the life which was now fleeing so rapidly away. It is this wild longing—it is this eager vehemence of desire for life—*but* for life—that I have no power to portray. . . .[28]

Morella dies leaving a daughter to haunt her tepid husband— on her deathbed she speaks rather like M. Valdemar, saying, 'I am dying, yet shall I live'—and when the husband, belatedly and by some strange prompting, gives the mother's name to the daughter, the living girl is possessed by the dead woman, and very soon dies in her turn: 'she died; and with my own hands I bore her to the tomb; and I laughed with a long and bitter laugh as I found no traces of the first, in the charnel where I laid the second—Morella.' The daughter was loved as much as the mother was taken for granted: 'I loved her', the narrator says, 'with a love more fervent than I had believed it possible to feel for any denizen of earth.' Is this *because* she is his daughter and not his wife?

The end of 'Ligeia' is even more distressing. The husband takes to opium after Ligeia's death, and marries again. In this case too the second woman sickens and dies, and is possessed by the first, except that here the possession takes place *after* death. The second wife, Rowena, amid much sighing and several relapses, her renewed breathing hampered by 'the bandages and draperies of the grave', enacts a 'hideous drama of revivification', and returns to life as Ligeia, her fair hair and blue eyes transposed into the black hair and eyes of her predecessor. We can if we wish (and a number of critics have wished) see this reincarnation as a guilt-ridden opium dream of the narrator's rather than a 'real' change in the fictional corpse. I don't think it matters greatly whether Ligeia's return is the narrator's fantasy or Poe's metaphor—although perhaps it is stronger if it is the latter. What is striking about this brooding story, Poe's own favourite among his tales, is the sheer terror of this resurrection. The shroud and the rest are Gothic trappings, relatives of M. Valdemar's putrid body. But the eyes which the corpse finally opens are like M. Valdemar's voice, and similarly complicate the horror with a sense of unthinkable trespass:

> And now slowly opened *the eyes* of the figure which stood before me. 'Here then, at least,' I shrieked aloud, 'can I never—can I never be mistaken—these are the full, and the black, and the wild eyes—of my lost love—of the lady—of the LADY LIGEIA!'

The lady has conquered death through her love for him and her love for life, but all he can do is shriek, and all we are left with is helpless dismay. It is not so much that the love remains lost, as the narrator says and as Harold Bloom reminds us. It is that it is not lost *enough*, that it will not go away, even in death; it unravels the sombre perfection of 'nevermore'.

Poe had himself dreamed of Ligeia's eyes apparently,[29] and his narrator finds in the material world a 'circle of analogies' to their expression:

> I recognized it . . . sometimes in the survey of a rapidly-growing vine—in the contemplation of a moth, a butterfly, a chrysalis, a stream of running water. I have felt it in the ocean; in the falling of a meteor. I have felt it in the glances of unusually aged people. And there are one or two stars in heaven . . . in a telescopic scrutiny of which I have been made aware of the feeling. I have been filled with it by certain sounds from stringed instruments, and not unfrequently by passages from books.

There are obvious links here to Baudelaire's theory of correspondences, and to the hints and secrets Proust's hero found in steeples and hawthorn bushes and the glint of a roof in the sunshine. But Poe's narrator can meditate on his analogies only when Ligeia's eyes are closed on earth, when her beauty, as he puts it, has 'passed into my spirit, there dwelling as in a shrine'. The end of the story opens the shrine, topples the spirit back into the world, and destroys what Henry James, writing of Poe, called the peace of art.

Poe is consciously playing with two philosophical problems in 'Morella' and 'Ligeia'—or rather attacking our constructed universe by means of two such problems. Both are evoked in prophecies from the dying women. Morella says she will live in her child, a familiar enough trope, except that she means it quite literally. What is questioned then is identity: 'the *principium individuationis*—the notion of that identity which at death is or is not lost forever'. The narrator shudders at the 'too perfect *identity*' of the daughter's smile with the mother's. Ligeia quotes a remark she attributes to Joseph Glanvill: 'who knoweth the mysteries of the will in its vigor? Man doth not yield him to the angels, *nor unto death utterly*, save only through the weakness of his feeble will.' Death ends our identity; our will ends with death. Poe plainly believes these things as much as the next man (and more than some). Yet he makes Morella and Ligeia overturn these fundamental notions, and the terror of their reappearances is more metaphysical than Gothic. Poe's imagination, seeking out the scarcely visible cracks in

23

our confidence about what we know for sure (what we cannot *not* know, as James said), momentarily abolishes the impossible for us. Anything becomes possible. The thought is thrilling for an instant; then it unnerves us completely. 'Ligeia', as David Halliburton suggests, is the strongest of testimonials to 'the indestructibility of life'.[30] That this should be what is scaring in the story rather than what is comforting, is Poe's particular touch. If life is a crime, then the afterlife is not another realm, but a dogged and infinitely tormenting prolongation of the life we have.

But how is life a crime? We need to glance here at the mawkish 'Eleonora', which retells the story of 'Morella' and 'Ligeia' *without* the haunting. The narrator enjoys an idyll with a girl who then dies. He vows just before her departure that he will never marry another, and invokes the curse of 'the Mighty Ruler of the Universe' should he break his faith. But he does break it, and is not afraid of the curse, and the curse is not visited on him, because 'the Spirit of Love reigneth and ruleth', and absolves him of his vow.[31] I am not sure this odd release is not as disturbing as the punishment might have been. The eyes of Ligeia seem to have been wished away rather than really closed. Certainly the pardon in 'Eleonora' resembles the escapes from certain death in the other group of stories we have looked at, and the resemblance might be worth pursuing. For the moment I want to suggest that all these tales imply a guilt which can either be heightened or hidden, like a bet that can be doubled or withdrawn. What you cannot do is not place the bet in the first instance. That would be the equivalent of the heroes in these stories loving their wives sufficiently while they were alive, or of the narrator in 'Eleonora' remaining faithful to her memory without making a vow. One road from this territory leads straight into Poe's biography, of course; but another stays very close to the fiction. I think Davidson is right to insist on the moral dislocation of Poe's imagined world, and on the compulsive behaviour of Poe's guilty men:

> No one understands or can interpret, in this moral region of Poe's lost souls, why he must be punished; yet the penalty . . . is frightful. . . . No other god but the self as god can wreak such a vengeance. . . .

Poe's narrators, Davidson says, 'are like Kafka's man in *The Trial* who never knows the charges contained in his indictment'.[32] I would add only that they do not need to know the charges. All they need is the indictment, since what is indicted is life itself, life seen as a failure to answer an imperious call. To live, in Poe's writing, is to place a horribly risky bet, to embark on a perilous and flimsy bluff. The crime, so to speak, is always already committed. The question is whether it will be found out, and whether it will lead to more crimes. Those who are *not* bluffing, those brave and terrifying women who think life is worth coming back from death for, are the merciless, loving judges.

I have not yet mentioned 'The Fall of the House of Usher', which very much fits into this pattern. It has been well discussed elsewhere, and I shall only point to the critics' near-unanimous eagerness to keep Madeline Usher alive till the last minute.[33] On the standard reading of the story, Madeline has sunk into a cataleptic coma, and her brother Roderick, anxious to get her out of the way, has buried her alive. Not without some hesitation, however, since he decides to keep her coffin in a vault for a fortnight, prior to consigning it to its 'final interment'. Resisting this treatment, Madeline comes crashing back through the ancient architecture, and Roderick, sensing her return, cries, '*We have put her living in the tromb!*' But what if this response is just Roderick's morbid scruple? What if Madeline is dead, and like Poe's other heroines cannot stay away from the life she has lost?

> without those doors there *did* stand the lofty and enshrouded figure of the lady Madeline of Usher. There was blood upon her white robes, and the evidence of some bitter struggle upon every portion of her emaciated frame. For a moment she remained trembling and reeling to and fro upon the threshold—then, with a low moaning cry, fell heavily inward upon the person of her brother. . . .[34]

'Bitter struggle' is nicely equivocal. Has Madeline been battling with death itself or with a screwed-down coffin lid and a massive iron door? I am not asking what 'really' happened, but what the force of the image is. Certainly Poe talks enough about catalepsy for the standard reading to be sensible, and even attractive. But then the story is about Roderick's anxious haste to end his worries, and not about Madeline's relentless will to live. The wilder reading has its appeal because it collects both strands: Madeline is Roderick's unfinished and perhaps unfinishable life; she returns from the dead for him, and his world caves in.

3

'And thus', Poe wrote in 'The Man of the Crowd', 'the essence of all crime is undivulged.'

> There are some secrets which do not permit themselves to be told. Men die nightly in their beds, wringing the hands of ghostly confessors, and looking them piteously in the eyes—die with despair of heart and convulsion of throat, on account of the hideousness of mysteries which will not *suffer themselves* to be revealed.[35]

Since so many of Poe's stories suggest exactly the opposite of this, insist on crimes which cry out in the beating of a heart or the howling of a cat, or the mournful return of the insufficiently loved to haunt emotional defaulters, the thought of an essentially undivulged, undivulgable crime is worth pausing over. The story in which the remark appears is both powerful and baffling. The narrator observes a London crowd, 'reading' faces and manners as he says certain books *cannot* be read. Then he spots an unreadable old man, whose countenance is remarkable for the 'absolute idiosyncrasy of its expression':

> Any thing even remotely resembling that expression I had never seen before. . . . As I endeavored . . . to form some analysis of the meaning conveyed, there arose confusedly and paradoxically within my mind, the ideas of vast mental power, of caution, of penuriousness, of avarice, of coolness, of malice, of bloodthirstiness, of triumph, of merriment, of excessive terror, of intense—of supreme despair.

The narrator follows the man for a night and a day, and learns only that he does not sleep and that he seeks out crowds wherever they are to be found. The narrator can guess 'how wild, a history . . . is written in that bosom', but it is not a history he can decipher. He concludes only that 'This old man . . . is the type and genius of deep crime. He refuses to be alone. *He is the man of the crowd.*'

It looks as if it ought to be possible here to decide which of his ideas Poe believes and which he entertains. Either crime is essentially undivulged (behind every known crime lurks a worse, unconfessed one), or it is essentially self-betraying, horribly anxious to give its game away. It would be safest to say Poe entertains both ideas, or oscillates between the two. I am tempted to suggest that he is afraid he believes the second, while the first is a fantasy of immunity—a desolate and lonely immunity, but an immunity all the same. Certainly most of Poe's fiction emphatically asserts the legibility of the world, either because the corpse comes back to unravel the mystery, or because a lynx-eyed detective sees what has escaped everyone else but is nevertheless *there.* Is Poe hinting at the double-edged nature of his idea: at the attractions of reading, the dangers of being read? A peculiar posture for a writer, unless it is a sort of definition of literature, that signing of messages for readers you don't know, an act simultaneously of display and disguise.

The logic of Poe's detective tales is pitiless, closes every fissure which other stories seek to open. 'It is not too much to say', Dupin remarks to his friend in 'The Murders in the Rue Morgue', 'that neither of us believe in praeternatural events. Madame and Mademoiselle L'Espanaye were not destroyed by spirits. The doers of the deed were material and escaped materially.'[36] Dupin would not be a fan of Poe's horror stories. The doers of the deed were in fact material, but they were not plural, and Dupin concludes, for several cogent reasons, that they were not human. He is right. They were an orang-outang. Similarly in 'The Gold-Bug', another character with a French name remorselessly argues himself into the apparent dead end where the solution lies. The drawing of a skull has appeared on a piece of parchment where Legrand has sketched a scarab. At first Legrand thinks of coincidence. He has drawn his beetle on a parchment which has on its reverse side a skull rather resembling a scarab. But coincidence always dissolves in Poe. In Poe, as in Freud's unconscious, there are no accidents.[37] Then Legrand remembers there was *nothing* on the parchment when he drew the scarab, since he actually looked at both sides. He is satisfied that his friend did not sneakily draw the skull, 'and no one else was present to do it. Then it was not done by human agency. And nevertheless it was done.'[38]

The answer to the riddle, as answers always are in these cases, is a disappointment: invisible ink, a remote control human agency. The pay-offs in Poe's mysteries—the cracked code, the buried treasure, the orang-outang, the repossession of the purloined letter—are never interesting, and Poe's invention of the detective story is relevant here. The whole genre rests on chases not on catches. Asking who cares who killed Roger Ackroyd, Edmund Wilson missed the point, which is that no one cares. What we care about is the apparent impossibility of all solution to the mystery until the mundane solution is found. Poe's detective stories, and those of others, are related to tales like 'A Descent into the Maelstrom', with their apparent impossibility of survival, and like 'Ligeia', where the human will ruins the very idea of the impossible. This is to say that what matters in detective stories is the detective rather than the crime; or more precisely, what matters is the movement of the detective's mind: 'that moral activity', as Poe says, 'which *disentangles*'.[39]

Poe is curiously hesitant about the nature of his forays into detection. 'I am not now writing a treatise,' he says at the beginning of 'The Murders in the Rue Morgue', 'but simply prefacing a somewhat peculiar narrative by observations very much at random.' The implication is that the mystery (the peculiar narrative) is the point, and that the reflections it provokes are merely to serve as a context. At the end of what amounts to a remarkable essay on the interconnections of the analytical and the imaginative faculties of the mind, Poe (or his narrator) reverses his argument: 'The narrative which follows will appear to the reader somewhat in the light of a commentary upon the propositions just advanced.' In the second of his tales highlighting the disentangling talents of the Chevalier C. Auguste Dupin, 'The Mystery of Marie Rogêt', Poe remarks that depicting Dupin's 'mental character . . . constituted my design'.[40]

Is Dupin's mind a proof that the world can be read, at least by an exceptional intelligence? Could Dupin have read the wild history in the face of the man of the crowd? Or is Dupin's mind the topic, and the world merely his laboratory? Is Dupin's mind an example, a commentary, as Poe says, on more abstract propositions? Poe seems not to want to make a decision here. He is entertaining Dupin and his skills as he entertained the voice of M. Valdemar and the eyes of Ligeia: metaphors, let us say, which make us wonder about much of what we take literally. It will help if we remember that Dupin is just as much a fantasy for Poe (for us) as an identity which survives death or a will which overwhelms it. Patrick F. Quinn distinguishes between victims and pursuers in Poe, giving them the names of Roderick Usher and Auguste Dupin: 'Poe could not be the detective, the hunter, for he was too radically the criminal, the prey.'[41] This is plausible as biographical speculation. Poe wanted to be Dupin, perhaps, but felt he was Usher. But surely this does not go far enough. Poe played the rôle of Usher in life, but he played both rôles with relish in his fiction, and the rôles may not be so far apart as they look. Poe's narrator speaks of Dupin's 'excited, or perhaps . . . diseased intelligence'; and Dupin too is a member of an old and decaying family, and a man full of whims, who inhabits 'a time-eaten and grotesque mansion'—the phrase is applied to Dupin's place in the Faubourg St. Germain, not to the House of Usher. Eliot drily reminds us of Sherlock Holmes's visit to Usher's territory:

> Holmes was deceiving Watson when he told him that he had bought his Stradivarius violin for a few shillings at a second-hand shop in the Tottenham Court Road. He found that violin in the ruins of the house of Usher.[42]

Dupin's disease is what he can see, his 'peculiar analytic ability':

> He boasted to me, with a low chuckling laugh, that most men, in respect to himself, wore windows in their bosoms, and was wont to follow up such assertions by direct and very startling proofs of his intimate knowledge of my own. His manner at these moments was frigid and abstract; his eyes were vacant in expression; while his voice, usually a rich tenor, rose into a treble which would have sounded petulantly but for the deliberateness and entire distinctness of the enunciation.

I am not sure there is a great difference between Dupin's trance and the nervousness of Poe's criminals and haunted husbands. In all cases a mystery is about to be revealed, what is hidden or interred is about to leap out into the open air of the world. All of these characters are troubled or thrilled by what we might call the failure of burial. What distinguishes Dupin is his resolute refusal to believe in the inexplicable, while the others are constantly ambushed by it. Dupin, like all great detectives, is thoroughly insufferable in his self-confidence. He sleeps through the Prefect's account of things in 'The Mystery of Marie Rogêt' because he knows it all already. He has a fair idea of where the purloined letter is even before he goes to look. The Minister who has stolen it has been 'driven to simplicity', Dupin says in a fine phrase: 'to conceal this letter, the Minister . . . resorted to the comprehensive and sagacious expedient of not attempting to conceal it at all.'[43] The letter is in full view in the Minister's apartment, and that is why it could not be seen by policemen looking for *hidden* things. I have already hinted at the relevance of this little fable for criticism.

Dupin's views are often of exceptional interest in themselves, and worth further exploration. Only a subtle mind would understand the complications that might drive a man to simplicity. But we need also to note Dupin's limitations, because in this way we can get the full sense of him as a mask, a rôle, an idea being entertained. The narrator of 'MS found in a Bottle' is a reasoner of Dupin's type who finds himself flung into the thoroughly unimaginable, the thoroughly unamenable to reason. What would have happened to Dupin in such circumstances? 'Hereafter', the killer in 'The Black Cat' says, 'perhaps some intellect may be found which will reduce my phantasm to the commonplace—some intellect more calm, more logical, and far less excitable than my own. . . .'[44] He seems to be invoking Dupin. But Dupin would be wrong to reduce this wild story to the commonplace, and would not be able to do it in any case if he were not so safely removed from the sphere of human passions. Dupin is the intellect facing a world made clear for it. He cannot stumble because all hindrances, save those his analytic powers require for their exercise, have been cleared away. And this is why he is only part of Poe's story. With the partial exception of the purloined letter, Dupin has no personal stake in the crimes he uncovers, and in the light of one of Poe's most brilliant and most cherished ideas, Dupin's faith in reason seems a very precarious protection against confusion. Dupin can have no understanding of the perverse, and the perverse, Poe liked to suggest, is what makes the world go round; and round; and round.

4

For Baudelaire, Poe's lesson was that 'we are all born marked for evil.' He taught 'the great forgotten truth—the primordial perversity of man'; he 'imperturbably affirmed' our 'natural wickedness'.[45] These phrases suggest how far Baudelaire really was from the man he felt to be his American twin. Poe was not the moral dandy the word 'imperturbably' implies. He was not the satanic theologian that Baudelaire himself so incisively became. He was *shallower* than that, and this is his peculiar virtue. It is why he can make our skin crawl. Perversity in Poe is *sheer* perversity: not a devious consequence of the fall but a motiveless, amoral appetite for ruin, a 'spirit of perverseness', an 'unfathomable longing of the soul *to vex itself*'.

I do not know whether we can believe in such an appetite except as a *boutade*, a fantastic refusal of all available explanations for behaviour. Do not we always find real motives, even for perverseness, if we dig deep enough? Baudelaire's view was that we simply had to dig to the very bottom of our nature. Psychoanalysis, like most modes of interpretation, refuses the purely random as a matter of principle. The absence of motive for the murders in the Rue Morgue is what allows Dupin to conclude that the murderer is not human. But Poe wishes to propose to us a perfectly arbitrary perverseness. This is as deep as shallowness can get, and ought to make us wonder whether we find motives because they are invariably there or because we can't bear to go without them. Truth is not always in a well; indeed the well may be empty. 'Perverseness', Poe says, 'is one of the primitive impulses of the human heart—one of the indivisible primary faculties, or sentiments, which give direction to the character of Man.'

31

It is true that Poe flirts with what was to become Baudelaire's reading of this impulse. The narrator of 'The Black Cat', having gouged out one of his pet's eyes in a drunken fury, hangs the poor creature 'in cool blood' as he says, 'with the tears streaming from my eyes, and with the bitterest remorse at my heart'. He does this

> *because* I knew that in so doing I was committing a sin—a deadly sin that would so jeopardize my immortal soul as to place it—if such a thing were possible—even beyond the reach of the infinite mercy of the Most Merciful and Most Terrible God.

This is a man after Baudelaire's heart, daring God to damn him. But the narrator's other reasons for killing his cat are less spectacular, and I find, more disturbing: '*because* I knew that it had loved me, and *because* I felt it had given me no reason of offence'. This is as much as to say that the lack of a reason is reason enough: genuine, motiveless perversity. The alcoholism and violence which come up in this story are similarly ungrounded, and are described as if they might simply settle on a man like snow. Poe was very good at this effect when he wanted to be, as in 'Loss of Breath': ' "Thou wretch!—though vixen!—thou shrew!" said I to my wife on the morning after our wedding. . . .'[46] What happened during the night? Why did he marry her? Has anything provoked this outburst? Does the narrator himself know why he is so angry? We cannot tell, since Poe, after a mock-philosophical opening, just starts his story there. We may feel in such cases that Poe is withholding information, and that this is what gives his fiction its contrived air. But we can scarcely fail to see that he is withholding the information on purpose, and we must wonder, I think, what sort of information would really help in the situations Poe has set up. A man kills his wife with an axe because she happens to get in his way when he wants to kill a cat. A reasonable account of this lurid event would surely be even crazier than a reasonless one. Poe is our hysteria, as Harold Bloom and Yvor Winters say. But he is also our scepticism, our preference (at times) for the freely pointless over the impeccably plausible.

'The Imp of the Perverse', like 'The Murders in the Rue Morgue', is part-tale and part-essay, and raises the question of motive and explanation in its form as well as in its topic. It continues the proposition about perverseness from 'The Black Cat', although here the element of parody is stronger, the flavour of the scientific pastiche. Phrenologists and moralists, Poe says, have overlooked 'a radical, primitive, irreducible sentiment', which is 'a *mobile* without motive, a motive not *motivirt*': 'I am not more certain that I breathe, than that the assurance of the wrong or error of any action is often the one unconquerable *force* which impels us, and alone impels us to its prosecution.'[47] Far from being a distortion or displacement of our desire to defend ourselves, this impulse fundamentally seeks out what will damage us. We want to impress someone, are afraid of his anger, and know just what will arouse it. 'That single thought is enough', Poe says. We do precisely what is necessary to produce the anger we dread. 'We have a task before us which must be speedily performed. We know that it will be ruinous to make delay.' Enough said again. We delay all we can, until time runs out: 'The clock strikes, and is the knell of our welfare. . . . The old energy returns. We will labour *now*. Alas, it is *too late!*' We stand on the edge of a high cliff, scared of falling, and we want to fall because we are scared. Why do we do, or fail to do these things? 'There is no answer, except that we feel *perverse*. . . .'

> Examine these and similar actions as we will, we shall find them resulting solely from the spirit of the *Perverse*. We perpetrate them merely because we feel that we should *not*. Beyond this or behind this, there is no intelligible principle.

It is at this point that Poe delivers one of his finest jokes. The narrator of this philosophical tale is a murderer driven by the imp of the perverse not to his crime—that was entirely reasonable, a mere matter of wanting to get his hands on a comfortable inheritance—but to confessing it. No sooner does he think that no one can divulge his crime if he doesn't, than he craves to betray himself; and he does betray himself, *because* he knows it is what he must not do.

> And now my own casual self-suggestion, that I might possibly be fool enough to confess the murder of which I had been guilty, confronted me, as if the very ghost of him whom I had murdered—and beckoned me on to death.

On a casual reading it is easy to moralize this story. The narrator's theory of perverseness is a manifestation of crazy pride, an elaborate denial of the conscience which has nagged him all along, an 'intelligible principle' he cannot bear to acknowledge. Read more closely, and taken in conjunction with 'The Black Cat', the tale is more unsettling, and an impressive illustration of the narrator's argument as it stands. That the perverse may serve the cause of good as readily as it serves the cause of evil, that it can make you confess a murder as promptly as it can make you commit one, proves its genuine moral neutrality. Its only rule is that we must do what we know we should not do—by any criteria, moral or otherwise. The essence of crime, like the essence of all action, may be not hidden but meaningless, a capricious preference for harm.

Does Poe believe this? He entertains the thought, for its intellectual challenge, and for the havoc it creates among received ideas. For the check it places on Dupin's omniscience too. If the perverse were a primary impulse it would introduce into the trial of Poe's life a sophisticated plea for diminished responsibility, would even hint at a sophisticated form of innocence: I was completely at the mercy of the imp, as we all are. It is in this same spirit, I think, that Poe so regularly places his characters on the borders of madness. They insist, crazily, on their normality: 'you might have fancied me mad', 'mad am I not'. They complain of our suspicions: 'why *will* you say that I am mad?' They occasionally concede the point: 'We will say, then, that I am mad.'[48] Poe's aim, I suggest, is not to explore madness—the recurring show is too formal and too literary for that—but to rattle the windows of sanity. In the very funny story 'The System of Dr. Tarr and Professor Fether', the inmates of an asylum have taken over, locking their keepers away, and the whole joke rests not on the rather flat-footed quirks of the patients—one thinks he is a tea-pot, another a donkey, another a bottle of champagne, and so on—but on the ease with which the barmiest behaviour can be made to seem reasonable if you have the right theory. The Parisian visitor to the upturned asylum thinks some of the goings-on there rather strange, but reflects that he is in the provinces after all, and that 'the world is made up of all kinds of persons, with all modes of thought, and all sorts of conventional customs. I had travelled, too, so much as to be quite an adept in the *nil admirari* . . .' He is completely dazed, as well he might be, by the chief madman's discourse on the cunning of the lunatic:

> the dexterity with which he counterfeits sanity, presents, to the metaphysician, one of the most singular problems in the study of mind. When a madman appears *thoroughly* sane, indeed, it is high time to put him in a straight jacket.[49]

And when the rest of us appear thoroughly sane? The gag here attacks not the actual, practical distinction between madness and sanity, which is shifting and difficult enough, but the unreliability of the *signs* of madness. Madness, like much else in Poe, is not always where we look for it. Sanity itself, for example, may be littered with licensed madness, hidden on the surface, like the purloined letter, ample evidence of the primacy of the perverse.

.5

American writers in the nineteenth century, as A. Robert Lee has reminded us, loved sequences and cycles. Irving, Bierce, Hawthorne, Twain, Melville, Poe and others produced collections of stories in the way that Whitman produced lists, and perhaps for much the same reasons. They asserted identity while demonstrating heterogeneity. But Poe also needed his collections to underline the provisional nature of his propositions. 'I may', he wrote in his preface to *Tales of the Grotesque and Arabesque*, 'have written with an eye to this republication in volume form, and may, therefore, have desired to preserve, as far as a certain point, a certain unity of design.'[50] The *may* is odd, implies a hypothesis where none exists, since Poe goes on to say 'This is, indeed, the fact . . .'. 'Unity of design', in this context, is not a value in its own right, but a claim to a style made by a man who has other styles, or intends to have them. 'These many pieces are yet one book' is not an argument about a secret architecture, such as Baudelaire hinted at for *Les Fleurs du mal*, but a reminder that this is only *one* book; there were other writings before, will be others after.

The two volumes of *Tales of the Grotesque and Arabesque* included comic and lugubrious and speculative pieces, as did the *Tales* of 1845. The projected *Prose Romances of Edgar A. Poe* ran to only one volume (1843), but that one contained 'The Murders in the Rue Morgue' and 'The Man That Was Used Up'. Critics have assumed that Poe saw his lighter stories as grotesque and his darker ones as arabesque, but such a stiff distinction would have defeated his more sinuous purpose, and he seems in practice to have used both words to mean much the same thing: not exactly as synonyms, perhaps, but as near relations. The masqueraders in 'The Masque of the Red Death', for example, are said to be both grotesque and arabesque. Still, there is a slight, unsettling alternation in the terms. The grotesque surely is a touch more violent or extravagant; the arabesque slightly more elegant or convoluted or brooding. The chief point, of course, and this was the signal Poe's title clearly sent, is that *grotesque* and *arabesque*, like *terror* or *horror* or *the fantastic*, indicate the familiar norm even as they prepare to abandon it. The norm survives in such regions as a shadow or a memory, an unshakable part of the definition of the strange.

Poe's tales are *fictions* in the sense we have come to associate with the work of Jorge Luis Borges: constructions which question the often quite casual agreements we have converted into stable-seeming truths. The ideas Poe entertains—that the dead do not die, that the world is legible, that perversity is a primary impulse—are clearly very dubious, much better entertained than believed, but I hope I have said enough about them to suggest that their dubiousness is part of their performance and their power. The first and the third of the ideas I have looked at are, strictly, nonsense. If the dead do not die, they are not *dead*; a reaction to a provocation, however violent or unintelligible, cannot be a *primary* movement. The second is not nonsense, since the world is legible in all kinds of ways, and we read it daily. But the notion of a perfect legibility is apt to provoke nervous smiles rather than complacency. When Dupin identifies a knot in a small piece of ribbon as 'one which few besides sailors can tie, and is peculiar to the Maltese', we seem to have stepped not only into the chambers of Sherlock Holmes but into a world where the ambitions of deductive logic are parodied.[51] In Nabokov's play *The Event* an improbable detective greets a man he does not know with these words:

> Judging by certain outward signs intelligible only to an experienced eye, I can tell you that you have served in the navy, are childless, have recently been to the doctor, and are fond of music.

The other man replies, 'Wrong on all counts'.[52]

Poe's nonsense and parodies, like many enduring jokes and much philosophy, ask us not whether certain thoughts are true but why we can't make them go away. Even the solipsist, Wittgenstein said, does not expect the chair to be missing when he sits down. Poe did not expect his young wife back from the tomb. He did not believe that the world is perfectly legible, or that perversity is primary. He did wonder why we cannot lay our dead to rest, why we want so much to strip the world of its secrets, why perversity so often looks like the only explanation for uncontrollable and self-destructive human behaviour. He is like his hero in the story 'Mystification', who always seems laudably to be trying to prevent the very confusions he is causing. This is the 'beauty . . . of his *art mystifique*', and his face at such moments is 'radiant with the quizzical expression which was its natural character . . .'.[53]

We see Poe's tricks, but we do not easily see his radiance, because it is everywhere, because it is hidden on the surface. His shifting masks and registers should alert us to the thoroughly theoretical nature of his fictional enterprise. His impossibilities make us worry about what we have done with the notion of the possible. Are we sure the corpses we have buried still lie where we left them?

NOTES

1. Allen Tate, 'Our Cousin, Mr. Poe', in R. Regan (ed.), *Poe* (Englewood Cliffs: Prentice-Hall, 1972); T. S. Eliot, 'From Poe to Valéry', in E. W. Carlson (ed.), *The Recognition of Edgar Allan Poe* (Ann Arbor: University of Michigan Press, 1966); Harold Bloom, 'Inescapable Poe', *New York Review of Books*, 11 October 1984.

2. 'The Sleeper', *Poetry and Tales* (Library of America, 1984), p. 64. All further references to Poe's work are to this edition.
3. Jacques Lacan, 'Le Séminaire sur "La Lettre volée" ', *Ecrits I* (Paris: Editions du Seuil, 1970), p. 35.
4. T. S. Eliot, in Carlson, pp. 212–13.
5. Allen Tate, in Regan, p. 48.
6. 'Silence—a Fable', *Poetry and Tales*, p. 221.
7. 'The Facts in the Case of M. Valdemar', *Poetry and Tales*, p. 833.
8. 'Why the Little Frenchman Wears His Hand in a Sling', *Poetry and Tales*, p. 364.
9. 'Four Beasts in One—The Homo-Cameleopard', *Poetry and Tales*, pp. 184–85.
10. 'How to Write a Blackwood Article', *Poetry and Tales*, p. 282.
11. James W. Gargano, 'The Question of Poe's Narrators', in E. W. Carlson (ed.), *The Recognition of Edgar Allan Poe* (op. cit.). James M. Cox, 'Edgar Poe: style as pose', in Thomas Woodson (ed.), *Twentieth-Century Interpretations of "The Fall of the House of Usher"* (Englewood Cliffs: Prentice-Hall, 1969). Cox's essay is the subtlest piece of criticism of Poe I have come across.
12. 'Ligeia', *Poetry and Tales*, p. 262; 'Eleonora', *Poetry and Tales*, p. 472.
13. 'The Murders in the Rue Morgue', *Poetry and Tales*, p. 412.
14. Claude Lévi-Strauss, *Tristes Tropiques* (Paris, 1962), p. 44: *'tous trois démontrent que comprendre consiste à réduire un type de réalité à un autre; que la réalité vraie n'est jamais la plus manifeste; et que la nature du vrai transparaît déjà dans le soin qu'il met à se dérober.'* Jacques Lacan, 'Le Séminaire sur "La Lettre volée" ', p. 46.
15. Julian Symons, *The Tell-Tale Heart* (London: Faber and Faber, 1978), p. 207.
16. Stéphane Mallarmé, 'Le Tombeau d'Edgar Poe', *Oeuvres complètes* (Paris, 1945), p. 70.
17. E. H. Davidson, *Poe: A Critical Study* (Cambridge, Mass.: Harvard University Press, 1966), p. 106.
18. David Galloway (ed.), *The Other Poe* (Harmondsworth: Penguin Books, 1983), p. 13.
19. 'The Facts in the Case of M. Valdemar', *Poetry and Tales*, pp. 833–42.
20. James Joyce, *Ulysses* (London, 1960), p. 240.
21. 'The Black Cat', *Poetry and Tales*, p. 606.
22. See 'Sonnet—to Zante', 'Sonnet—Silence' and 'The Raven', *Poetry and Tales*, pp. 75, 77, 81–6.
23. 'A Descent into the Maelstrom', *Poetry and Tales*, p. 432.
24. 'The Man That Was Used Up', *Poetry and Tales*, p. 316.
25. 'The Man of the Crowd', *Poetry and Tales*, p. 388.
26. Harry Levin, *The Power of Blackness* (New York: Knopf, 1958), p. 156.
27. 'Morella', *Poetry and Tales*, p. 234. My later quotations from this story are to be found on pp. 239, 237, 235, 238.
28. 'Ligeia', *Poetry and Tales*, pp. 265–66. My later quotations from this story are to be found on pp. 277, 265, 269.

29. Marie Bonaparte, *The Life and Works of Edgar Allan Poe* (London: Imago Publishing, 1949), p. 130n.
30. David Halliburton, *Edgar Allan Poe: A Phenomenological View* (Princeton: Princeton University Press, 1973), p. 209.
31. 'Eleonora', *Poetry and Tales*, p. 473.
32. E. H. Davidson, op. cit., pp. 189, 190, 206.
33. See, for example, Davidson, p. 197; Leo Spitzer, 'A Reinterpretation of "The Fall of the House of Usher"', in Woodson, p. 60; Patrick F. Quinn, *The French Face of Edgar Poe*, quoted in Woodson, p. 88.
34. 'The Fall of the House of Usher', *Poetry and Tales*, p. 335.
35. 'The Man of the Crowd', *Poetry and Tales*, p. 388. Later quotations from this story are to be found on pp. 392 and 396.
36. 'The Murders in the Rue Morgue', *Poetry and Tales*, pp. 416–17.
37. Except when Poe needs to cheat a little, as with the window the orang-outang closes on its way out in 'The Murders in the Rue Morgue', or the broken nail in the same window.
38. 'The Gold-Bug', *Poetry and Tales*, p. 584.
39. 'The Murders in the Rue Morgue', *Poetry and Tales*, p. 397. Subsequent quotations from this story are found on pp. 397, 400, 401–2.
40. 'The Mystery of Marie Rogêt', *Poetry and Tales*, p. 507.
41. Patrick F. Quinn, in Woodson, p. 83.
42. T. S. Eliot, in Carlson, p. 208.
43. 'The Purloined Letter', *Poetry and Tales*, p. 695.
44. 'The Black Cat', *Poetry and Tales*, p. 597. Further quotations from this story are to be found on pp. 599, 599–600.
45. Charles Baudelaire, 'Notes nouvelles sur Edgar Poe', in Carlson, p. 47.
46. 'Loss of Breath', *Poetry and Tales*, p. 151.
47. 'The Imp of the Perverse', *Poetry and Tales*, pp. 826, 827. Further quotations from this story are to be found on pp. 828, 829, 831.
48. 'The Imp of the Perverse', 'The Black Cat', 'The Tell-Tale Heart', 'Eleonora', *Poetry and Tales*, pp. 830, 597, 555, 468.
49. 'The System of Dr. Tarr and Professor Fether', *Poetry and Tales*, pp. 702, 713.
50. 'Preface', *Poetry and Tales*, p. 129.
51. 'The Murders in the Rue Morgue', *Poetry and Tales*, p. 425.
52. Vladimir Nabokov, *The Man from the U.S.S.R. and Other Plays* (London, Weidenfeld and Nicholson, 1985), p. 259.
53. 'Mystification', *Poetry and Tales*, pp. 254, 257.

2

Washington Irving and the Land of Was

by HOWELL DANIELS

1

The first thing to say about Irving the short story writer is that he would probably not have recognized the term. Despite his now assured place as the inaugurator of a distinctively and in some ways peculiarly American literary genre, Irving did not regard himself primarily as a writer of short stories, and he seems to have been but fleetingly aware of the literary potentialities of the form.[1] Paradoxically, his reputation rests now, as it did in his lifetime, upon his undisputed masterpiece 'Rip Van Winkle' and, to a lesser extent, 'The Legend of Sleepy Hollow' which with 'The Spectre Bridegroom' are the only easily identifiable short stories in *The Sketch Book of Geoffrey Crayon, Gent.* (1820). *Bracebridge Hall* (1822) contains but four examples of the genre. Two years later, however, in *Tales of a Traveller* (1824) Irving published a series of stories of which the last three sections are set in England, Italy and the United States respectively. Irving expected much of this volume but its critical reception ensured that it was many years before he turned again to this particular narrative form. While *The Alhambra* (1832) includes a number of charming anecdotes and legends, it was not until the end of his life that Irving brought together a number of tales and longer fictions in a prolix and uneven miscellany entitled *Wolfert's Roost and*

Other Papers (1855). The revised collected edition of Irving's
works contained twenty-one volumes, but he had in effect
ceased to practise the form of the short story in 1824.

2

At the beginning of his career in England Irving may have
been reasonably secure in his identity as an American, but he
was profoundly if unsurprisingly unsure of his rôle as the first
American author to envisage writing as a profession. The
defensive ironies in his work (particularly evident in 'The
Author's Account of Himself' in *The Sketch Book*), the personae
of Diedrich Knickerbocker and Geoffrey Crayon (who in turn
invent other narrators), the adoption of framing devices, the
simultaneous seeking of authenticity and the undermining of
it, all point to a distinct unease in his situation. In terms of
form, Irving had no established tradition to draw upon; the
serial publications which his successors made use of and which
in turn affected the form of prose narratives were not available
to him. Something of this uncertainty is reflected in his letters:

> I notice what you say on the subject of getting up an original
> work, but I am very squeamish on that point. Whatever my
> literary reputation may be worth, it is very dear to me, and I
> cannot bring myself to risk it by working up books for mere
> profit.[2]

When submitting the first sketches by Geoffrey Crayon, he
wrote to his brother: 'Do not show the Mss. to any one, nor say
any thing about it. Write to Thomas [his publisher] *confi-
dentially*. It is better to awaken no expectations.'[3] In a later
letter he confided:

> I have attempted no lofty theme nor sought to look wise and
> learned. . . . I have preferred addressing myself to the feeling
> and fancy of the reader, more than to his judgement—My
> writings may appear therefore light and trifling in our Country
> of philosophers and politicians—but . . . I seek only to blow a
> flute accompanient in the national concert, and leave others to
> the fiddle and frenchorn.[4]

In his correspondence Irving refers not to the short story
but to 'various literary materials', a 'variety of writings'[5] and,

on occasion, seems to regard sketch and tale as interchange-able. It was not until *The Sketch Book* and *Bracebridge Hall* brought commercial success and public attention that he began to reveal something of his attitude towards his art. A letter of September 1823 to Peter Irving, referring to the 'quantities of these legendary and romantic tales now littering from the press in England and Germany', stresses that he wishes to avoid 'the commonplace of the day' and

> strike out some way of my own, suited to my own way of thinking and writing. I wish, in everything I do, to write in such a manner that any particulars may have something more than the mere interest of adventure to recommend them, which is very evanescent. . . .[6]

Irving's attitude to the writing of fiction is best expressed in his often-quoted letter of December 1824 to Henry Brevoort:

> I fancy much of what I value myself upon in writing, escapes the observation of the great mass of my readers: who are intent more upon the story than the way in which it is told. For my part I consider a story merely as a frame on which to stretch my materials. It is the play of thought, and sentiment and language; the weaving in of characters, lightly yet expressively delineated; the familiar and faithful exhibition of scenes in common life; and the half concealed vein of humour that is often playing through the whole—these are among what I aim at, and upon which I felicitate myself in proportion as I think I succeed. I have preferred adopting the mode of sketches and short tales rather than long works, because I chose to take a line of writing peculiar to myself; rather than fall into the manner or school of any other writer; and there is constant activity of thought and a nicety of execution required in writings of the kind, more than the world appears to imagine.[7]

Irving's letters also demonstrate that if he was uncertain of the rôle and the rewards of being a professional author, he was in no doubt as to his temperamental unsuitability for public office. To Brevoort, in 1821, he wrote somewhat tartly:

> How else am I to serve my country—by coming home and begging an office of it; which I should not have the kind of talent or the business habits requisite to fill?—If I can do any good in this world it is with my pen. . . . As to the idea you hold out of being provided for *sooner or later* in our *fortunate* city—I

can only say that I see no way in which I could be provided for, not being a man of business, a man of Science, or in fact any thing but a mere belles lettres writer.[8]

In rejecting commercial and political life for the solitary status of a professional author, Irving does not elaborate on the 'kind of talent' that he might bring to the literary life or, by implication, the importance of the imagination in that career. At the end of 1824, however, after some pungent reviews of *Tales of a Traveller* had appeared in the previous months, Irving wrote to his nephew Pierre P. Irving a long letter which effectively seeks to dissuade the young man from following in his footsteps and advises him to concentrate upon the law:

> I hope that none of those whose interests and happiness are dear to me will be induced to follow my footsteps and wander into the seductive but treacherous paths of literature. There is no life more precarious in its profits and fallacious in its enjoyments than that of an author. . . . I look forward with impatience to the time, when a moderate competency will place me above the necessity of writing for the press.

Despite the very considerable sums of money that his writings had procured for him, Irving's pointing out of the economic hazards in the life of the author is understandable; less easy to reconcile with Irving's own literary success are his remarks on the imagination which are expressed with a vehemence uncharacteristic of the author:

> Do not meddle much with the works of imagination. . . . Many and many a time have I regretted that at my early outset in life I had not been imperiously bound down to some regular and useful mode of life and been thoroughly inured to habits of business and I have a thousand time regretted with bitterness that ever I was led away by my imagination.[9]

The debate between the claims of the imaginative life and those of the larger world is also reflected in some of Irving's sketches and stories. 'Roscoe' considers with sympathy the position of the scholar-author in a commercial city; another business failure, on this occasion in America, is recorded in 'The Angler' where the bachelor fisherman lives contentedly in retirement on the pension which the loss of a leg in a naval battle brings him; some of the tales in 'Buckthorne and His

Friends' examine sceptically the nature of literary life and, in particular, the London literary scene. Reflected alike in his fiction and his letters are the landscapes of Irving's childhood and youth. Even in Buckthorne's account of his childhood one notes the intensity of feeling with which a generalized *English* landscape, complete with blue hills, is presented.

3

Two of the entries in Irving's notebook for 1817 read:

> Let me wander along the streams of beautiful England and dream of my native rivers [—] of my beautiful native country.

> The Lazy luxury of a summer day in the country—to lie in a bed of red clover with a book and look down on the Hudson. Sloops with sails flapping against the mast.[10]

America may constantly have been in his thoughts as he travelled around Britain, but there is nothing in Irving's literary career up to 1819 that either presages or explains the two masterpieces that he included in *The Sketch Book*: 'Rip Van Winkle' and 'The Legend of Sleepy Hollow'. The influence and popularity of these stories have been permanent and profound. At least sixty different editions of *The Sketch Book* were available before Irving's death in 1859[11]; indeed, it was estimated well over half a million copies of his works had been sold in the last decade of his life.[12] As an essayist, historian and biographer Irving was acclaimed in his lifetime, but ultimately he is remembered as the author of 'Rip Van Winkle'. With this one story Irving gave to Americans an identifiable and usable past; to the world he presented the first autonomous figure, as it were, of the American literary imagination.[13]

The two stories represent Irving's American version of the dream of order reflected in larger fashion in the book of which they form a part. In *The Sketch Book* Irving constructed, even invented, a static, timeless England at precisely the point in the history of the United States when his countrymen required a feudal rather than imperial Britain, a pre-1776 past which imperturbably blends the natural and historical picturesque. At the same time by grafting European legends on to a familiar

American landscape he offered American readers a recognizable past of their own. The key to 'Rip Van Winkle' is the escape from time, and it is also the dominant motif of *The Sketch Book*.

In the unchanging landscape of the Catskills Rip sleeps through twenty years of violent political transformation and social change. On his return to the village the portrait of King George on the inn sign has been replaced by that of another George who carries a sword and not a sceptre; even the 'very character of the people seemed changed. There was a busy, bustling disputatious tone about it, instead of the accustomed phlegm and drowsy tranquillity.' But despite the larger historical upheaval it is worth stressing that Rip's domestic scene has emphatically changed for the better: the death of his tyrannical wife enables him to be 'idle, with impunity' on the inn bench, an old widower who is also an historian and teller of tales of times before the war. Rip is now a man without woman in his nameless village at the foot of the Catskills, the 'fairy mountains', the 'blue highlands', in which he has been dislocated in time as effectively as the Catskills have been 'dismembered' in space.[14] Through supernatural agencies he has been denied the passing of time and the acts of history which take place in time. To him the political changes are finally without meaning. Within his narrow domestic and social circle order has not merely been restored; it has been improved upon.

Another assured and poised version of the recent American past is found in 'The Legend of Sleepy Hollow', a more leisurely and discursive tale which lacks some of the resonances of 'Rip Van Winkle'. Once again Knickerbocker's pen offers a quasi-historical (or pseudo-fictional) account, but the descriptions of Sleepy Hollow, that haunted and haunting region, suggest that the valley is Irving's version of the great good place which resists the relentless pressures exerted by time. The narrator comments:

> If ever I should wish for a retreat, whither I might steal from the world and its distractions, and dream quietly away the remnant of a troubled life, I know of none more promising than this little valley.

A 'drowsy, dreamy influence seems to hang over the land, and to pervade the very atmosphere' of this 'enchanted region', which provides fertile ground for the development of the imaginative faculties; even those who enter the valley 'are sure, in a little time, to inhale the witching influence of the air, and begin to grow imaginative, to dream dreams, and see apparitions'.[15]

In effect, Sleepy Hollow remains untouched by time and social change; 'population, manners, and customs, remain fixed, while the great torrent of migration and improvement, which is making such incessant changes in other parts of this restless country, sweeps by them unobserved.' A similar observation is made in different form later in the story:

> Local tales and superstitions thrive best in these sheltered, long-settled retreats; but are trampled under foot, by the shifting throng that forms the population of most of our country places. Besides, there is no encouragement for ghosts in most of our villages, for they have scarcely had time to finish their first nap and turn themselves in their graves, before their surviving friends have travelled away from the neighborhood. . . .[16]

Sleepy Hollow is the chief repository of such accumulated folklore: there 'was a contagion in the very air that blew from that haunted region; it breathed forth an atmosphere of dreams and fancies infecting all the land.' Recent history in the form of tales of the Revolutionary War abounds in the neighbourhood of the Van Tassel farm but not in Sleepy Hollow where the inhabitants 'walk in a continual reverie'.[17] The valley is as remote from reality as the portrait of pre-industrial England that emerges from other pages in *The Sketch Book*; and if, unlike Europe, the region is unable to offer 'the masterpieces of art, the refinements of highly cultivated society', it certainly provides 'the quaint peculiarities of ancient and local custom' that Irving refers to in 'The Author's Account of Himself'.[18]

The leisurely, ordered days, the profusion of animal and vegetable life, the sense of plenitude engendered by a benevolent nature, all suggest that Irving, albeit in a comic mode, is constructing a version of pastoral. The descriptions of the abundance offered by the Van Tassel farm and the products of its kitchens are particularly relevant, despite their primary appeal to Ichabod Crane's stomach. The lanky figure of Crane is the typical intruder into the established pastoral scene. As a schoolmaster, he is considered to be of 'vastly superior taste and accomplishment to the rough country swains'; neither of Dutch descent nor a native New Yorker, he comes from Connecticut, the state which 'supplies the Union with pioneers for the mind as well as the forest'.[19] Indeed, after his expulsion from the enchanted area—which adds another legend to the collection—this schoolmaster becomes progressively a lawyer, a politician, a judge, participating fully in the public life of the state but excluded for ever from the land of Cockaigne.

4

In these two tales fiction masquerades as history. 'Rip Van Winkle', we are told, was found among the papers of the 'late Diedrich Knickerbocker' whose researches included 'the legendary lore so invaluable to true history'. Irving the author causes Crayon, the primary narrator, to comment on the work of the secondary narrator, Knickerbocker, in such a way as both to establish authenticity and to question it. *The History of New York*, we are obliquely informed, possessed 'scrupulous accuracy . . . as a book of unquestionable authority'.[20] In the Note appended to the story Knickerbocker claims it is 'too well authenticated to admit of a doubt' and, having himself talked with Rip, the 'story therefore is beyond the possibility of doubt'. But in the narrative an alternative explanation is hinted at:

> He was observed, at first, to vary on some points every time he told it, which was, doubtless, owing to his having so recently awakened. . . . Some always pretended to doubt the reality of it, and insisted that Rip had been out of his head, and that this was one point on which he always remained flighty.[21]

'The Legend of Sleepy Hollow', according to the postscript, is related to Knickerbocker by 'a pleasant, shabby, gentlemanly old fellow' who on being taxed as to the truth of the tale replies, 'I don't believe one-half of it myself.'[22]

The multiplicity of narrators in Irving's work, the creation of personae, the defensive ironies, the attempted substitution of history for fiction, all point to an author profoundly insecure as to the legitimacy of fiction. In 'Rip Van Winkle' and 'The Legend of Sleepy Hollow' the idea of unreliable narration is largely external to the action of the stories; in his third collection, *Tales of a Traveller*, and especially in its first section 'Strange Stories by a Nervous Gentleman', Irving self-consciously plays with reader expectation and exploits the assumed response which the form and language of the narrative would seem to indicate. In effect, he subverts the short story as he invents it—but in the manner of the eighteenth rather than the twentieth century.

In these stories Irving parodies the typical concerns of the Gothic school of fiction. The choice of narrators and the formal linkages between the tales are skilfully done and, on occasion, as in 'The Bold Dragoon', a distinctive narrative voice is heard. But probably the best illustration of Irving's method is found in the short 'Adventure of the German Student', a powerful and eminently Romantic story told by 'the old gentleman with the haunted head' who has complained of the 'burlesque tendency' in the tales already given. The adventure, 'for the truth of which I can undertake to vouch, and which is of a very grave and singular nature', concerns a melancholy young man in Paris at the time of the Revolution who one night brings home a woman he finds at the foot of the guillotine. The next morning she lies dead in the student's bed, and it is revealed that she had been guillotined the day before. As the black collar around the neck of the corpse is untied, the head rolls onto the floor. The story ends:

> 'And is this really a fact?' said the inquisitive gentleman.
> 'A fact not to be doubted,' replied the other. 'I had it from the best authority. The student told it me himself. I saw him in a mad-house in Paris.'[23]

Unreliable narration is here close to entering the tale itself as the assurances of authenticity collapse.

Another form of questioning of conventional narrative is found in some of the tales of 'The Italian Banditti' (the ribaldry and subject-matter of which little pleased contemporary audiences), most notably in 'The Story of the Young Robber' where an account of multiple rape and murder is incapable of being travestied. The realism of this story causes it to fit uncomfortably into the comic mode which dominates this section. In particular, the English abroad are treated humorously. In his affectionately ironic portraits of the phlegmatic English in supremely picturesque Italy, Irving makes use of the freedom afforded by the expatriate perspective and anticipates the way in which in some of Henry James's fiction nationality functions as an index to character.

Knickerbocker is again resurrected to claim responsibility for the five stories which end *Tales of a Traveller*. Once again the reader is presented with some of the remembered landscapes of Irving's early years, 'a region of fable and romance' to him. The best of the stories is 'The Devil and Tom Walker', set just outside Boston in the year 1727 where the terrain is as flinty as the hearts of Tom Walker and his wife. Ultimately, however, the story tends to remain on the level of allegory, despite the narrator's attempt, almost as a sort of narrative tic, to claim historical veracity for it. His story is in turn followed by 'Wolfert Webber' which is told by 'one of the most authentic narrators in the province'.[24]

Examples of unreliable narration occur in Irving not because of any self-conscious belief in the validity and autonomy of fictional narrative but because of his profound misgivings concerning the genre, which arise in part from the lack of a literary tradition to guide him, from his own temperament, and from his situation as an American in a strange land. Meta-fictional elements in his prose derive from his attempts to historicize his stories, to give them the authenticity of fact, usually by means of frame narratives but occasionally by assertions within the text. Hazlitt was basically correct when in a perspicacious essay in *The Spirit of the Age* he commented that Irving's writings were

> literary *anachronisms* . . . Instead of looking round to see what *we are*, he sets to work to describe us as *we were*—at second hand. . . . Instead of tracing the changes that have taken place in society since Addison or Fielding wrote, he transcribes their account in a different handwriting, and thus keeps us stationary, at least in our most attractive and praise-worthy qualities of simplicity, poverty, hospitality, modesty and good-nature. This is a flattering mode of turning fiction into history, or history into fiction. . . .[25]

Despite the presence of glancing references to the contemporary in Irving's work, his writings lack the clear moral
and intellectual purpose evident in Fenimore Cooper's parallel
career in the 1820s and 1830s when he employed a variety of
literary forms to instruct as well as entertain his American
readers. The difference between the portraits of England in
Gleanings in Europe: England (1837) and *The Sketch Book* is far
greater than the seventeen years between their publication
would suggest. Something of the reticent Irving's own sense of
his ambiguous position emerges in a little-known story which
he included in *Bracebridge Hall*.

5

'The Stout Gentleman', written approximately mid-way
through the period 1819–24 when Irving was experimenting
with the form of sketch and story,[26] is a very short tale, an
account of a 'rainy Sunday in the gloomy month of November'
spent at an inn in Derby. As the sound of the rain mingles with
that of the bells, the narrator, 'a thin, pale, weazen-faced man,
extremely nervous', seeks 'to amuse the eye'; one window,
however, yields only a panorama of roofs and chimneys while
the other looks out over the stable-yard in which all nature has
been seemingly infected by the cafard that a wet English
Sunday induces. Even the eye attuned to the picturesque can
make little of this scene, one of the very few in Irving's writings
on England which attempts realistic description. Rain no
more falls upon his selected landscapes than it does on the
blue remembered hills of his American childhood.

The consolations offered by society are as inadequate as
those provided by the aesthetic impulse; the commercial
travellers in the public room of the inn disappear, as do the girls
at a window of a home opposite the inn, 'summoned away by a
vigilant vinegar-faced mother, and I had nothing further from
without to amuse me'. Accordingly, the narrator turns inward
to the imagination. Old books, newspapers, even graffiti all fail
to console, and the almanac contains the assurance 'expect-
much-rain-about-this time'.[27]

At this point in the story the presence of the stout gentleman,
newly arrived by coach, makes itself felt as the inn bustles to serve

him. For the narrator there is at last 'ample exercise' for his imagination as he speculates on the identity and the weight of the occupant of Room 13. From time to time the narrator is forced to modify the imaginary portrait for as fast as 'I wove one system of belief, some movement of the unknown would completely overturn it, and throw all my thoughts again into confusion'.[28]

The day passes; the rain continues to fall. A process which had begun as playful speculation to counter boredom now becomes an intensive attempt to unravel the mystery of the 'mysterious unknown'. Even the return of the salesmen fails to halt the narrator's quest: 'He had kept my fancy in chase during a long day, and it was not now to be diverted from the scent.' As midnight passes the narrator is determined to catch a glimpse of the occupant of Room 13, but the open door reveals only a chair at a table 'on which was an empty tumbler, and a "Times" newspaper, and the room smelt powerfully of Stilton cheese'.

The narrator sleeps badly, 'still haunted in my dreams by the idea of the stout gentleman and his wax-topped boots'. Late the following morning he is awakened by the sounds of the coach preparing to depart and rushing to the window he catches

> a glimpse of the rear of a person getting in at the coach-door. The skirts of a brown coat parted behind, and gave one a full view of the broad disk of a pair of drab breeches. The door closed—'all right!' was the word—the coach whirled off:—and that was all I ever saw of the stout gentleman![29]

In the reception of 'The Stout Gentleman' fiction and history begin to combine in a strange fashion. After the publication of *Bracebridge Hall* it was rumoured that the owner of the 'broad disk' was none other than Sir Walter Scott. Indeed, the prefatory letter, dated Michaelmas Day, 1822, to Scott's *Peveril of the Peak* describes the physical appearance of the author:

> a bulky and tall man, in a travelling great-coat, which covered a suit of snuff-brown . . . there was somewhat of a sarcastic shrewdness and sense, which sat on the heavy pent-house of his shaggy grey eyebrows. . . . A stout walking-stick stayed in his hand . . . his breeches were substantial thick-set—and a pair of

51

top boots which were slipped down to ease his sturdy calves did not conceal his comfortable travelling stockings. . . .

It struck me forcibly, as I gazed on this portly person, that he realised, in my imagination, the Stout Gentleman in No.11 [*sic*] who afforded such subject of varying speculation to our most amusing and elegant Utopian traveller, Master Geoffrey Crayon.[30]

Crayon, in turn, responded by commenting in 'The Great Unknown', a preface to the first story in *Tales of a Traveller*, that the narrator was not he but the nervous gentleman who had become 'excessively annoyed' at being asked to exhibit himself 'for no other reason than that of being "the gentleman who has had a glimpse of the author of *Waverley*" '.[31] As a consequence of Scott's contribution to the debate, a fictional character (who may or may not have been based upon an actual sighting of the novelist's rump) is given a semi-factual as well as fabular basis before reappearing in the comments of a fictional character (the nervous gentleman) who is in turn the creation of another fictional character (Crayon) created by Irving. The attempted validation of authenticity could hardly go further.

The details given concerning the stout gentleman are tantalizingly few but telling. He wears a brown coat over drab breeches; his room contains an empty tumbler, a *Times* newspaper and the smell of Stilton cheese, while outside stands a pair of boots with waxed tops. Two years earlier, in his essay 'John Bull', Irving had described an equally stout but mythical gentleman, based upon the caricatures of the figure of John Bull exhibited in London shops. The essay, influenced by the allegorical portrait in *The Diverting History of John Bull and Brother Jonathan* (1812) by James Kirke Paulding, Irving's brother-in-law, presents the familiar features of Bull: 'a sturdy, corpulent old fellow, with a three cornered hat, red waistcoat, leather breeches, and stout oaken cudgel'.[32] Although Irving points out that Bull has shrunk somewhat since his prime, his basic outline is not unlike that of Walter Scott. Indeed, part of Scott's description of himself might well fit comfortably into Irving's essay:

His age seemed to be considerably above fifty but could not amount to three-score, which I observed with pleasure, trusting that there may be a good deal of work had out of him yet; especially as a general haleness of appearance—the compass and strength of his voice—the steadiness of his step—the rotundity of his calf—the depth of his hem, and the sonorous emphasis of his sneeze, were all signs of a constitution built for permanence.[33]

Scott's features are 'rather heavy, than promising wit or genius'[34]; John Bull has 'little of romance in his nature but a vast deal of strong, natural feeling. He excels in humour, more than in wit. . . .' For all Bull's 'odd humours, and obstinate prejudices, he is a sterling-hearted old blade'.[35] Irving, after meeting Scott for the first time, wrote to his brother Peter: 'as to Scott, I cannot express my delight at his character and manners—he is a sterling golden hearted old worthy.'[36] The phrase is echoed many years later in Irving's preface to the revised edition of *The Sketch Book* where he pays his tribute 'to the memory of that golden-hearted man'.[37] The literal figure of Scott, then, seems to personify some of the physical and psychological characteristics of the traditional image of John Bull.

There is no reason to doubt the sincerity or warmth of Irving's feelings towards Scott. At the same time, it cannot be over-emphasized that Irving was deeply insecure, both as an American in England and as an American author seeking to earn a living by his pen in a foreign country. Despite the reception of the first volume of *The Sketch Book*, Irving in 'L'Envoy' at the end of the second felt it necessary to apologize for 'the numerous faults and imperfections' of his work, the 'deficiences' of which are exacerbated by his situation:

> He finds himself writing in a strange land and appearing before a public which he has been accustomed, from childhood, to regard with the highest feelings of awe and reverence. He is full of solicitude to deserve their approbation, yet finds that very solicitude continually embarrassing his powers, and depriving him of that ease and confidence which are necessary to successful exertion.[38]

In *Bracebridge Hall* Irving can even attribute his success to his exotic status:

> It has been a matter of marvel, that a man from the wilds of America, should express himself in tolerable English. I was

looked upon as something new and strange in literature; a kind of demi-savage, with a feather in his hand, instead of on his head; and there was a curiosity to hear what such a being had to say about civilized society.[39]

'The Stout Gentleman' may well be a parody of the process of 'associated ideas' which occurs with regularity in Irving's work. Expectations aroused by the tale and by the supremely bathetic conclusion at one level are a comment on the genre of mystery stories which the guests at Bracebridge Hall indulge in. The sub-title, 'A Stage-coach Romance', the epigraph from *Hamlet*, 'I'll cross it though it blast me!' (a reference to the ghost), and Crayon's introduction of the 'extraordinary narrative' with the sentence 'I think it has in it all the elements of that mysterious and romantic narrative so greedily sought after at the present day',[40] all suggest that Irving is here exploiting readers' responses to a literary convention in much the same way as several stories in *Tales of a Traveller* play with expectations aroused by certain types of narrative.

But, while it is certainly possible to enjoy the tale as a variant of the literary shaggy-dog story, it may also be regarded as an oblique statement of Irving's secret fears of rejection by the country which he had the temerity to portray in his writings. In this connection we recall the theme of the interloper in 'The Legend of Sleepy Hollow' and in 'Rip Van Winkle' where the ninepin players stare at Rip 'with such fixed, statue-like gaze, and such strange, uncouth, lack-lustre countenances, that his heart shook within him and his knees smote together'. We remember, too, Rip's confusion and bewilderment after his awakening when he finds himself a stranger in a hostile community. On this reading the final comic but also offensive gesture of the stout gentleman depicts the imagined response not merely of an anonymous—or distinguished—individual but of an entire society to all the anxieties and doubts with which Irving was afflicted. Two years later, at the end of 'The Strolling Manager', Buckthorne retires to a country estate as a result of an inheritance: ' "I've done with authorship. That for the critics!" said he, snapping his fingers.'[41] Irving after the reception of *Tales of a Traveller* indulged in a different sort of retreat as he moved from fiction into history and published in succession *A History of the Life and Voyages of Christopher Columbus* and *A Chronicle of the Conquest of Granada.* The decision, however, may already have been made in 'The Stout Gentleman' whose conclusion represents the most fundamental response that life can make to art.

NOTES

1. 'The American short story began in 1819 with Washington Irving.' This is the opening sentence of the first chapter of F. L. Pattee's pioneering study *The Development of the American Short Story* (1923). Pattee listed forty-eight short narratives which to him qualified as short stories; Charles Neider in his edition of *The Complete Tales of Washington Irving* (1975) stretches an admittedly elastic term and reprints sixty-two 'stories'.
2. Ralph M. Aderman, Herbert L. Kleinfield and Jenifer S. Banks (eds.), *Washington Irving: Letters* (Boston: Twayne Publishers, 1978), Vol. 1, p. 520.
3. Ibid., p. 539.
4. Ibid., p. 543.
5. Ibid., pp. 614, 647.
6. *Letters* (Boston: Twayne Publishers, 1979), Vol. 2, p. 5.
7. Ibid., p. 90.
8. *Letters*, Vol. 1, p. 614.
9. *Letters*, Vol. 2, pp. 84, 85.
10. Walter A. Reichart and Lillian Schlissel (eds.), *Washington Irving: Journals and Notebooks* (Boston: Twayne Publishers, 1981), Vol. 2, pp. 182, 197.
11. Stanley T. Williams and Mary Ellen Edge, *A Bibliography of the Writings of Washington Irving: A Check List* (New York: Oxford University Press, 1936), p. xii.
12. Carl Bode, *The Anatomy of American Popular Culture* (Berkeley and Los Angeles: University of California Press, 1959), p. 203.
13. Although the tale together with its companion piece has been much reprinted and frequently illustrated, the history of the relationship between picture and text has yet to be systematically examined. Since Philip Young's richly suggestive article, 'Fallen from Time: The Mythic Rip Van Winkle', *Kenyon Review*, XXII (1960), 547–73, the story has been profitably examined from a variety of viewpoints.
14. Haskell Springer (ed.), *The Sketch Book of Geoffrey Crayon, Gent.* (Boston: Twayne Publishers, 1979), pp. 37, 40, [29].
15. Ibid., pp. 272, 273.
16. Ibid., pp. 274, 289.
17. Ibid., pp. 289, 273.

18. Ibid., p. 9.
19. Ibid., pp. 276, 274.
20. Ibid., p. 28.
21. Ibid., p. 41.
22. Ibid., pp. 296, 297.
23. Charles Neider (ed.), *The Complete Tales of Washington Irving* (Garden City, New York: Doubleday, 1975), pp. 222, 227.
24. Ibid., pp. 430, 448.
25. *The Spirit of the Age* (London: Henry Colburn, 1825), pp. 421–22.
26. In his admirable *Washington Irving: An American Study, 1802–1832* (1965) William L. Hedges analyses in detail Irving's literary experiments during these years.
27. Herbert F. Smith (ed.), *Bracebridge Hall or The Humourists. A Medley by Geoffrey Crayon, Gent.* (Boston: Twayne Publishers, 1977), pp. 50, 51.
28. Ibid., p. 54.
29. Ibid., pp. 54, 55, 56.
30. Walter Scott, *Peveril of the Peak* (Edinburgh: Adam and Charles Black, 1871), pp. 9–10.
31. *Complete Tales*, p. [195].
32. *Sketch Book*, p. 248.
33. Scott, p. 10.
34. Ibid.
35. *Sketch Book*, pp. 249, 255–56.
36. Letters, Vol. 1, p. 501.
37. *Sketch Book*, p. 7.
38. Ibid., p. 299.
39. *Bracebridge Hall*, p. 3.
40. Ibid., p. 48.
41. *Complete Tales*, p. 357.

3

Authorship and Authoritarianism in Hawthorne's Tales

by DAVID TIMMS

by DAVID TIMMS

1

It is paradoxical that while Hawthorne's early efforts in the short story were directed at making explicit collections, unified thematically or formally, the collections that were actually published were not conceived as such.[1] Most of the tales and sketches from *Twice Told Tales* (1837, 1842), *Mosses from an Old Manse* (1846) and *The Snow Image* (1851) in effect were reprints, having already appeared in periodicals and Christmas annuals and the like. *The Snow Image* in particular was compiled from extremely miscellaneous sources,[2] comprising both Hawthorne's earliest work as well as tales written subsequent to the appearance of *Mosses from an Old Manse*.

In view of their publishing history, then, it is not surprising that despite their urge to extrapolate a unified authorial personality from the collections of tales before them, Hawthorne's contemporary critics should have found a paradoxical and complicated figure. The most famous formulation of this multifacetedness is of course Melville's:

> In spite of all the Indian-summer sunlight on the hither side of Hawthorne's soul, the other side—like the dark side of the physical sphere—is shrouded in a blackness, ten times black.[3]

Others noticed the same quality, including the man who commissioned Melville's review, Evert Duyckinck:

> Imagine a man of a rugged frame of body and a fancy within airy, fragile and sensitive as a maiden's; the rough hairy rind of the cocoa-nut enclosing its sweet whiteness; fancy all this as a type of Nathaniel Hawthorne, and you have some idea of the peculiarities which impart their strength and their weakness to his writings.[4]

The idea of a mixture of male and female is almost a commonplace of nineteenth-century Hawthorne criticism. Reviewers did not notice, however, that the tendency to diametrical opposites itself subverts the idea of looking for the author behind the book. But this split characterization of the voice of the tales is instructive; Hawthorne's narrative voices are not uniform; there is no sure authorial personality immediately evident in them. I wish to argue in what follows that this is consonant with a distrust of authority observable in Hawthorne's works as a whole. For Hawthorne, some kinds of authorship imply authoritarianism, and what is sought in his texts is a relationship with the reader that is collaborative, not dictatorial.

2

Several figures in the tales show Hawthorne's awareness that the profession of authorship involved the risk of losing proper contact with the rest of humanity or of dominating others. An example of the first risk is Oberon in 'The Devil in Manuscript'. The story is narrated by Oberon's friend, who visits him one snowy evening to find the author in a mood of deep melancholy. His stories have not been taken up by the booksellers to whom he has sent them, and he proposes to burn the manuscripts and renounce authorship for ever. As the flames rise, he describes the hold authorship has had upon his brain, and says that his muse is a 'fiend' that has kept him in thrall. The fire is a purgation. But suddenly the two men are roused by a commotion outside: the flames have set the chimney ablaze. Oberon does not realize the cause of the fire, but is exultant because the scene will furnish literary material:

'In an hour, this wooden town would be one great bonfire!
What a glorious scene for my next—Pshaw!'[5]

Oberon catches himself, but not before we have seen the fact
that the human sympathies he should have had for those who
might lose life and livelihood in the blaze are replaced by a
love of the picturesque. When he sees that his own manuscripts are the cause of the fire it is clear that his taste for a
literary dénouement has similarly supplanted his concern for
humanity: 'Here I stand—a triumphant author! Huzzah!
Huzzah! My brain has set the town on fire! Huzzah! (*SI*, 178).
But another author is involved in this, for someone other than
Oberon is telling us the story. The narrator is extraordinarily
equivocal. From what he says to his friend, Oberon certainly
does not believe him to have any literary leanings of his own:
'my peace is gone, and all by these accursed manuscripts.
Have you felt nothing of the same influence?' (*SI*, 171). The
narrator replies 'Nothing', but he has a curious reaction to
Oberon's act. He thinks on the one hand that he would be
pleased if Oberon's tales were 'out of [his] sight', and that they
'would make a more brilliant appearance in the fire than
anywhere else'. But on the other, he tries to stay his friend at
the moment the manuscripts go on the flames: 'But, all at
once, I remembered passages of high imagination, deep
pathos, original thoughts, and points of such varied excellence,
that the vastness of the sacrifice struck me most forcibly' (*SI*,
175). He confesses jokingly that he has himself felt the urge to
turn novelist on reading Oberon's stories, and recognizes to
the reader that in writing, being 'the victim of [one's] own
enchantments', there is 'a strange sort of happiness' and that
he is 'smitten with a strange longing to make proof of it' (*SI*,
174). Is the story itself proof that the 'strange longing' has
been fulfilled? Certainly the speaker is not simply a medium
for Oberon: his opening description of the snowy night goes
beyond mere scene-setting into the epideictic, a fact which he
notices himself: 'After this picture of an inclement night . . .'
(*SI*, 170). Just as Oberon forgets the misfortunes he has visited
upon his neighbours when he sees the fire as grist to his
story-telling mill, the narrator forgets the derangement of his
friend, and perhaps, shows the jealousies of the aspirant
author in his early denigration of Oberon's efforts.

An author may become domineering, as may be seen in the early 'Alice Doane's Appeal'. It is a curious story-within-a-story, or perhaps more properly a story-outside-a-story. It is told by a narrator who is a man of letters, and who has written, years ago, a story about witchcraft and high passions and murder in which a malevolent wizard had contrived a confrontation between a young man, Leonard Doane, and one Walter Brome, who is afterwards revealed to have been his brother, on the subject of their sister. Brome, without knowledge of their kinship, has tempted his sister to 'shame' (*SI*, 272). The confrontation results in the murder of Brome by Doane. Afterwards the guilt-stricken murderer and his sister visit a graveyard where spectres in Purgatory have come to bear witness to the crime; the sister, Alice of the title, makes an appeal to Walter, who 'absolve[s] her of every stain', on which 'ghost and devil fled, as from the sinless presence of an angel' (*SI*, 277). This story is revealed to us sometimes as extracts and sometimes in the form of summary by the narrator, who is describing the effects of his telling it while out on a walk one June afternoon to two 'young ladies' of his acquaintance. He has chosen the venue of the walk, Gallows Hill, even though, as he recognizes, a nearby place called 'Paradise' would have been a more fitting setting for his companions; he says gallantly that they would have been 'at home there'. He himself, he tells us, 'often courted the historic influence of the spot', but it is part of his text that he is unusual, and the general 'are people of the present and have no heartfelt interest in the olden times' (*SI*, 266–67). His companions are clearly more 'of the present' than he would like, for try as he will he cannot make them shudder at his grisly tale. Even after he has told them of the spectral gathering among the gravestones, they 'began to laugh, while the breeze took a livelier motion, as if responsive to their mirth' (*SI*, 278). He is 'piqued' at this, and decides to conjure up a procession in their imaginations, describing a hypothetical crowd of all those persecuted in 'old witch times', and at last succeeds:

> I strove to realize and faintly communicate, the deep, unutterable loathing and horror, the indignation, the affrighted wonder, that wrinkled on every brow, and filled the universal

heart. . . . But here my companions seized an arm on each side;
their nerves were trembling; and sweeter victory still, I had
reached the seldom trodden places of their hearts, and found
the well-spring of their tears. (*SI*, 278–80)

The narrator's glee is clearly evident, and his vocabulary
underlines the violence of his experiment; it is a 'victory' and
he has 'trodden' in new places in their hearts. In the end, this
story-teller, with his indecent urge to reduce young women to
tears, is really no different from the stern-faced Cotton Mather
in whose 'figure on horseback, so darkly conspicuous, so
sternly triumphant' 'were concentrated those vices of spirit
and errors of opinion, that sufficed to madden the whole
surrounding multitude' (*SI*, 279). Here we see the story-teller
in his worst guise, allied with the egocentric mob-rouser, the
one who preys on people's emotions and manipulates people's
feelings for a sense of personal triumph.

Hawthorne is critical of the egocentric author, then, but he
also subverts his personal status as author in the tales and
sketches. Many of them contain matter that is extrinsic to the
stories proper but present their authorial origin in a way that
undermines its authority. The very title *Twice Told Tales* could
be understood to mean that they do not originate from the
person whose name is on the title-page, and in fact Hawthorne
did not add his explanation that they are 'twice-told' because
they had appeared earlier in magazine form until the edition of
1851. Some of the stories have sub-titles or 'editorial' addenda
that cast doubt upon the creative capacities of the author.
'Egotism; or The Bosom Serpent', and 'The Christmas
Banquet' are both identified as being from 'the Unpublished
"Allegories of the Heart" ', and 'Ethan Brand' is called 'A
Chapter from an Abortive Romance'. One group of pieces is
called 'Passages from a Relinquished Work'. Other matter
ridicules the author himself. One of the darkest tales,
'Rappaccini's Daughter', has a mocking preface from a
supposed editor announcing that the tale following is trans-
lated from the French works of one M. Aubépine. He describes
this Aubépine in terms exactly like those the speaker uses of
himself in 'The Old Manse', except that Aubépine's works are
apparently voluminous where Hawthorne's are slender. His

opinion of Aubépine is as critical as Hawthorne's of himself: reading through Aubépine's work has been 'wearisome'; he can find 'affection' for his author, but not 'admiration' (*MM*, 92). An editorial footnote in 'Time's Portraiture' criticizes the modern bearer of the old New England name of 'Hathorne' for adding a supernumerary 'w' (*SI*, 331).

Moreover, the creative status of many of the pieces is dubious, for the line between genres is blurred. Poe referred to this in reviewing *Twice Told Tales* when he complained that the title is a misnomer since the inclusions 'are by no means *all* tales, either in the ordinary or the legitimate understanding of the term. Many of them are pure essays. . . .'[6] He might also have said that many of them are 'impure' essays, in the sense that it is often very difficult to decide whether we are being offered something for consideration as a fiction or as a descriptive piece. 'Little Annie's Ramble', for instance, is a piece that Poe calls an 'essay', and which Hawthorne's contemporaries found a

> sketch, simple, natural, full of child-like feeling, of a child's stroll with her friend through the gay streets of the town, by the printshops and the toy-shops, through all the little worlds of gorgeous sights, which arrest infancy's lingering steps on its earliest walks.[7]

Much of the 'sketch' is certainly taken up with descriptive matter as the narrator and his companion pause before the sights. But it is also a purely fictional piece about the speaker. He claims that he has taken his walk with the little girl—which we learn at the end has caused much distress to her mother, since he failed to tell her that he was taking Annie away—because 'the pure breath of children revives the life of aged men' whose 'moral nature [is] revived by their free and simple thoughts, their airy mirth, their grief, soon roused and soon allayed' (*TT*, 129). In fact, the narrator does his best throughout the story to draw Annie's attention to the miseries of existence; he wonders if in the busy streets the 'rattling gigs . . . will be smashed to pieces before our eyes' (*TT*, 122) and points out to her 'a shrill voice of affliction, the scream of a little child, rising louder with every repetition of that smart, sharp, slapping sound, produced by an open hand on tender flesh' (*TT*, 128). Annie is not herself allowed a single word in the story to lighten it. Surely this narrator has something of the quality of Dimmesdale as he re-enters Boston after agreeing with Hester to run away to Europe; he has the urge to corrupt the innocent and blight their happiness. And the deliberateness and 'poetic' quality of the description of the slaps, alliterative and overlexicalized, suggests the narrator's unwholesome and prurient mentality. 'Little Annie's Ramble', then, is as much a psychological study as a representation of the shop windows of a provincial New England town; the nature of the creative act that produced it is neither wholly one thing nor the other.

There is also a blurring of the distinction between what the reader takes to be fact and what he or she takes to be a fiction. Roderick Elliston is the unfortunate sufferer who has the snake in his bosom in 'The Bosom Serpent', and he is the narrator of 'The Christmas Banquet'. But he has very much the manner, style and method of introducing his tale as has the omniscient narrator of, say, 'David Swan' or 'Fancy's Show Box'. Many of the characters in the stories whose profession is writing have very similar lineaments to those Hawthorne gives himself in his prefaces: rather obscure and unsuccessful, and with an inveterate tendency to allegorizing. Are we listening to 'Hawthorne', or to his creation?

Within the tales themselves too Hawthorne often withdraws from those elements of authorial/narratorial function that most clearly suggest authoritativeness. His reliable narrators are very reluctant to assert any superiority. We find very little in their stories of what Barthes calls the 'cultural' or 'reference code', that is, comments by the narrator on the world outside the story, artistic-scientific, moral. Barthes's description of this 'code' is made during his discussion of Balzac's *Sarrazine* in *S/Z*, where he quotes two 'lexies' from Balzac's text: 'I was deep in one of those daydreams which overtake even the shallowest of men, in the midst of the most tumultuous parties.' He comments: 'The statement is made in a collective and anony-mous voice originating in traditional human experience.'[8] Roger Fowler expands: 'The narrative stance created by the invocation of these cultural codes joins narrator and reader in a compact of knowing discourse.'[9] Barthes is surely right and wrong. Right to the extent that Fowler implies in his gloss; such comments appeal to a human experience that is assumed to be shared. But the voice itself is anything but anonymous, it clearly characterizes a narrator. And further, even though it does as Fowler says create an in-group who are 'in the know', set off against an 'out-group' that comprises most significantly the subject of the story being retailed, it is not an in-group of equals. The narrator has to make a considerable rhetorical effort not to sound didactic. George Eliot, for instance, manages it, though many would disagree; Balzac, to my view, does not, and it is surely this that James was thinking of when he complained that in Balzac you have to scan 'elaborate messes of folly' before you reach 'one little flower of available truth'.[10] One of the rhetorical intentions of using this 'reference code' is to build up a foundation of authority so that as Fowler says, 'from this base the narrator can claim general acceptance of the judgements he makes on the world within the story.'[11]

'Young Goodman Brown' is like Sarrazine one of the naïve. But in Hawthorne's story the 'reference code' is virtually absent. I can find only three clear examples; they are references to a shared moral world rather than an artistic or scientific or legendary. They are: (a) '. . . the instinct that guides moral man to evil' (*MM*, 83); (b) 'The fiend in his own shape is less hideous than when he rages in the breast of man' (*MM*, 84); and (c) 'Unfathomable to mere mortals is the lore of fiends' (*MM*, 85). It is significant that the first of these does not come until the story is more than half way through; it comes at a point in the story at which the narratorial stance shifts dramatically. The plot of story is simple: Young Goodman Brown, previously pious inhabitant of a colonial New England village, leaves his wife of three months, Faith, to keep an appointment in the forest with devil worshippers. He is shocked to find on the journey and when he sees the worshippers that all those he had previously held in high regard, including his new wife, are also of the devil's party. At the end we are left in some doubt as to whether Brown's experience is a dream or an actuality, but the effect is the same: to turn Brown into a gloomy misanthrope for the rest of his life.

The reference code, as I comment above, allies narrator and implied reader and excludes the subject of the story. The reason that there are no examples of the reference code in the early part of the story is that the narrator's rhetorical effort is to ally himself with the reader *and* Brown, and use of the reference code at this point would have broken down this attempt. Where the narrator judges rather than merely reports, the judgement is such a one as might have been made by Brown himself, or by the as yet uninformed reader if he/she had been within the story; the narrator does not remind us of his special status. This feature is marked when Brown meets a mysterious figure along the path:

> As nearly as could be discerned, the second traveller was about fifty years old, apparently in the same rank of life as Goodman Brown, and bearing a considerable resemblance to him though perhaps more in expression than in features. Still, they might have been taken for father and son. And yet, though the elder person was as simply clad as the younger, and as simple in manner, too, he had an indescribable air of one who knew the world. . . . (*MM*, 76)

Description is a narrative function that does not make the narrator as 'visible' as summary, or the kind of commentary contained in the 'reference code'. Nonetheless, it is as Barthes says allied to the epideictic, and can be used to show off the descriptive skills of the narrator.[12] Stephen Crane's descriptive paragraphs are prime examples of this. But here, rather than put himself forward as authority, Hawthorne's narrator conceals himself behind Brown. The description is full of qualifications and uncertainty: 'apparently . . . perhaps . . . might have been . . . indescribable'. The narrator himself never clears up the riddle of the strange gentleman's resemblance to Brown; it is left to one of his accolytes whom we meet along the way.

The first example of the reference code we meet is at the point in the story at which Brown ceases to vacillate, and declares 'My Faith is gone. . . . There is no good on earth, and sin is but a name.'

> And maddened by despair, so that he laughed loud and long, did Goodman Brown grasp his staff and set forth again, at such a rate, that he seemed to fly along the forest path, rather than to walk or run. The road grew wilder and drearier, and more faintly traced, and vanished at length, leaving him in the heart

of the dark wilderness, still rushing onward, with the instinct that guides mortal man to evil. (*MM*, 83)

It is only at this point that the narrator implies that he and the reader share a moral world not inhabited by Brown: but the hero has deserted us rather than vice versa; the narrator asserts moral superiority not on the grounds of authority, but on the grounds of a demonstrated failure on the part of his subject.

But is the narrator now instructing the reader? Again, this passage, and the story in general, shows Hawthorne withdrawing from one of the positions of narratorial authority. The narrator never resolves for us the problem of whether or not the whole episode is a figment of Brown's imagination; but further, he undermines the status even of those elements in the story that might be supposed to have 'really' happened to Brown, particularly the trip into the forest. The idea of the journey representing a spiritual journey is of course a conventional one, and here its potential as allegory is reinforced by the vocabulary Hawthorne uses of it, particularly the Biblical 'wilderness'. The status of the episode as literal fact is also shaken by the narrator's imputations of uncertainty: 'he *seemed* to fly. . . .' It is not that behind the flight through the forest we can discern an allegory; rather its double nature is asserted so that it is both real and symbolic at once, the narrator pressing neither as a 'primary' reading.

3

Throughout Hawthorne's fiction there is a deep scepticism about the motives of authority figures, even though such figures appear in very different forms. Perhaps the mildest is the obtuse father in 'The Snow Image' who, failing to believe his children when they insist that their playmate is made of snow and cannot stand the heat of the stove, forces her into the warm and melts her. Sometimes they are figures whose motives might be laudable in other contexts, but whom an obsession has made monstrous. Aylmer in 'The Birthmark' is such a figure, who in trying to eradicate what he sees as the one fault in his wife's otherwise perfect beauty kills her. Such figures might be seen as tragic, but their endeavours are at best misguided, and at worst evil.

But there is another class of these figures, who appear in the tales of New England history: colonial governors or leaders, religious and military, and Hawthorne's presentation of them suggests his complete belief in the adage that power corrupts. There is a small gallery of these figures: Richard Digby in 'The Man of Adamant', Governor Andros who appears in 'The Grey Champion' and is mentioned elsewhere as a 'tyrant', Cotton Mather, described as the foremost persecutor of witches in 'Alice Doane's Appeal'. The most interesting of them is John Endicott; interesting not simply because he appears at least three times in Hawthorne's stories, twice as a major figure, but also because his rôle is problematical, for this argument. In 'Endicott and the Red Cross' he appears superficially to be for all his sternness an anti-authority figure, a New England patriot resisting the dictates of an English monarch. 'Endicott and the Red Cross' is a version of an episode from New England history. John Endicott, a Puritan leader, on receiving notice that Charles I was to send an Anglican governor to New England, tore the red cross from the English ensign to show his contempt for British rule and for the high-church religion the cross suggests. 'Endicott and the Red Cross' recounts his hearing the news and his rebellious act, and incidentally offers a 'sketch' of the New England township in which the act was performed. In the first paragraph the narrator offers an outline suggesting an increasingly difficult political situation between the colonies and the Crown, which the King and his chief minister were trying to remedy by violence and main strength. It is clear that the narrator in no way supports the efforts of Charles and Laud to dictate to the American people. The final paragraph is a coda in which the narrator hails Endicott's act as the first in a series which was to culminate in the American Revolution, and which he says entitles the name of Endicott to be 'for ever honoured' (*TT*, 441).

Between the opening abstract and the coda that finishes 'Endicott and the Red Cross' there are three distinct sections. The first describes Endicott and digresses from him to what can be seen reflected in his highly polished breast plate, and from these scenes to, first, the 'engines' of 'puritanic authority': whipping post, pillory and stocks, with malefactors suffering punishment; and second, to the crowd of inhabitants, among whom are singled out those who still bear the marks of this authority having been exercised in the past:

> . . . some, whose ears had been cropt, like those of puppy dogs; others, whose cheeks had been branded with the initials of their misdemeanors; one, with his nostrils slit and seared; and another, with a halter about his neck, which he was forbidden ever to take off, or to conceal beneath his garments. (*TT*, 435)

The second part is concerned with Endicott's conversation with an arrival, the Puritan divine Roger Williams, who brings the letter announcing the Anglican governor. The third deals with Endicott's refusal to abide by the injunction of Governor Winthrop and Williams himself not to stir up any commotion which might give the King 'a handle' against his subjects; his rousing speech to the assembled crowd; and his climactic tearing of the red cross from the flag.

In each section Endicott's status as the champion of liberty and freedom hailed by the coda is undermined. Endicott is described solely in terms of his grey beard and the iron breastplate singled out as his most salient feature in 'The Maypole of Merry Mount'. And its suggestions of aggression are heightened by the fact that in its highly reflective surface can be seen the dripping bloody head of a wolf nailed to the porch of the Puritan meting house: a neat way of connecting the bloody symbol directly with both the habitation of the Puritan religion and its embodiment in one man. The contiguity of the description of the physical machinery of Puritan oppression to the description of Endicott metonymically associates the two, and lest we might think that this is an unusual day in the colony's history, the description of the maimed in the crowd reminds us of the fact that this oppression is perennial and not occasional.

In the next section, the opposition of Endicott and Roger Williams is significant. Williams was known all his life as a promulgator of the most democratic aspects of the religion the Pilgrim Fathers took to the New World, and he was himself persecuted for his attempts to put into practice his beliefs that church government and civil government should be based on the consent and equality of individuals. Endicott is made here not only to flout directly the advice of the Governor and Williams, but 'imperiously' to silence the preacher when he remonstrates against Endicott's inflammatory and dangerous insults to the English royal line. The third section is Endicott's speech, full of absurd hyperbole about the outcome of the efforts of the proposed Anglican Governor: 'We shall hear the sacring-bell, and the voices of Romish priests saying the mass' (*TT*, 440). In tearing out the red cross he again makes use of his sword, underlining his position as a warlike Puritan of a very different stamp from Roger Williams. When Endicott takes his stand on 'civil rights' and 'the liberty to worship God according to our conscience', we hardly need the outburst of the 'Wanton Gospeller' who is being punished for exercising exactly that right, or the 'sad and quiet smile' that 'flitted across the mild visage of Roger Williams' (*TT*, 439) to understand that Endicott is a bigot of the worst order for whom liberty means only the freedom to believe as he believes.

What then are we to make of the nationalistic coda which applauds Endicott? Even Frederick Crews, who reads the bulk of the tale as I do, and who recognizes that the story 'has been taken by most critics as a glorification of the Revolutionary spirit' feels that 'Hawthorne's opening and closing paragraphs . . . provide the basis for this straightforward reading.'[13] But this is to see the central parts of the story as separate from the opening and coda, and to see them solely in terms of what they refer to rather than how things are referred to. In fact, the *narrator* of 'Endicott and the Red Cross' is a nationalist throughout; it is the implied author of the tale who is sceptical, and who includes the narrator in his scepticism. For all his evident bigotry, Endicott is never described in other than heroic terms by this narrator, and the criticisms of his words and deeds that beg to be made are made where they are made at all by characters within the story, like the Wanton Gospeller and Roger Williams. The narrator's catalogue of the appalling cruelties perpetrated on the various members of the populace contains not a single note that suggests pity for them or thankfulness that such things are no longer done. At one point the text threatens to modulate into such a condemnation:

> Let not the reader argue, from any of these evidences of
> iniquity, that the times of the Puritans were more vicious than
> our own, when, as we pass along the very street of this sketch,
> we discern no badge of infamy on man or woman. (*TT*, 435)

As we read this we surely expect the 'iniquity' in question to
be the iniquity of punishing offenders in so monstrous a way.
But in fact we are the victims of a semantic confusion; the
iniquity the narrator refers to is the iniquity the Puritans
punish, and he reflects that if his own contemporaries had
methods of outward punishment as visible as those the
Puritans used, they should still see scarlet letters and cropped
ears and halters on the streets! He seems regretful as a man of
letters that such picturesque sights are denied to modern
times, an attitude that has already been announced in his
comment that 'by a singular good fortune for our sketch, the
head of an Episcopalian and suspected Catholic was gro-
tesquely encased' (*TT*, 434) in the pillory. The hard-
heartedness Endicott puts to the service of his religion and his
country this narrator puts to the service of his art and his
country; his coda is really no surprise, for he has implied that
he is rather like Endicott all along, as much by what he does
not say as by what he does. Endicott, despite the coda, is as
much a tyrant and egotistical authoritarian as the royal power
he seeks to pull down—and if this narrator does not notice it,
the implied author of the tale certainly does. Part of his
message must be that even when authoritarians seem to be on
your side, they are nonetheless to be distrusted for their
egotism.

4

It is clear that Hawthorne saw himself as out of step in
authorial practice with his contemporaries. His presentation of
himself in his prefaces emphasizes the fact that he lived in a
backwater, was 'the obscurest man of letters in America' (*TT*,
3). And the fact that he felt he had to explain the nature of his
fictions, which he does in preface after preface, indicates that
he did not want his books read with conventional expectations. His insistence that his readers should not expect his
fictions to follow 'the probable and ordinary course of man's

experience'[14] implies that he wanted to distinguish his mode of writing carefully from the mode most salient in his lifetime: realism.

Contemporary commentators on nineteenth-century realism underline its authoritarian implications. Jonathan Culler's restatement of Sartre's view of the nineteenth-century novel is that it is 'told from the viewpoint of wisdom and experience and listened to from the viewpoint of order'.[15] The language of realism, according to John Ellis and Rosalind Coward, is 'the language of mastery'.[16]

According to Marshall McLuhan, it is only after the isolation of the sense of sight induced by print culture that the idea of the author, the 'fixed point of view' becomes possible.[17] That fixed point of view is surely the basis of the insistence on 'order' that Sartre refers to, for the foundation of realism as a literary mode is that conviction that there is a common world of phenomena referred to by the author the broad outlines of which we must accept as being independent of our individual perception. The author formulates truth in the realist novel and the reader consumes it. The Age of Realism is also the age in which it became convention for the author of a novel to be named on its title page. And author, according to Foucault, implies authoritarianism:

> The author allows a limitation of the cancerous and dangerous proliferation of significations within a world where one is thrifty not only with one's resources and riches, but also with discourses and their significations. The author is the principle of thrift in the proliferation of meaning.[18]

We can see what Foucault means by looking at the conclusion of Trollope's *Barchester Towers* (1857). 'The end of a novel,' says Trollope, 'like the end of a children's dinner party, must be made up of sweetmeats and sugar-plums.'[19] Trollope dispenses, reassures, comforts; he is not exactly thrifty in terms of content here, but he is in terms of principle; he is paternal and so authoritarian, he not we will determine what we as readers are to get.

Hawthorne's presentation of himself in his prefaces is not designed either to establish his credentials as a litterateur or to impress himself upon the world as a personality. Though 'The

Old Manse' was read by some of Hawthorne's contemporaries as a piece that sets itself up as autobiography, as a kind of apology for the author, Hawthorne clearly thought that such critics had missed the point. He comments in *The Snow Image* that 'a little preliminary talk about his external habits, his abode, his casual associates, and other matters entirely on the surface . . . hide the man, instead of displaying him' and he warns that the only way to 'detect any . . . essential traits' of the author is to 'look through the whole range of his fictitious characters, good and evil' (*SI*, 14). And indeed what 'The Old Manse' offers is not any genuine biographical information about Hawthorne; it might rather be seen as *Mosses from an Old Manse* in little, for it is itself a series of mini-tales and sketches suggested by certain features of the history and geography of the immediate locale of his house. A recollection of a mossy gravestone causes him to break off and tell a very short story of the Revolution, when a local lad roused from woodchopping by the sound of muskets rushed to the source of the sound and killed an English soldier with his axe. A mention of the lily pond makes him speculate on the paradox that the same milieu produces one kind of lily that is pure white and sweet smelling and another that is yellow and stinks. This is clearly the stuff the tales proper are made of, and what 'The Old Manse' achieves is not autobiography but rather a model for how the tales should be read.

'Nobody', says one of the characters in Hawthorne's last completed novel, *The Marble Faun*, 'ought to read poetry, or look at pictures or statues, who cannot find in them a great deal more than the artist has expressed. Their highest merit is suggestiveness.'[20] This is certainly an expression of Hawthorne's own views, as his comments on painting and story throughout the *French and Italian Notebooks* makes clear. It stresses the belief articulated in Hawthorne's anti-authoritarian stance that the relationship of author and writer is not one of teacher and taught. That stance throughout the tales is different from the one implied by conventional realist texts of his time. Hawthorne encourages his reader to be a producer rather than a consumer of meanings.

In 'Ethan Brand', which a sub-title declares to be 'A

Chapter from an Unfinished Romance', Hawthorne's narrator describes his hero's fate:

> . . . where was the heart? That, indeed, had withered—had contracted—had perished! It had ceased to partake of the universal throb. He had lost his hold of the magnetic chain of humanity. He was no longer a brother man, opening the chambers of the dungeons of our common nature by the key of holy sympathy, which gave him a right to share in all its secrets; he was now a cold observer, looking on mankind as the subject of his experiment, and, at length, converting man and woman to be his puppets, and pulling the wires that moved them to such degrees of crime as were demanded for his study. (*SI*, 99)

Hawthorne's terminology here is very suggestive. The word 'observer' and its derivatives is one that tolls through nineteenth-century criticism of the novel as the keynote of realist writing, the faculty that the realist writer must cultivate to succeed, and on which all realist writing was declared to rest. The description of Brand looking on mankind as a subject of experiment calls to mind Zola's comparison in 'The Experimental Novel' between the new 'naturalist' novelist and the scientist. This formulation of Brand's 'Unpardonable Sin' makes Brand as clear an authoritarian as Endicott, and his great fault rests on a similar basis: an egotism that cuts him off from others. Seen in this light, Hawthorne's rejection of authoritarianism and his corollary modification of the conventional authorial stance of most of his contemporaries are intimately related. His wish to make his reader a producer of meaning rather than a passive recipient of it becomes more than a technique by which his texts achieve meaning. He consistently mentions in his prefaces that the chief merit of the stories is that they served to 'open an intercourse with the world' (*TT*, 16), that they led to 'the formation of imperishable friendships' (*TT*, 7) and that he prefers to think of his readers as 'a circle of friends' (*MM*, 34). The engagement of storyteller and reader he engineers is itself an instance of 'friendship' and imaginative sympathy that Hawthorne identifies as the basis of our moral and social life.

NOTES

1. For an account of Hawthorne's early attempts to make collections, see Arlin Turner, *Nathaniel Hawthorne: A Biography* (New York and Oxford: Oxford University Press, 1980), pp. 69–79.
2. See 'Historical Commentary', in *The Centenary Edition of the Works of Nathaniel Hawthorne, Vol. XI: The Snow Image and Uncollected Tales*, ed. William Charvat, Roy Harvey Pearce, and Claude M. Simpson (Columbus, Ohio: Ohio State University Press, 1974), pp. 379–409.
3. Herman Melville, 'Hawthorne and his Mosses' (1850, in J. Donald Crowley (ed.), *Hawthorne: The Critical Heritage* (London: Routledge and Kegan Paul, 1970), p. 115.
4. Evert Duyckinck, 'Nathaniel Hawthorne' (1845) in *Hawthorne: The Critical Heritage*, p. 97.
5. 'The Devil in Manuscript', *The Centenary Edition of the Works of Nathaniel Hawthorne, Vol. XI: The Snow Image and Uncollected Tales*, p. 177. Future references will all be to the volumes of tales in this edition, which includes, besides *The Snow Image*, Vol. IX, *Twice Told Tales* (1974) and Vol. X, *Mosses from an Old Manse* (1974). I will make such references in abbreviated form (*SI, TT, MM*) in the body of the text.
6. Edgar Allan Poe, Untitled Review (1842), in *Hawthorne: The Critical Heritage*, p. 87.
7. Andrew Preston Peabody, Untitled Review (1838), in *Hawthorne: The Critical Heritage*, p. 65.
8. Roland Barthes, *S/Z*, trans. Richard Miller (New York: Hill and Wang, 1974), p. 18.
9. Roger Fowler, *Literature as Social Discourse: The Practice of Linguistic Criticism* (London: Batsford, 1981), p. 101.
10. Henry James, *French Poets and Novelists* (London: Macmillan, 1876), p. 88.
11. Fowler, p. 101.
12. Roland Barthes, 'L'effet du Réel', *Communications*, 11 (1968), p. 88. Quoted by Seymour Chatman, *Story and Discourse: Narrative Structure in Fiction and Film* (Ithaca and London: Cornell University Press, 1978), p. 144.
13. Frederick Crews, *The Sins of the Fathers: Hawthorne's Psychological Themes* (London: Oxford University Press, 1966), p. 41.
14. 'Preface', *Centenary Edition . . ., Vol. II: The House of the Seven Gables* (1965), p. 1.
15. Jonathan Culler, *Structuralist Poetics: Structuralism, Linguistics and the Study of Literature* (London: Routledge and Kegan Paul, 1975), p. 195.
16. Rosalind Coward and John Ellis, *Language and Materialism: Developments in Semiology and the Theory of the Subject* (London: Routledge and Kegan Paul, 1977), p. 49.
17. Marshall McLuhan, *The Gutenberg Galaxy: The Making of Typographic Man* (London: Routledge and Kegan Paul, 1962), p. 136.
18. Michel Foucault, 'What Is An Author?', in *Textual Strategies: Perspectives*

in *Post-Structuralist Criticism*, ed. Josué V. Harari (London: Methuen, 1979), pp. 158–59.

19. Anthony Trollope, *Barchester Towers* (1857; Harmondsworth: Penguin Books, 1982), p. 495,

20. *Centenary Edition . . ., Vol. IV: The Marble Faun* (1968), p. 379.

4

Voices Off and On: Melville's Piazza and Other Stories

by A. ROBERT LEE

> In summer, too, Canute-like, one is often reminded of the
> sea. For not only do long ground-swells roll the slanting grain,
> and little wavelets of the grass ripple over upon the low
> piazza, as their beach, and the blown down of dandelions is
> wafted like the spray, and the purple of the mountains is just
> the purple of the billows, and a still August noon broods upon
> the deep meadows, as a calm upon the Line; but the vastness
> and the lonesomeness are so oceanic, and the silence and the
> sameness, too, that the first peep of a strange house, rising
> beyond the trees, is for all the world like spying, on the Barbary
> coast, an unknown sail.
>
> And this recalls my inland voyage to fairy-land. A true
> voyage; but, take it all in all, interesting as if invented.
>
> —'The Piazza', *Piazza Tales* (1856)

1

So, part-way into 'The Piazza', Melville has his narrator
assume the voice of an evidently poetical ex-mariner. Just
previously, he has had him speak in turn as a piazza-builder, a
weather-gazer, and a quirky source of gossip to his country
neighbours. Such the teller; the tale, a promised 'inland
voyage to fairy-land', beckons quite as engagingly. We could

hardly ask for a more inventive call to attention, a more enticing invitation into Melville's short fiction. Or at least into the stories which make up his only collection, *Piazza Tales* (1856), those selected from the sixteen which with one exception he first published between 1853 and 1856 in *Putnam's Monthly Magazine* and *Harper's New Monthly Magazine*.[1]

But as so often in Melville's story-telling, on pursuing 'The Piazza' further any temptation to complacency or too confident a sense of direction begins to give way to unease and ambiguity. Not only will this 'voyage to fairyland' turn darkly unbucolic, but the narrator himself by the end will have been driven to lonely night-thoughts, 'haunted' pacings of his piazza deck. What by his own terms might have been a 'Midsummer's Night Dream', a quest for 'rainbow's end', becomes cankered, a stark, isolating process of disillusion. Equally, the quintet of tales to which 'The Piazza' acts as prologue will be anything but 'summery', incidental diversions to be read in the spirit of 'a still August noon'. Quite the contrary: a more unsettling fictional realm of displacement, loss, exile and illusion would be hard to imagine. And just as 'The Piazza' and its story of the narrator's encounter with the mountain girl Marianna begins as would-be 'romance' (duly buttressed by references to Spenser and *Cymbeline*) only to end a bleak, cautionary tale, so, too, all of Melville's Piazza and other short fiction will offer narrative which turns in on itself, seeming to tell the one thing while telling in fact quite another. 'True . . . but . . . interesting as if invented' supplies the perfect gloss. For like the Hawthorne whose 'wild, witch voice' he has 'ring through' his 'Virginian Spending July in Vermont', the ostensible writer-narrator of his deeply admiring 'Hawthorne and his Mosses' published in August 1850 as a two-part review in the *Literary World*,[2] Melville also rarely deploys a story-voice which does not dissimulate or unfold stories only outwardly the 'inventions' they appear. His narrators, whether first- or third-person, accordingly have to be heard several ways at once, the voices of Melville's sense of the world as conundrum and endlessly cross-plied and contradictory.

'Voices off and on', thus, is meant as a directional fix on Melville's manner of making us 'hear' his stories, his styles of narrative disclosure. Whereas writers like Hawthorne or James have long been admired, not to say analysed, for their tactics of voice—be it as 'point of view', or tone, or the creation of the reader—Melville far less so.[3] Yet whether, as is overwhelmingly the case, we listen to him in his guise of a purposely fashioned authorial 'I', or as an objectified, third-person voice, the general effect is strikingly of a kind. Our sense of both telling and tale has to be extraordinarily acute, in the case of the former because it resorts to voices which can dazzlingly mislead or deceive, and in the latter because Melville's virtually every story amounts to a 'story-within-a-story', 'inside narrative' to quote the half-title of *Billy Budd, Sailor* (1888–91). Both constitute crucial dynamics in Melville's short fiction, the means behind his inspired accounts of the hidden, often desperate and certainly unexpected, edges to human behaviour.

Little wonder, in retrospect, that to his initial American-Victorian readership, Melville's stories where encountered at all were taken to confirm that he had gone askew. The one-time season's find who had launched himself with *Typee* (1846), all sailorly adventure and South Seas warmth and Rousseauism, was no more. The warning-signs were to show ominously in the other full-length work which followed, in sequence *Omoo* (1847), *Mardi* (1849), *Redburn* (1849), *White-Jacket* (1850), *Moby-Dick* (1851), and an especial cause of dismay, *Pierre* (1852). Melville the mariner-turned-teller had become ever more difficult, full of unwanted metaphysics and perversity of pose. How could the stories be thought other than mid-career eccentricity, a falling-away? And certainly by the time of *The Confidence-Man* (1857), the last of the full-length narratives to be published in his lifetime, and of his poetry, 'eminently adapted for unpopularity' as he once ruefully described it,[4] the evidence looked conclusive. Obscurity had become all and Melville himself a spent, inaccessible force.

Even Melville's rehabilitation in the 1920s, worthy as it was, did little to supply new focus or support for the stories, perhaps unavoidably as it tended to centre on the essential adventureliness of *Moby-Dick* and of his other different Atlantic and Pacific sea narratives. The stories, in one sense, could not avoid seeming a reduction of power as much as scale. Then, too, to have thought him a short-fiction writer as against the expansive chronicler of ocean and shipboard life— and one especially gifted in subtleties of voice—would have meant some partial abandonment of his legend as yet another American literary 'life' figure. No longer could he be thought simply the artless, ingenuous literary sailor home from the seas, any more than Mark Twain (at any rate the genius behind his great river novels *Huckleberry Finn* and *Pudd'nhead Wilson*) could be thought simply the former steamboat pilot who had done no more than transpose a few boyhood Missouri tall tales into written narrative form.

Melville has slowly won his due as a far more conscious writer than once perceived, and nowhere better than in *Moby-Dick* itself. Despite its exhilarating 'sea-room'[5] and 'hell-broiled'[6] voyaging-out, it clearly represented a more complex conception and telling than its first promoters ever acknowledged. Its celebrated 'careful disorderliness'[7] in truth masked a most careful orderliness. Over time, too, this has led on to a still growing respect across the board for Melville's fiction both long and short. So that whether it has been the arresting nature of Melville's visions in his stories—the apparitional appearance of an anorexic law-copyist in Wall Street, the Galápagos islands as a 'hell' of reptilianism and burnt-out cases, or a Spanish slave-ship over-run by its black human cargo and under the mock-command of its prisoner captain, to give the best-known instances—or whether it has been because the stories demonstrate his skills of narration in briefer compass, they have undoubtedly gained in the process. Rightly so, too, we might feel moved to add. They offer instances of his best, most challenging and demanding, work.[8]

In a connected way, the stories have also frequently been thought Melville's covert way of answering-back, *exercices de style* by which to avenge himself on, or at least to complain and grumble at, an age which once had lauded but later repudiated him. The move-over to short fiction probably did have something in it of a defensive nature, prompted in addition by Melville's rising need for cash and a more regularized income to support his wife Elizabeth and their young family. But none of these factors, whether the eclipsing effect of *Moby-Dick*, or his reputation as before all else a Man of the Sea, or the view of the stories as merely ancillary to the longer work and altogether too querulous and off-centre, need any longer seriously detain us. None of which is to deny unevenness, some obviously lesser work, and one or two near-failures. But key stories like 'Bartleby' (1853), 'The Encantadas' (1854) and 'Benito Cereno' (1855), to which this essay gives its main attention, show him utterly in the first rank of story-telling, dramatic further endorsement were it still needed of his place both as a major figure of the American Renaissance and a Master of the Revels far beyond.

2

Before turning to the Piazza fiction proper, I want to pause over a story which illustrates perfectly Melville's mastery of voice—'The Town Ho's Story', first issued in *Harper's* in October 1851, then in two subsequent publications, and incorporated into *Moby-Dick* as Chapter 54.[10] When read as part of the latter, it accretes a run of implications. It functions as a 'gam' episode, one among nine others; it contains a prophetic warning of how the *Pequod*'s journey will end; and in as far as it is kept from Ahab it serves as another hidden text in a narrative renowned for its secret nooks and crannies. But however best read, as a chapter of *Moby-Dick* or of and for itself, it offers a vintage exhibition of story-telling voice. It indeed puts before us the crucial intervention of the white whale; but at the same time it makes quite another order of appeal. We are left in no doubt that this is but one telling of many given by Ishmael, and possibly by others, yet a telling wholly unique and singular.

We are alerted at the outset that some more than 'objective' narration is about to unfold when Ishmael sets up a frame for his reader/listener to respond to:

> For my humor's sake, I shall preserve the style in which I once narrated it at Lima, to a lounging circle of my Spanish friends, one saint's eve, smoking upon the thick-gilt tiled piazza of the Golden Inn.

At one level we hear a sea-story, that of the Mate Radney's 'down' on the Lakeman Steelkilt, the latter's revenge, punishment and escape, and the destruction of the Mate by the white whale, eventfulness in plenty one might think. We also hear of the tale's earliest transmission; it seemingly began as 'the private property' of three white sailors, 'confederated' with an otherwise Polynesian crew, who told it to the harpooner Tashtego to binding oaths of secrecy. But he, unwittingly, rambled in his sleep, 'and revealed so much of it that way, that when he awakened he could not well withhold the rest'. Intervening at this point as the authorial 'I', Ishmael then vows to put on 'lasting record' 'the whole of this strange affair'. 'For my honor's sake', be that a story-telling gesture of good faith or something else, he now re-tells it as he alleges he once did for a group of high-born Peruvian drinking cronies, a story thus poised between English and Spanish and confessedly just one of many past ways it has been narrated. Interrupted a dozen times by these 'Spanish' listeners, asked to define words like 'Lakeman' and 'canallers', and required to play his part in jibing at priests and acknowledging the parallel between New World Hispanic Lima and Old World Italian Venice, Ishmael is moved consciously to tilt and 'stage' his story for the occasion. He assumes a voice of witness as it were, an 'I was there' authentication, yet also a voice utterly aware of its present showmanship. But that should not really surprise in a narrator who begins his larger story with the words 'Call me Ishmael', as direct yet actually as indirect and pseudonymous a piece of self-staging as any in Western fiction.

Moved eventually by sun, drink, and the rising momentum of the Dons' question and his own story-telling keenness to meet them fully and persuasively, he calls half-heretically but in the manner of any good tap-room orator for a 'copy of the Holy Evangelists' to 'prove' the 'truth' of his account. And this despite the manifest ambiguity of his story's genesis, its recognized legacy of different conflicting and reworked tellings, and his own unabashed relish of the rôle of performer. Ishmael's 'style of narration' almost to a fault signals Melville's command of voice: the narrator's assumption of story-telling authority, his readiness to improvise and ride with each interruption, his throat-clearing and different tics of style. Melville also so appeals to us as *his* reader, responding to a factitious narrator, inviting us to watch and hear Ishmael's every oratorical trick of the trade, and obliging us to acknowledge that the whole occasion belongs in the gift of himself as behind-the-scenes author. For Melville the manner of a story's telling palpably deserves equal status with the story itself, an equation in which voice is of the essence. In all these respects 'The Town Ho's Story' offers a marker for the voicing of the *Harper's* and *Putnam's* magazine fiction which shortly was to follow.

3

Of all Melville's Piazza stories, probably none seeks a more exacting response to voice than 'Bartleby'. Most of the explicatory accounts have become familiar enough, especially 'Bartleby' as a parable of the dead-letter fate of his own books with the scrivener the surrogate figure of his own rejection. Melville, too, had refused to 'check his copy', to go on writing in imitation of an agreed, rule-of-thumb reality. Other accounts can be readily added.[11] Bartleby offers a 'parable of walls', an existential, eerily modern story in which an alienated humankind would 'prefer not' to inhabit its unsought 'absurdity' of being.[12] Or 'Bartleby' tells a religious fable of sorts, Bartleby as the spurned Christ or Buddha driven to a muteness akin to that of the 'fleecy' Eastern stranger who appears aboard the *Fidèle* in *The Confidence-Man*, Melville's unknowable, voiceless avatar who chalks up quotations on Charity from Corinthians, 1, 13.[13] Slightly less cosmically, 'Bartleby' offers a classic portrait of personality disorder, catatonia perhaps, or schizophrenia, in which lawyer and clerk constitute divided facets of a single temperament, a story not dissimilar in kind to Henry James's 'The Jolly Corner'. Or 'Bartleby' tells a Wall Street story almost to the letter, the epicentre of business America seen as murderous to the human creative spirit. Yet however persuasive these and related other readings, they have been concerned with thematic analysis. 'Bartleby' can as profitably be read through its operative means, none more so than voice.

For a start, it begins as almost nothing *but* voice, the narrator lawyer at pains to make us listen to everything on his terms, he as subject and Bartleby as object. He it is,

82

accordingly, who sets the parameters within which we are to understand this strange drama of walls and exile. His parade of credentials, which I contract slightly, could not be more insistent, especially about his self-effacement and discretion:

> I am a rather elderly man. The nature of my avocations, for the last thirty years, has brought me into more than ordinary contact with what would seem an interesting and somewhat singular set of men, of whom, as yet, nothing that I know of, has ever been written—I mean, the law-copyists, or scriveners. I have known very many of them, professionally and privately, and, if I pleased, could relate divers histories, at which good-natured gentlemen might smile, and sentimental souls might weep. But I waive the biographies of all other scriveners, for a few passages in the life of Bartleby, who was a scrivener, the strangest I ever saw, or heard of. While, of other law-copyists, I might write the complete life, of Bartleby nothing of that sort can be done. . . .
>
> Ere introducing the scrivener, as he first appeared to me, it is fit I make some mention of myself, my *employés*, my business, my chambers, and general surroundings; because some such description is indispensable to an adequate understanding of the chief character about to be presented. Imprimis: I am a man who, from his youth upwards, has been filled with a profound conviction that the easiest way of life is best. Hence, though I belong to a profession proverbially energetic and nervous, even to turbulence, at times, yet nothing of that sort have I ever suffered to invade my peace. I am one of those unambitious lawyers who never addresses a jury, or in any way draws down public applause; but, in the cool tranquillity of a snug retreat, do a snug business among rich men's bonds, and mortgages, and title-deeds. All who know me, consider me an eminently *safe* man. The late John Jacob Astor, a personage little given to poetic enthusiasm, had no hesitation in pronouncing my first grand point to be prudence; my next, method. I do not speak it in vanity, but simply record the fact, that I was not unemployed in my profession by the late John Jacob Astor; a name which, I admit, I love to repeat; for it hath a rounded and orbicular sound to it, and rings like bullion. I will freely add, that I was not insensible to the late John Jacob Astor's good opinion.

How, in fact, are we to take this voice? Is it what it purports, gentle, well-meaning, discreet, that of a walker in the shadow of others and to be taken completely at its word as 'un-ambitious', 'eminently *safe*' and unprone to 'dangerous indignation at wrongs and outrages'? Is it, to the contrary, smug, unctuous, quite as walled-in as Bartleby's by its fetishistic love of the Wall Street order of things? Is it not, also, a voice telling its story as of the present and at the same time in retrospect, regretting the abolition of the Master of Chancery sinecure, and not so much passingly 'affected' by Bartleby as completely turned about and traumatized by his arrival? About the only thing of which we can be absolutely certain is that of an already 'singular set of men', law-copyists, Bartleby will indeed be 'the strangest I ever met'. The more, then, the lawyer sets out his credentials—a lawyer never given to addressing a jury, 'snug', the three-times repeater of the name of John Jacob Astor—the less we can be sure that he will say all there is to say about Bartleby. One moment he sounds a voice confident of its own axis, the next disoriented, uncertain how best to act. Should he give voice to, or act on, sensations which lie outside of his cherished realms of 'safety'?

However, in fact, we do hear his voice, in one important sense we cannot avoid hearing in it the assumption of consensus, the self-appointed tone of the centre. He speaks as an intimate of business's rules and rhetoric, capitalism not as the hard clash of market competition but as a 'bonded' and legalized right order—be it of 'work', conduct, society, the very rhythm of the day, week, sabbath or year. His is the voice of a would-be standard of ordinariness, whether he speaks as of 'now' or with a paining backward glance. In situating the narrator at the greatest temperamental remove from the forlorn, barely audible, 'unreasonable' Bartleby, Melville can the more convincingly register his lawyer's rising hysteria at each successive 'prefer not to' and refusal to copy. Whatever else, the lawyer's is a voice riding for a fall, a check to its own certainty.

We meet, too, other voices, all of which help to contextualize that of the lawyer. The story offers the testimonies of Turkey and Nippers, half-baked 'morning' and 'afternoon' scriveners—writers prepared to settle for half at least—with correspondingly half-baked opinions. There is available, just about, the testimony of Ginger Nut, the dollar-a-week office boy anxious to emulate and placate his elders. We hear, too, in order, the angry remonstration of the lawyer's successor in his shafted, Wall Street office, the complaint of his former landlord, and the rumour of clients leaving and a possible mob, all brought on by Bartleby's 'stationary' and unspeaking sentinelship. With Bartleby removed to the Tombs, still other voices testify. One of the turnkeys wonderingly calls him 'the silent man'. The grub-man who thinks Bartleby 'odd' and 'a gentleman forger', amazes at his refusal of dinner, the world's everyday nutrition. We hear, too, of the lawyer's baffled resort to the voices of philosophic authority. 'Edwards on the Will' and 'Priestly on Necessity'.

Above all, we hear Bartleby's own voice, descending from a whisper to voicelessness and preferring not to copy, not to check, not in any way to affirm or validate the world of the lawyer. His is the exquisite but intransigent voice of withdrawal into silence. Not for nothing has he on occasion been interpreted as Thoreauvian passive resistance or dissent taken to its ultimate expression. 'I know you . . . and I want nothing to say to you', he 'says' to his one-time, risingly desperate, employer. Curled foetally at the foot of the Tombs prison wall, his eyes open and gaze-like, he opts or recedes into wordlessness, extrication from his own and all the voices about him. In this, 'a bit of a wreck in mid-Atlantic' as the lawyer patronizingly and only in part comprehendingly calls him, he incarnates nothing less than the Dead Letters—once 'errands of life'—which formerly were in his charge. For him all language, all copy, all letters, and assuredly all voice, have become void: *tout le reste est silence*. He can offer only unvoiced witness, the testimony of the unspoken. Lawyer and scrivener thus end bound one into the other, perhaps different and opposite, perhaps two dimensions of a single self. One has aspired 'safely' to the world's eloquence, the other 'unsafely' to a terrifying eloquence of silence. Melville so tells 'Bartleby' as a colloquy, or colloquium, and with as sure a grasp of the tactics of voicing as anything he wrote.

85

4

Melville's other triumph of first-person voicing lies in 'The Encantadas', his sequence of ten allegorized story sketches of the Galápagos, each with its Spenserian heading and each at once free-standing and a part of the sequence as an integrated whole. To read them as a single stretch of narrative, however, is again to become powerfully aware of Melville's ventriloquy, his control of story-telling register. Within the one voice we cannot but hear others: Melville as veteran whalerman and one-time man-of-war enlistee, or as antic Darwinian naturalist (*The Origin of Species*, that other Galápagos classic, appears in 1859), or as the self-posturing teller of seeming tall tales and gimcrack doggerel, or, and more soberly, as the haunted witness to the stories of Hunilla and Oberlus and all the other recurring population who have washed up on these volcanic outposts of the Pacific. Melville modulates into a run of sub-voices, each an aspect of the voice at the centre but each incrementally different. The sub-voice, for instance, in which he opens Sketch First, might be thought humouresque, a dare to its 'landsmen' (to employ a term from *Moby-Dick*)[14] readers to try even imagining a world as apparently infernal and spent as the Galápagos:

> Take five-and-twenty cinders dumped here and there in an outside city lot; imagine some of them magnified into mountains and the vacant lot the sea; and you will have a fair idea of the general aspect of The Encantadas, or Enchanted Isles. A group rather of extinct volcanoes than of isles; looking much as the world at large might, after a penal conflagration.

Melville maps this 'vacant lot' like an inspired impressionist. Formed out of 'cinders', 'dross', 'dark clefts' and 'ashes', the isles offer 'a Plutonian sight', at once 'uninhabitable' and 'woe-begone'. Air and sea conspire into 'dark, vitrified masses'. 'Screaming' flights of unearthly birds hover ominously. Sea-wrecks are to be found, 'relics' and 'charred wood'. And as if the inheritors of this 'fallen' terrain there exist but 'mosses', 'wiry shrubs' and crawling things—'tortoises, lizards, immense spiders, snakes, and that strangest anomaly of outlandish nature, the *iguana*'. Apart, too, from the off-shore birds, on *terra* *firma* only 'voiceless' reptile noise is to be encountered ('no voice, no low, no howl is heard; the chief sound of life here is a hiss'). Melville's successive descriptions, provocative to both eye and ear, speak unnervingly, a hell-on-earth born of elemental convulsions in the larval bowels of the planet. He has his narrator allude to his own muteness before the isles, and his Bartlebyesque 'fixed gaze'. He imagines, too, 'the ghost of a gigantic tortoise', 'crawling along the floor' with the words 'Memento *******' upon its shell, unspoken, eternal sign-language as to the dead estate of all about. As a co-opting act of voice, Sketch First ('The Isles at large') works brilliantly, Melville quite at the top of his narrational form.

In Sketches Second, Third and Fourth, Melville's voice becomes one of recollection, things once seen, wondered at, and re-invoked as if having belonged to a near fantastical world. Sketch Second begins with the memory of three Galápagos turtles caught 'off the South Head of Albermarle' and brought aboard for food. The narrator's remembering imagination again works vividly. He speaks of 'these really wondrous tortoises', their shells 'black as widower's weeds'. He dubs them 'mystic creatures' whose movement on deck 'affected me in a manner not easy to unfold'. They in their turn become for him actors in some primordial drama:

> With a lantern I inspected them more closely. Such worshipful venerableness of aspect! Such furry greenness mantling the rude peelings and healing the fissures of their shattered shells. I no more saw three tortoises. They expanded— became transfigured. I seemed to see three Roman Coliseums in magnificent decay.

Scarred and full of hieroglyph-like markings they strike him as ancient messengers of time whose 'crowning curse is their drudging impulse to straightforwardness in a belittered world'. And hearing them scrape and fall foul of all the tackle on deck, he falls asleep below only to experience a 'wild nightmare':

> Listening to these draggings and concussions, I thought me of the haunt from which they came; an isle full of metallic ravines and gulches, sunk bottomlessly into the hearts of splintered mountains, and covered for many miles with

inextricable thickets. I then pictured these three straightforward monsters, century after century, writhing through the
shades, grim as blacksmiths; crawling so slowly and ponder-
ously, that not only did toad-stools and all fungus things grow
beneath their feet, but a sooty moss sprouted upon their backs.
With them I lost myself in volcanic mazes; brushed away
endless boughs of rotting thickets; till finally in a dream I found
myself sitting crosslegged upon the foremost, a Brahmin
similarly mounted upon either side, forming a tripod of
foreheads which upheld the universal cope.

It would be difficult not to hear a more charged voice-within-
a-voice, the dream or poet voice of the narrator who, 'next
evening', his nightmare behind him, nevertheless 'sat down
with my shipmates, and made a merry repast from tortoise
steaks and tortoise stews'.

Sketch Third depicts Rock Rodondo, to the narrator's
transforming perception a 'famous Campanile or detached
Bell Tower of St. Mark', and an upright formation which acts
as 'the aviary of the ocean'. Around it surge flocks of sea-fowl,
a 'demonic din'. He singles out especially the penguins as
'neither fish, flesh, nor fowl'. Of the pelicans he asks 'what sea
Friars of Orders Gray?' Rodondo, in one perspective 'dead
desert rock', doubles as an array of others—bird-sanctuary, a
chain of 'fish-caves', 'a tall light-house', 'the lofty sails of a
cruiser'. It takes its place, however, in what Sketch Fourth
calls 'A Pisgah view from the rock', a panorama of 'yonder
Burnt District of the Enchanted Isles' which also contains this
splendidly spoof statistical table:

Men	none
Ant-eaters	unknown
Man-haters	unknown
Lizards	500,000
Snakes	500,000
Spiders	10,000,000
Salamanders	unknown
Devils	do.
Making a clean total of	11,000,000

Sketches Fifth, Sixth and Seventh reveal Melville as historian,
though a historian who offers himself as a mix of census-taker

and memorialist. He recalls the whaleship *Essex* (as he had in *Moby-Dick*) nearly wrecked at Rodondo; he calls up those one-time Elizabethan exotics, the buccaneers; and he describes the Charles's Isle kingdom of a Cuban Creole made sole monarch for his services in the Peruvian liberation from Spain. Deposed by his citizenry, the drop-outs of every navy at sea, the Creole is forced to return to Peru leaving behind a 'permanent *Riotocracy*', 'the unassailed lurking-place of all sorts of desperadoes'.

Sketch Eighth, 'Norfolk Isle and the Chola Widow', Melville tells in a hitherto absent voice of the tragic. He pronounces the isle to have been 'made sacred by the strangest trials of humanity', the abandonment, pain and eventual re-discovery of Hunilla, 'the dark-damasked Chola widow'. Bereft of her 'pure Castilian' husband, Felipe, and her 'only Indian brother, Truxill', she is found by the narrator's ship 'marooned', 'lost' in her 'labyrinth' of grief. The death of husband and brother have left her in 'nameless misery', cheated by the captain who left them there in the first place; she is described as 'this lone shipwrecked soul', 'the vanquished one' who arouses 'worship'. Melville has his narrator's voice also speak of a necessary 'reticence' ('it may be libelous to speak some truths'), the imposition of authorial discretion in the face of another's unbreachable moral privacy. Hunilla may have been raped, may have been seen but passed by, or may simply have endured infinitely more than any narration can say. Appropriately, therefore, the narrator testifies that 'during the telling of her story the mariners formed a voiceless circle round Hunilla and the Captain. . . .' Her story she so tells herself, to have it told in turn by the narrator, and that in turn by Melville: again, each layer of voice building into a story-telling whole. Our last sight of Hunilla, observed noiselessly by the narrator 'prostrate upon the grave' of her family, and then at Payta, Peru, 'lone' and fixed upon the 'armorial cross' on the ass she is riding, is told as though from an even further distance—by a narrator who now opts to withdraw having become as alert as she to the cheat of words. Hunilla, in this, links directly to the figure Melville might have depicted as Agatha had he written up the story he once offered to Hawthorne in 1852.[15]

Sketch Ninth, 'Hood's Isle and the Hermit Oberlus', moves into slightly less sombre idiom: the depiction of the hermit Oberlus, another island tyrant once ill-done by but in revenge become a murderous ill-doer himself. The narration directs us towards myth, Oberlus as a Caliban (in fact he is a Creole, also, who claims Sycorax for his mother), 'an insulted misanthrope' and 'volcanic creature thrown up by the same convulsion which exploded into sight the isle'. He ends up 'a central figure of a mongrel and assassin band' in a Peruvian jail, a one-time island monarch of 'cindery solitude' and another of the antic population of the Galápagos. The final sketch, Sketch Tenth, 'Runaways, Castaways, Solitaries, Grave-stones, etc', offers a summarizing observation: 'Probably few parts of earth, in modern times, sheltered so many solitaries.' Melville has the narration refer to the isles as 'hermit' and 'refugee' terrain, places 'dreary' and full of 'relics'. But in closing, his tone also becomes wry and Yankee-ironic once more. Reference is made to the practice of leaving 'a stake and a bottle' as a kind of South Seas 'post-office'. In time 'the stake rots and falls, presenting no very exhilarating object'. The decaying post-box might have been a detail which also carries over from Melville's putative Agatha story. But it might, too, have been Melville's ironic prediction of the fate of his own 'Letters from the Galápagos'. That would have been ironic prediction indeed: for 'The Encantadas' not merely contain some of his sharpest observational writing, they show him consummately at strength in the handling of voice.

5

Particularity of voice also marks out Melville's lesser first-person narratives, three with 'domestic' flavours more than most—'I and My Chimney', 'The Lightning-Rod Man' and 'The Apple-Tree Table'. In the first, in the inflection of the beleaguered husband, the voice is all edginess, that of the seeming curmudgeon at once on the attack and the defensive. The story centres on the narrator's protection of his 'corpulent old Harry VIII of a chimney', the image of his own selfhood under siege. His wife and daughters press him to move out of the country back into town. Surveyors and architects recommend changes of design to the chimney. Neighbours and kin urge more 'reasonable' behaviour. In response the narrator dodges and weaves, jokes, writes mock-formal letters, and retreats into convenient absences and silences about the house. The chimney becomes an *alter ego* ('I and my chimney, two gray-headed old smokers'), the threatened self 'that will never surrender'. The story voice relies upon its own sustaining mannerisms, a speaking self adroitly full of quirks and twitches. In 'The Lightning-Rod Man', the quickness of temper that threatened in 'I and My Chimney' actually snaps into utterance. Melville takes aim at all 'salesmen' of false panaceas against the 'grand irregular thunder' of things, those who offer (and get the profit from) palliatives, bromides, each and every manner of false comfort. Whether angled at American hucksterism, or at deeper metaphysical confidence-trickery, Melville has the rod salesman represent a 'latest form of infidelity' or devilry. Such the implication at least of his throwing his 'tri-forked thing' at the narrator's heart. The story matchingly is told as an elliptical duet, two voices tensely in counterpoint. In 'The Apple-Tree Table', he again has us listen to a put-upon narrator, the story of a bug 'miraculously' released from captivity which has the family inclining towards superstition and the narrator in consequence towards mock-despair. A light enough piece, it nonetheless shows Melville attempting a further array of voices: suspense, spoofery, family small-talk and the Thurberish complaint of its paterfamilias narrator.

In another related cluster of stories—'Cock-A-Doodle-Doo', 'The Happy Failure', 'The Fiddler' and 'Jimmy Rose'—Melville uses narrators almost exaggeratedly concerned to flourish their authority, their claimed superiority of witness to events and behaviour out of the ordinary. Melville, however, everywhere slips in grounds for doubt, as if the very unordinariness of the experience under relation unavoidably imposes a margin between story-teller and story. But then how could any story fully account for events like the death of a country family whose defiant emblem is a crowing cockerel, or the reversal to sanity of a crackpot Hudson River inventor, or the rise and fall of a literary prodigy who takes to the fiddle, or the mad-alec hibernation of a once-successful New York merchant? Each of these stories offers more Melvilleian 'inside narrative', off-beat possible envisionings of his own condition and writerly fate. Each, too, makes a point about the times, 1850s America as abrim with human oddness and eccentricity— a 'masquerade' which in *The Confidence-Man* he would turn to masterly satiric advantage. And each, too, again shows Melville an adept in the voicing of his fiction, the posturing, slightly guyed-up exaggeration of the telling at one with the tale.

An even darker vein of satire runs through Melville's three paired tales, or diptychs. In these a single voice discloses mutually commenting and inverse worlds. In 'The Two Temples', Melville's theme is charity, firstly charity anything but begun at home and parodied in the denial of admission to worship at a genteel New York church, and secondly charity instinctively given in the form of an unlooked-for London theatre ticket to hear the actor Macready perform. The contrasts come over sharply: American church snobbery as against British secular generosity; the closedness of one institution as against the openness of the other; and the mutual and parallel 'dramas' of both. 'Poor Man's Pudding and Rich Man's Crumbs' deflates the view of poverty when seen from affluence. In the first part, Melville's critical gaze falls upon the falsely benign view of Nature as always 'the blessed almoner', a story of starvation told as the dialogue between a townsman narrator and 'Poet Blandmour'. In the second, an indictment is made of 'philanthropy' as the donation of demeaning banquet left-overs to London beggars. Both offer stories in themselves; but they tell, too, their narrator's own inward moral arousal and education. 'The Paradise of Bachelors and The Tartarus Maids' again uses one story-telling voice to tell two linked but counterposed stories. In the first life is all protected cakes-and-ale congeniality, a fraternity of male unmarrieds taking dinner at the Temple— the world, work, Eros put in abeyance. In the second, equally a 'bachelor' story, life is all threatening uncongeniality, female impregnation and reproduction told under camouflage of a visit to a paper-mill near 'Woedolor Mountains in New England' being run by pale spinster workers each responsible to a 'dark-complexioned, well-wrapped personage' and his ironically named boy aid Cupid. Melville has his narrator speak twice-in-one, a 'bachelor' voice describing respectively its own imagined pleasures and fears, its own visions of an a-sexual Heaven and a sexual Hell.

6

Both 'The Bell Tower' and 'Benito Cereno' move into third-person narration, though to greatly differing effect. The former, insistently stylized and not dissimilar in theme to Hawthorne's 'Ethan Brand', issues a warning against the elevation of the head over the heart, the worship of perfect technology over imperfect humanity. The story of Bannadonna, a 'great mechanician' but 'unblest foundling', it shows how a 'splinter' of human bone (from a workman struck down by Bannadonna), 'a defect, deceptively minute', puts his otherwise flawless edifice at risk. The flaw in fact leads to his undoing, as one of the molten 'domino' figures in his baroque apparatus strikes him upon his 'intervening brain'. At his funeral, in the same Italian cathedral, the belfry in turn crashes down like some 'lone Alpine land-slide'. A story told in the intended voice of prophecy, Melville pitches 'The Bell-Tower', however, too gnomically, too explicitly as warning. The last paragraph simply says too much: 'So the creator was killed by his creature. . . . And so pride went before the fall.'

Fortunately no over-insistence of this kind mars 'Benito Cereno', Melville's third virtuoso Piazza Tale and the companion-piece in imaginative reach to 'Bartleby' and 'The Encantadas'. Its chill, tense, exhilarating story of slave insurrection off the Chilean coast-line relies throughout upon tactics of indirection, a quite masterly display of voice and counter-voice. In the first instance we are put to judge two versions: the first told as the narrative *per se*, the second as 'sworn' deposition, a fiction of fact as against a supposed non-fiction of facts. Within this, Melville has us encounter the triangular exchanges of Amaso Delano, Benito Cereno and Babo, a speaking tableau of dissimulation, lies, and uncomprehending response. He also makes the *San Dominick*, on whose decks the drama is first played out, as against Delano's ship the *Bachelor's Delight*, a 'hubbub of voices', an echoing, near fantastical African sound-chamber and 'Heart of Darkness' within which to enact this singular confrontation of black and white, slavery and freedom, repression and revolution. Then, too, he textures his story with a complex run of *unspoken* gestures and emblems, mutely coded signs which require the reader's decipherment.

If the story does offer a voice beyond any of these, we meet it at the outset, cautioning against too absolute, too black-and-white, an interpretation of any single set of appearances:

> The morning was one peculiar to that coast. Everything was mute and calm; everything gray. The sea, though undulated into long roods of swells, seemed fixed, and was sleeked at the surface like waved lead that has cooled and set in the smelter's mould. The sky seemed a gray surtout. Flights of troubled gray fowl, kith and kin with flights of troubled gray vapours among which they were mixed, skimmed low and fitfully over the waters, as swallows over meadows before storms. Shadows present, foreshadowing deeper shadows to come.

With this as touchstone, Melville tells his story through the vantage-point of Amaso Delano, sealer-captain of Duxbury, Massachusetts, 'a person of a singularly undistrustful good nature' but also kin to the 'white noddy', the 'somnambulistic' sea-bird 'frequently caught by hand at sea'. He it will be who must decipher, and we through him, the *San Dominick*'s maze of sights and sounds: the likeness of the ship to a Pyrenean 'white-washed monastery after a thunder-storm' patrolled by its inquisitional 'Black Friars'; the 'shield-like stern-piece' which depicts 'a dark satyr in a mask, holding his foot on the prostrate neck of a writhing figure, likewise masked'; the covered replacement figurehead which is the bleached skeleton of the co-owner Alexandro Aranda; the striking of the white boy by the black; the parodic imperial dumb-show of padlock and key as Atufal makes his ritual appearances before Cereno; the different hints and nods of the imprisoned white crew; the intricate Gordian knot ('a combination of double-bowline-knot, treble-crown-knot, back-handed-well knot, knot-in-and-out-knot, and jamming-knot') of which he is enjoined to 'Undo it, cut it, quick'; and Babo's body-servant impersonation which Delano misreads even through to

Cereno's last jump into the departing whale-boat. His confusions become ours; his, too, the voice through which doubt and suspicion are made to gather and resonate before experiencing the final 'flash of revelation'.

Cereno and Babo represent counter-voices. Delano—New World, Yankee, Protestant, 'bachelor' yet blithely racist and quite capable of bidding for Babo—we hear only as played off theirs. For they both speak from wholly opposite and inverse assumptions, compounded by the rôle-playing they enact before him. Cereno, paradoxically, is made to impersonate himself, to speak as though still in command, the Old World, Castillian and Catholic Don who carries forth the standard of slave-trading and empire into the Pacific. Babo, the Senegalese ring-leader, assumes the voice of slave-sycophancy, the doubling inflection of one who 'acts out' his required historical script. Their two voices invert Delano's, themselves inverted puppeteer and puppet voices of the slave equation, at once particular and specific to this story yet tied to a far larger Western racial-historical drama.

Only as the 'rescue' is achieved can Cereno speak in his own true voice, one enfeebled, maskless, and hollow.

> You were with me all day; stood with me, sat with me, talked with me, looked at me, ate with me, drank with me; and yet, your last act was to clutch for a monster, not only an innocent man, but the most pitiable of men.

His last exchange with Delano, equally, refers us to the core, the very axis, on which the tale has turned:

> 'You are saved,' cried Captain Delano, more and more astonished and pained; 'you are saved: what has cast such a shadow upon you?'
> 'The negro.'
> There was silence. . . .

Whether 'the negro' designates only Babo, or all black slavery, or blackness as a metaphysics ('el negro'), the story leaves poised as ambiguity. But 'silence', the willed refusal to say anything to or in a world which has first stolen and then denied him identity, is Babo's final captive testimony: 'Seeing all was over, he uttered no sound, and could not be forced to. His aspect seemed to say, since I cannot do deeds, I will not speak

95

words.' His fate is execution, with his head ('that hive of subtlety') sat upon a pole in the plaza at Lima, there to meet 'unabashed', 'the gaze of the whites'. That defiant voiceless-ness, portending, awesome, freighted with meaning, represents the true 'voice' of 'Benito Cereno', Melville's 'inside narrative' of the calamity of slavery as fatal human division.

7

Although the stories so far mentioned make up the accepted corpus of Melville's short fiction—allowing that *Israel Potter* (1855) and *Billy Budd, Sailor* are to be thought novellas—he did write others. These include his two-part 'Fragments from a Writing Desk', published in the *Democratic Press & Lansingburgh Advertiser* for May 1839, a piece of juvenilia which tells the near self-parodic Gothic fantasy of a beautiful deaf-and-dumb mystery woman; 'The Gees', Melville's portrait of tough Cape Verde Portuguese sailors which he issued in *Harper's* in March 1856; 'Daniel Orme' and 'John Marr', two sailor sketches written essentially to accompany his sea poetry; and miscellaneous other late snippets like 'The Marquis of Grandvin' and 'Three "Jack Gentian Sketches" ', further visions of the cavalier good life. But there are grounds for thinking yet one other composition, not ordinarily read as fiction, ought to be added to the roster. That is 'Hawthorne and his Mosses', Melville's exuberant, self-revealing 'shock of recognition' on encountering as though for the first time the stories of his slightly older New England contemporary and written up in review form for the *Literary World*.[16]

Declaring Hawthorne to be a national literary figure, 'this Portuguese diamond in our American literature', Melville at the same time clearly believed he had met with his own first true philosophical stable-mate, his fellow dissenter from the Age's yea-saying and especially its American manifestation as Emersonian Transcendentalism.[17] But for all that his 'essay' offers eulogy to 'this most excellent Man of Mosses', an outpouring of rare, unstinting acclaim which as much reveals Melville's recent reading of Shakespeare as of Hawthorne, it also assumes the form of a story. Like the 'narrative' of Melville's Agatha correspondence, told but untold as it were,

'Mosses' unfolds to nothing less than a story-like rhythm with appropriate setting, decor and above all narrator. Melville could not have begun 'Mosses' in fact more as a story, given the creation of his 'Virginian Spending July in Vermont', the effete, magnolia-bathed Southerner idling his time in a New England barn only to be taken daemonic possession of by Hawthorne's Northern, Calvinized 'magic' as he calls it. As so often in his short fiction proper, we hear first a voice—in this case one full of seclusion, private awakening, and pleasure:

> A papered chamber in a fine old farm-house—a mile from any other dwelling, and dipped to the eaves in foliage—surrounded by mountains, old woods, and Indian ponds—this, surely, is the place to write of Hawthorne. Some charm is in this northern air, for love and duty seem both impelling to the task. A man of a deep and noble nature has seized me in this seclusion. His wild, witch voice rings through me; or, in softer cadences, I seem to hear it in the songs of the hillside birds that sing in the larch trees at my window.

The 'Virginian' serves as Hawthorne's 'ideal reader', coming to see *Mosses from an Old Manse* as 'something far better' than *Travels in New England* (actually published in four volumes in 1821–22 as *Travels in New England and New York* by the Connecticut wit Timothy Dwight (1752–1817)). His voice, quite as much as Hawthorne's, becomes slightly 'wild' and witch-like. He testifies to 'how magically stole over me this Mossy Man!' He speaks of 'soft ravishments', Hawthorne as all too simple-mindedly thought 'a pleasant writer, with a pleasant style', 'a sequestered, harmless man, from whom any deep and weighty thing could hardly be anticipated'. In a quite seamless transition, he accordingly points to another Hawthorne, 'Calvinistic', possessed of the 'power of blackness', 'thunderous' and no less than Shakespearean in profundity and feats of expression ('Some may start to read of Shakespeare and Hawthorne on the same page'). Melville's review-story so turns from setting the reader at ease to challenge, 'Mosses' as a narrative of personal transformation but also an act of critical provocation.

Other dimensions of voice play into this story. If the eulogist

Melville also plays practical critic, calling attention to different effects of voice in Hawthorne's own stories—'The Intelligence Office', for example, as 'wondrous symbolizing', 'Young Goodman Brown' as 'allegorical pursuit' and 'deep as Dante', or 'A Select Party' as typically duplicitous and over-easily thought the writing of 'a "gentle" harmless man'. He speaks of Hawthorne's 'hoodwinking', his conjuration of 'lights and shades' and 'witchery'. He employs an intriguing affective vocabulary of 'cadence', 'magic', 'wondrous effects', and 'manifold, strange and diffusive beauties', all terms utterly applicable to his own short fiction. However much Hawthorne for him said 'NO! in thunder', he employed 'magical' resources of voices to match.[18]

'Mosses', however, does not stop there. It reveals Melville as a reader not only of Hawthorne but of Shakespeare, also a 'shock of recognition' for him as underlined resoundingly by his insights into tragedies like *Lear* ('the frantic king tears off the mask, and speaks the sane madness of vital truth') and into the Problem and Late plays. It reveals the innate literary nationalist in Melville, impatient with 'literary flunkyism' towards England and exhorting that 'America . . . prize and cherish her writers'. No doubt he was testifying to his own aspirations and to those of the 'Young America' circle in which Evert Duyckinck, his friend and the Editor of the *Literary World*, played a pre-eminent part.[19] With hindsight, Melville can also be seen in this to have been participating in the current more associated with Emerson in essays like *Nature* (1836) and 'The American Scholar' (1837), the call for a national literature to match the political independence won at the Revolution. 'Mosses' so, too, displays Melville the stylist, the equal in aphorism and acuteness of phrase not only of an Emerson but of a Hazlitt or Lamb.

In each and all of these respects, 'Mosses' establishes itself as 'story', Melville's 'Virginian' voice throughout that of the reader-author ever more deeply seduced and transported. Sexual analogies permeate the piece: the narrator speaks of 'strong New England roots' being 'shot down' into his 'hot' Southern soil (an unlooked-for anticipation of Roland Barthes's notion of reading as *jouissance*?). Sexual-creative double-talk in Melville to be sure is familiar enough. One has only to think of chapters in *Moby-Dick* like 'Heads or Tails' and 'The Cassock', or 'The Tartarus of Maids'. Here, it most purposefully plays into 'Mosses' as simulated story, an organizing imagery to accompany all the other story-telling tactics Melville employs. These, as I suggest, include the narrator as both reader and writer; the seduction and shock of discovering Hawthorne; the 'practical criticism' decoding of his stories; the call to literary nationalism and the ambiguous legacy of Shakespeare for an American author; the assured scene-setting and pacing of 'Mosses' ('Twenty-four hours have elapsed since writing the foregoing. I have just returned from the haymow, charged more and more with love and admiration of Hawthorne'); and the exhortatory leave-taking of the last paragraph. On this line of argument, 'Mosses' properly belongs in Melville's story canon, its voice as distinctive—and symptomatic—as any in his *Piazza* repertoire.

NOTES

1. These are in sequence: 'Bartleby, the Scrivener: A Story of Wall Street', *Putnam's Monthly Magazine*, November–December 1853; 'Cock-A-Doodle-Doo! or, The Crowing of the Noble Cock Benevantano', *Harper's New Monthly Magazine*, December 1853; 'The Encantadas or Enchanted Isles', *Putnam's Monthly Magazine*, March–May 1854; 'The Two Temples', 1854, unpublished until *The Works of Herman Melville* (London: Constable, 1922–24); 'Poor Man's Pudding and Rich Man's Crumbs', *Harper's New Monthly Magazine*, June 1854; 'The Happy Failure: A Story of the River Hudson', *Harper's New Monthly Magazine*, July 1854; 'The Lightning-Rod Man', *Putnam's Monthly Magazine*, July, 1854; 'The Fiddler' (A Sketch), *Harper's New Monthly Magazine*, September 1854; 'The Paradise of Bachelors and The Tartarus of Maids', *Harper's New Monthly Magazine*, April 1855; 'The Bell-Tower', *Putnam's Monthly Magazine*, August 1855; 'Benito Cereno', *Putnam's Monthly Magazine*, October–November 1855; 'Jimmy Rose', *Harper's New Monthly Magazine*, November 1855; 'I and My Chimney', *Putnam's Monthly Magazine*, March 1856; 'The 'Gees', *Harper's New Monthly Magazine*, March 1856; 'The Apple-Tree Table, or Original Spiritual Manifestations', *Putnam's Monthly Magazine*, May 1856. To this list of fifteen stories needs to be added: 'The Town Ho's Story', *Harper's New Monthly Magazine*, October 1851. Melville also wrote in this period *Israel Potter*, first published in nine instalments in *Harper's New Monthly Magazine*, July 1854–March 1855 and then in full-length novel form in

99

March 1855. Also unpublished until the Constable Edition were: 'The Marquis of Grandvin'; 'Three "Jack Gentian Sketches" '; 'John Marr' and 'Daniel Orme'; and of course, *Billy Budd, Sailor* (1888–91).

2. 'Hawthorne and his Mosses', *Literary World*, August 17 and 24 1850.
3. For a helpful study in this respect, see Allen Hayman: 'The Real and The Original: Herman Melville's Theory of Prose Fiction', *Modern Fiction Studies*, Vol. VIII, No. 3, Autumn 1962. There exist, too, a number of full-length studies of Melville which seek to establish his conscious artistry. The following, especially, I have benefited from: Edgar A. Dryden, *Melville's Thematics of Form: The Great Art of Telling the Truth* (Baltimore: Johns Hopkins Press, 1968); John Seelye, *Melville: The Ironic Diagram* (Evanston: Northwestern University Press, 1970); and Richard H. Brodhead, *Hawthorne, Melville and the Novel* (Chicago: University of Chicago Press, 1976).
4. Merrell R. Davis and William H. Gilman (eds.), *The Letters of Herman Melville* (New Haven: Yale University Press, 1960). Melville to James Billson, 10 October 1884. The reference is to *Clarel* and runs in full as follows: ' "Clarel," published by George P. Putnam's Sons, New York—a metrical affair, a pilgrimage or what not, of several thousand lines, eminently adapted for unpopularity.—The notification to you here is ambidexter, as it were: it may intimidate or allure.'
5. This phrase first appears in 'Hawthorne and his Mosses': 'You must have plenty of sea-room to tell the truth in. . . .'
6. *Letters* (op. cit.), Melville to Hawthorne, 29 June 1851.
7. 'There are some enterprises in which a careful disorderliness is the true method.' *Moby-Dick*, Chapter 82.
8. Exegesis of the stories has been prolific. For overall accounts see: Richard Harter Fogle, *Melville's Shorter Tales* (University of Oklahoma Press, 1960); Kingsley Widmer, *The Ways of Nihilism: Herman Melville's Short Novels* (Los Angeles: California State Colleges, 1970); R. Bruce Bickley, *The Method of Melville's Short Fiction* (Durham, N.C.: Duke University Press, 1975); Marvin Fisher, *Going Under: Melville's Short Fiction and the American 1850s* (Louisiana State University Press, 1977); and William B. Dillingham, *Melville's Short Fiction 1853–56* (Athens: University of Georgia Press, 1977).
9. In a recent essay John Updike makes a similar point: 'The stories of "The Piazza Tales" are, with "Moby-Dick", "Typee", and "Billy Budd", the most widely read of Melville's works. They evince a competence, even a mastery, that Melville chose not to exercise much. "I would prefer not to", Bartleby famously says, and there is in all these tales a certain reserve, a toning down into brown and sombre colors the sunny colors of the earlier work, a·desolation hauntingly figured forth by the eerie slave-seized ship of "Benito Cereno" and the cinderlike "The Encantadas". The style, though a triumphant recovery from the hectic tropes of "Pierre", is not quite the assured, playful, precociously fluent, and eagerly pitched voice of the sea novels. It is a slightly *chastened* style, with something a bit abrasive and latently aggressive about it. However admirable, these tales are not exactly comfortable; their surfaces are not

100

seductive and limpid, like those of Hawthorne's tales.' 'Melville's Withdrawal', *New Yorker*, 12 May 1982, pp. 120–47 (reprinted in *Hugging The Shore*, New York: Alfred Knopf, 1983).

10. Melville's manner of narration in 'The Town Ho's Story' I have called attention to before (and apologize for any slight overlap) in '*Moby-Dick*: The Tale and the Telling', in Faith Pullin (ed.), *New Perspectives on Melville* (Edinburgh University Press, 1978), pp. 86–127.

11. For a typical spectrum of readings of 'Bartleby', see Howard P. Vincent (ed.), *Bartleby The Scrivener, The Melville Annual 1965/Symposium* (Kent State University Press, 1966).

12. See especially Leo Marx: 'Melville's Parable of Walls', *Sewanee Review*, LXI, 1953, 602–27.

13. See, as a companion piece to the present essay, A. Robert Lee: 'Voices Off, On and Without: Ventriloquy in *The Confidence-Man*', in A. Robert Lee (ed.), *Herman Melville: Reassessments* (London: Vision Press, 1984).

14. *Moby-Dick*, Chapter 24. Ishmael says: 'I am all anxiety to convince ye, ye landsmen, of the injustice hereby done to us hunters of whales.'

15. *Letters* (op. cit.), Melville to Hawthorne, 13 August 1852; 25 August 1852 and 25 November 1852.

16. 'Hawthorne and his Mosses' (op. cit.).

17. The literal course of Melville's relationship with Hawthorne runs as follows: he reads *Mosses from an Old Manse* in July, 1850; joins Oliver Wendell Holmes, Evert Duyckinck, the Hawthornes and other literary friends for a picnic at Monument Mountain in early August 1850, and publishes his review 'Hawthorne and his Mosses' in the *Literary World* for 17 and 24 August 1850; there follow numerous to-ings and fro-ings between Pittsfield and Lenox and Melville's effusive, near-Keatsian letters to Hawthorne written through 1851–52 including the Agatha correspondence; Melville dedicates *Moby-Dick* to Hawthorne 'in token of my admiration for his genius' and warms especially to Sophia Hawthorne's kindly, intelligent interest in her new neighbour; the relationship with Hawthorne begins to cool no doubt as a consequence of Hawthorne's natural reticence and understandable slight alarm at Melville's offers of brotherhood and intimacy; Hawthorne moves on in 1853 to the Liverpool Consulship. We have, in addition, their respective journal-entries for the Lancashire shoreline discussion which took place when Melville called in on Hawthorne en route to the Levant in 1856 (see Howard C. Horsford (ed.), *Journal of a Visit to Europe and the Levant, October 11, 1856–May 6, 1857 by Herman Melville* (Princeton University Press, 1955), entries for 10, 11, 12 and 13 November (pp. 62–3), and Nathaniel Hawthorne, *Journal*, November 1856, reprinted in Jay Leyda, *The Melville Log: A Documentary Life of Herman Melville 1819–1892*, 2 vols. (New York: Harcourt, Brace and Co., 1951), Vol. 1, p. 529. Hawthorne was to help Melville with publication the following year of *The Confidence-Man*. There exist, too, a number of postscripts: the likely depiction of Hawthorne as Vine in *Clarel* (1876); the guarded and disturbing report of Julian Hawthorne when he visited Melville in Manhattan in 1883 in the course of writing the biography of his father (*The Melville Log* (op.

cit.), Vol. 11, pp. 782–83); and the poem 'Monody', Melville's late recollection of Hawthorne, as he put matters, both 'estranged in life,/ And neither in the wrong'. The relationship is also usefully set out in Howard P. Vincent (ed.), *Melville & Hawthorne in the Berkshires: A Symposium, Melville Annual* (Kent State University Press, 1966).

18. *Letters* (op. cit.), Melville to Hawthorne, 16? April? 1851. 'There is the grand truth about Nathaniel Hawthorne. He says NO! in thunder. . . .'

19. See Perry Miller, *The Raven and the Whale: The War of Words and Wits in the Era of Poe and Melville* (New York: Harcourt, Brace & World, Inc., 1956), pp. 69–117.

5

Reporting Reality:
Mark Twain's Short Stories

by ANDREW HOOK

1

The short story is as American as apple-pie, and of all American authors Mark Twain is the most archetypally American. The result must be that Twain's short stories are the end of the line, the last word. Strangely, however, Twain himself does not seem to have thought so. Mark Twain saw himself as a great many things: journalist, Literary Man, novelist, lecturer, financial wizard, but never, apparently, as short story writer. He wrote nothing in the way of a planned book of stories; he published no collection exclusively of his short stories. Apart from one short piece entitled 'How to Tell a Story' (and even there he insisted that what he had to say referred to the *oral* tradition of story-telling), he had almost nothing to say about the 'art' of short fiction. Yet, in that admirable tradition to which the great majority of America's prose masters belong, Twain did write a large number of short stories. Just how large a number it is impossible to say, because, peculiarly in Twain's case, it is often difficult to decide where something else ends and the short story begins, or where the short story ceases to be only that. Whatever the exact number, he certainly wrote them; and the general critical consensus would be, wrote them well. As the editor of a recent collection of critical essays on Twain's stories puts it:

'. . . without question Twain became one of our finest masters of short fiction in America.'[1]

Pace Twain himself, then, does my opening syllogism hold water? The initial premise is of course no more than a version of an historical and critical commonplace which one suspects readers of this volume of essays will never be allowed to forget. The only interesting question is why it should be so: why is it that the short story caught on in America in such a bigger way than elsewhere? Literary historians have tended to favour the arguments from popular taste, the economics of publishing, and the conditions of authorship: American readers enjoyed the kind of story they read in *Blackwood's Magazine*; native American magazines developed to satisfy that taste; such magazines provided economically-rewarding outlets for budding American writers. But in truth the development of the short story as the characteristic American form reflected deeper structures than these.

The novel as a literary form settled uneasily upon the American scene. Its major nineteenth-century practitioners are united on this if on little else. Cooper, Hawthorne, James (and there is no dissent from Poe or Melville), as everyone knows, agreed that the American novelist was constantly finding himself in a tight spot, as Twain would have put it, because of the nature of American society. Where was the social richness, density, and variety, where were the traditions of conduct, the conventions of manners and behaviour, where was the sense of a rich historical past, which the novelist needed to go to work upon? And indeed it is true that what emerged as the major examples of novel-writing in nineteenth-century America proved to have little enough in common with the great tradition of the Victorian novel in Great Britain. Hence the inevitable critical debate over whether the American 'novel' is not in fact a 'romance'; or over what Trollope called the American author's preference for 'dreams' rather than the 'beef and ale' which concerned English novelists. Hence, too, the widely-expressed feeling that the American novel lacks a sense of fullness and coherence; it is a thing of 'scenes', 'tableaux', 'sketches', 'episodes'; usually nothing is fully rendered, exhaustively 'done'.

In the short story, of course, nothing needs to be. Hence the sense in which it seems to offer a formal solution to the kinds of problem faced by the American novelist that Hawthorne and James felt so keenly. The short story is by definition not much more than a 'scene', a 'tableau', an 'episode' or 'sketch'. (Early in the nineteenth century Washington Irving's *The Sketchbook* was a key work in demonstrating to a sceptical English readership that American literature did actually exist.) Perhaps this then is why Irving, Poe, Hawthorne, Melville, James—and Twain—turned so readily to the shorter forms of fiction, and why even in their longer fictional essays the characteristics of the short story—or even the thing itself— recur so frequently.

Or does the explanation of the American-ness of the short story lie even deeper within the distinctive structures of American culture and society? The favourite three-decker novel of Victorian England is at every level bound up with the nature of Victorian society; its essentially realistic mode, its slow, unfolding movement, its leisurely entwining of the lives and characters of its protagonists with a basically stable and well-ordered society—all of these characteristics reflect and appeal to basic dimensions and assumptions of Victorian society. Take away that society and its given readership, and the necessity or attraction of the three-decker novel form is no longer self-evident. And this of course is the American case. In the nineteenth century, America is still a frontier society; it is changing, growing, moving, building, creating itself. If the East is settled, civilized, the West is not. America is still a world in motion. What is the artist to do? The work of art shapes, orders, patterns; but what if the artist's material resists, refuses, the fixities of order and definition? If he is a Whitman, say, he sets aside the shaping spirit of imagination, and embraces instead a new aesthetic of motion or process; that is, he identifies with his material, rather than imposing himself upon it. ('The United States themselves are the greatest poem', said Whitman.) Or the writer may abandon the attempt to create the larger structure, the more compre-hensive statement, and settle instead for the temporary arrest, the briefer moment of ordering—all the more appealing and aesthetically satisfying because of the context of confusion out of which it has been plucked. If he is a prose writer, that is, he opts for the short story. From this perspective the short story emerges as the most appropriate form through which the literary imagination can contain the American experience. The nature of American society—its dynamic of change and restlessness—creates the short story as its typical aesthetic product.

But the image of the short story that is built into an analysis of this kind is one of the well-wrought urn, or even of Wallace Stevens's poetic jar which 'took dominion everywhere', taming the wilderness in Tennessee. The story as high art, taming, shaping, ordering. Now some American stories are of this kind—one thinks immediately of Poe or Hawthorne, still more of the polished elegance of James or Hemingway. But what would Mark Twain have made of any comparison between Stevens's 'Anecdote of the Jar' and any of his stories? The answer is a raspberry. The tradition of story-telling to which Twain belongs has little or nothing to do with high art. It is a tradition which is sceptical about Art of any kind. Art means the pretentious, the high-flown, the superior; Art means the undemocratic, the élitist; Art means the morally upright and inoffensive; Art means Europe, the Old World, which America has cast aside. Twain, in his short stories, just as in the rest of his work, rejected Art in all these senses. The Dickens of American writers, Twain was above all a popular writer. Hence his art emerged out of popular American culture: out of that tradition of comic Western story-telling which, as everyone knows, Twain inherited, consummated, and eclipsed. That is one story that does not need to be rehearsed.

The Western tradition of story-telling to which Twain belongs rejects the notions of artistic polish and perfection which help to sustain the argument about the naturalness of the short story form in the context of the restless, dynamic nature of American society. Yet the alternative tradition may share with the first at least a considerable unease over the traditional forms of the novel. For some American writers at least Art may have come to mean the Novel. Perhaps this is why the most genuinely distinctive American contribution to the formal development of prose fiction lies in the area of the 'collection' of short stories. 'Collection' though is misleading; it suggests a random bringing together of disparate elements.

Rather in question is a group of stories, discrete in terms of action and plot, but unified in terms of over-all design. Hamlin Garland's *Main-Travelled Roads* (1891) is an early example of the genre; Sherwood Anderson's *Winesburg, Ohio* (1919) a slightly later one. Garland distrusted the novel form; its structure and plot were determined by the demands of a harmful, sentimental romanticism. In order to write about life as it was, the sketch or the short story were more satisfying. What he called the 'novelette' was 'the most perfect form of writing'.[2] Sherwood Anderson went further, more or less announcing that the novel was an unAmerican activity. Anderson felt that 'the novel form does not fit an American writer.' It was a form 'which had been brought in'. What was wanted was 'a new looseness'. 'In *Winesburg*', he wrote, 'I had made my own form.'[3] In the work of Faulkner, and other more recent writers, the attack on the novel form, and the search for a 'new looseness', has been carried still further.

Twain himself made no direct theoretical contribution to this debate over the form of the novel. As we noted at the beginning, he never even published a 'collection' of stories. However he did once suggest that 'the world grows tired of solid forms in all the arts'[4]—and in such a comment there is at least a hint of a link between Twain and those American writers who more consciously wished to move away from traditional notions of the novel form. In any event, for a writer practice is more important than theory. Twain's practice is crystal clear. A 'looseness' of form—whether 'new' or not—is entirely characteristic of all his major fiction.

Even the critics agree. Twain was in some respects a meticulous craftsman, a true word-smith. But always at the local level. What he lacked was the kind of imagination that shapes and forms an extended body of material; a sense of over-all design is what is least evident in his books. As George Feinstein puts it: 'Mark Twain values, not the architectonic effect of a tale, but the art of the paragraph, the sentence, the illuminating incident.' Even his humour 'is in essence paragraphic, episodic, inconsequential'.[5] William Gibson broadly agrees: Twain's 'talent, his span of attention and concentration perhaps, worked best and most unremittingly in relatively short pieces of writing'.[6] And Justin Kaplan makes the same point with confidence and authority:

> Sentence by sentence and paragraph by paragraph Mark Twain was an entirely deliberate and conscious craftsman; he insisted that the difference between the nearly right word and the right word was the difference between the lightning bug and the lightning; his ear for the rhythms of speech was unsurpassed, and he demanded in dialect and social notation nothing short of perfection. But his larger, structural methods were inspirational and instinctive.[7]

What is abundantly clear is that Twain worked instinctively in terms of the minute particular. This is why his books are all in a sense 'collections', assembling large bodies of material into a kind of loose grouping. 'Solid forms', as a result, are very largely absent from his writing. But in their very formlessness, Twain's longer fictions are at least gesturing towards a re-definition of the novel form—a re-definition that has its origins in some kind of perhaps only half-conscious sense that the American experience as Twain himself understood it—'the drive and push and rush and struggle of the raging, tearing, booming nineteenth century'[8]—was not containable within the traditional structures of the novel form.

Thus Twain's rejection of that genteel tradition which had sustained New England's hegemony over America's literary culture involved not only his use of vernacular forms of linguistic usage, and the deployment of the humorous Western tradition of the tall story, but also his preference for fictional forms which depended less for their effect upon an identifiable structural unity than upon the force of his own presence within them. Twain, then, does indeed belong to that tradition in American writing which is uneasy about the appropriateness of established English models to the creation of American fictions. Admittedly, he advanced little in the way of theory on the topic; and he certainly did not consciously see some version, some re-definition, of the idea of the collection of stories or sketches as one possible solution to the problems at issue. But the pattern that emerges from within his longer fictions does point generally in that direction.

2

As I have noted, Twain did once undertake a brief excursion into the theory of the short story. In 'How to Tell a Story' his interest is in the humorous tale which he regards as a distinctively American creation. The witty or comic story, he argues, should not be confused with the humorous one. Wit and comedy depend upon *matter*; humour is essentially a question of the *manner* of story-telling. It is because the humorous story is all about the method of its narration that it is in fact a work of art: 'the humorous story is strictly a work of art—high and delicate art—and only an artist can tell it.'[9] (Even if he is a Western farmer.) His art lies in the fact or pretence of innocence: he keeps a straight face throughout. 'To string incongruities and absurdities together in a wandering and sometimes purposeless way, and seem innocently unaware that they are absurdities, is the basis of the American art. . . .'[10] Other features specified by Twain are 'the slurring of the point', or 'the dropping of a studied remark apparently without knowing it, as if one were thinking aloud'—and the effective use of the pause.[11] (Twain is writing about telling a story aloud, not in print; but it is obvious that his own practice reveals a substantial carry over from the one medium to the other. None the less, one does well to remind oneself that throughout his life Twain was a magnificent stage, platform, and after-dinner performer. What he could earn from his readings and lectures, frequently provided him with a more stable financial return than his published writings. His capacity to hold and enthrall an audience did an immense amount to create and further his reputation. Twain, that is, did not learn how to tell a story from the example of earlier story-tellers such as Petroleum V. Nasby and Artemus Ward; he learned the hard way in front of live audiences.)

What is clear, though, is that the lesson was a deeply congenial one. Like Dickens, Twain clearly found some kind of profound reassurance in his capacity to hold an audience spell-bound. Like Dickens too, who over and over again ended his public readings with the murder of Nancy by Bill Sikes, Twain felt a compulsive need to repeat a successful story. His favourite was 'The Golden Arm', a Gothic horror story about an American black whose wife had a golden arm. When she dies, he opens her grave to get the golden arm for himself. The rest of the story concerns his growing awareness that his dead wife is pursuing him to get her arm back. The haunting voice draws nearer and nearer, asking who has got its arm; the black cowers under his bed clothes; but the question is asked more and more loudly; at the climax of the story, Twain uses his device of the pause—and then comes out with—'*You've* got it!' Twain said that every time he told this story, if he got the timing right, he could guarantee that some girl in his audience would at this point, scream and jump out of her shoes. Twain's daughter Susy hated this story, and when her father came to read at Bryn Mawr she begged him not to include it in his programme. He agreed. But when the time came, he could not resist it, and the story was told as usual.[12]

In formulating his ideas about 'how to tell a story' Twain then had his own immense experience to draw upon. And when he came to write his stories down, he undoubtedly had that oral experience very much in mind. Indeed many of his stories do possess all or some of the characteristics he set out in his brief theoretical essay. Tales like 'The Story of the Old Ram', 'A Medieval Romance', 'Tom Quartz' and 'What Stumped the Bluejays', with their stringing together of 'incongruities and absurdities' have a 'shaggy dog' quality. Other tales—such as the famous 'Notorious Jumping Frog of Calaveras County'—seem innocent in a similar sort of way, but in the end prove to be what Twain calls 'snappers', or stories which—like 'The Golden Arm'—do after all make a pretty sharp point.

Apart from 'How to Tell a Story'—and perhaps his 'Report to the Buffalo Female Academy', in which he recommends to his young audience, as the essentials of good writing, naturalness, simplicity, unpretentiousness, linguistic aptness, and above all, the avoidance of moral didacticism—Twain rarely chose to discuss the aesthetics of his own practice as a writer. However, towards the end of his career, when he was writing fragments of his autobiography, he defended his decision to dictate his material in terms that are highly illuminating in relation to his writing as a whole. The passage is a fascinating one, and deserves to be quoted at some length:

> Within the last eight or ten years I have made several attempts to do the autobiography in one way or another with a pen, but the

result was not satisfactory; it was too literary. With the pen in one's hand, narrative is a difficult art; narrative should flow as flows the brook down through the hills and the leafy woodlands, its course changed by every bowlder it comes across and by every grass-clad gravelly spur that projects into its path; its surface broken, but its course not stayed by rocks and gravel on the bottom in the shoal places; a brook that never goes straight for a minute, but goes, and goes briskly, sometimes ungrammatically, and sometimes fetching a horseshoe three-quarters of a mile around, and at the end of the circuit flowing within a yard of the path it traversed an hour before; but always going, and always following at least one law, always loyal to that law, the law of narrative, which has no law. Nothing to do but make the trip; the how of it is not important, so that the trip is made.

With a pen in the hand the narrative stream is a canal; it moves slowly, smoothly, decorously, sleepily, it has no blemish except that it is all blemish. It is too literary, too prim, too nice; the gait and style and movement are not suited to narrative. The canal stream is always reflecting; it is its nature, it can't help it. Its slick shiny surface is interested in everything it passes along the banks—cows, foliage, flowers, everything. And so it wastes a lot of time in reflections.[13]

Such an analysis of the nature of narrative surely finds its ideal within the context of oral narrative; the technique it is recommending is the technique of the ideal American storyteller of 'How to Tell a Story'. Surely too it cannot be mere accident that, in attempting to identify the fundamental nature of narrative movement, Twain reaches instinctively for metaphors of the brook, the stream, the canal. It is as though the Mississippi itself, so central to Twain's experience of life, insistently presents itself as the paradigm of art as well. Experience, that is, seems to order art. It is hard to imagine an aesthetic that more thoroughly overturns traditional models. Such an aesthetic, however, does give substance to the view that Twain was a key figure in moving American narrative prose away from notions of the necessity of conventional formal discipline and control. Substance, too, perhaps to the view that it was the American experience itself (the Mississippi) that did not lend itself to such discipline and control.

3

Twain, as we have seen, was not a theory man. He would be the first to agree that the proof of the apple pie is in the eating. What then is the verdict? In my view at least, to read all of Twain's shorter fictions—including the stories extracted from his longer works—is to experience a measure of disappointment. They do not quite live up to the man. Precisely why is not always easy to pin down. Paradoxically enough, the problem often seems to be one of form. Much of what has been said above amounts to an attempt to explain how the short story can escape from the discipline of its own given form. But not even Twain can go on writing stories the point of which is their own lack of point. Formal problems also persistently arise for Twain in the crucial area of point of view. Just as much as in his longer fictions, he often seems to have had difficulty in sustaining throughout a story a coherent narrative voice. The voice present in the stories is most frequently an authorial one. This is both a strength and a weakness: a strength in that Twain's own robust character, his own no-nonsense, satirical, humorous, perspective can be effectively communicated by it; a weakness in that a version of that moral didacticism or even social and aesthetic superiority which he despised so much, can begin to obtrude through it.

Even more damagingly, the narrative voice can begin to reflect unresolved tensions within Twain's own approach to his subjects. To write at his best, it was clearly necessary for Twain to feel a stable relationship with his material. In his 'Report to the Buffalo Female Academy' he told his audience to write straight from the heart, applying its own language and its own ideas to its subjects. In his own case this usually meant either writing about his own childhood and past, or, more frequently in the case of the stories, about issues or topics which deeply concerned him. The characteristic mode of such stories is of course satirical—which is why stories of a broadly satirical kind make up easily the largest category in Twain's total output of short fiction. The objects of Twain's satire are widely-ranging: the sentimental moral idealism purveyed by popular fiction; romantic fiction's distorting of reality; politics and bureaucracy; newspapers and journalism; economic and other types of 'experts'; science and speculation; detective writing—'A Double-Barreled Detective Story' has an interesting self-reflexive quality (the late *A Fake* even more so); money and human folly in a variety of forms. The greater or lesser degree of success achieved by these satirical tales has much to do with the pressure of moral feeling with which Twain regards the particular topics. In them, too, he often emerges as the critic of the world which, in other contexts, he was happily prepared to represent and recommend. Twain found it possible to be both satirist and spokesman for late nineteenth-century America; the inherent contradiction, nonetheless, was perhaps enough to prevent his satirical writing always achieving the deeper kinds of intensity, and it also helps to explain the kind of narrative uncertainties I have just referred to.

Probably most interesting are those stories—'The £1,000,000 Bank-Note', 'The $30,000 Bequest', and even 'The Man That Corrupted Hadleyburg' and 'The Mysterious Stranger'— which seem to tap deeper levels of Twain's own complicity with a deeply materialistic, financially corrupt society. Twain knew a lot about the power of money to corrupt, because he had experienced that power in his own life. He had the gambling instinct, the financial fever, the materialist impulse, which had made post-bellum America into what he himself had dubbed the Gilded Age. Stories like 'The Man That Corrupted Hadleyburg' and 'The Mysterious Stranger' make it clear that Twain saw money as the root of all evil. The protagonist of 'The £1,000,000 Bank-Note' is not corrupted by the money he is given; the couple in 'The $30,000 Bequest' are destroyed by the money they never even actually possess. In 'The Man That Corrupted Hadleyburg' and 'The Mysterious Stranger' human nature is shown to be prey to the basest kind of material self-interest and selfishness. In all these stories Twain is able to fuse personal experience with a widely-ranging social criticism. Twain's very first successful story— 'The Notorious Jumping Frog of Calaveras County'—with its mocking allusions to Daniel Webster and Andrew Jackson— has come increasingly to be seen as a comment on the American national scene from a post-Civil War perspective. Equally, the later stories of money and corruption, individual and universalist as they are, should not be seen as divorced from the context of late nineteenth-century American capitalism. Of that phenomenon, Twain after all had an inside view.

Whatever the particular context in which they are placed, 'The Man That Corrupted Hadleyburg' and 'The Mysterious Stranger' have become Twain's two best-known and most widely discussed stories. As has already been implied, Twain was in practice far from fussy about the definition of what for him amounted to a short story. When, in 1957, Charles Neider came to compile the book which was published as *The Complete Short Stories of Mark Twain* he culled five stories from *Roughing It*, two from *A Tramp Abroad*, three from *Life on the Mississippi*, and three from *Following the Equator*. But even within this kind of context, the case of 'The Mysterious Stranger' is a genuinely extraordinary one. In a strict sense, despite its fame and all the critical attention paid to it, Twain did not actually write 'The Mysterious Stranger' as a single, autonomous unit. The familiar version of the tale, published originally in 1917, was in fact compiled from three different, unpublished, and unfinished Twain manuscripts by Albert Bigelow Paine, Twain's official biographer, and Frederick A. Duneka, general manager of Harper's publishing house. The editors apparently even wrote some linking material to make the story seem complete. Earlier in his career, Twain had been humorously scathing about unauthorized English editions of his works which contained material attributed to him but in fact the work of other hands—one wonders what he would have to say about the status and posthumous fame of 'The Mysterious Stranger'.

Whatever its textual instability, 'The Mysterious Stranger' has come to be regarded as the definitive statement of the pessimism and despair which overtook Twain in the latter part of his life. Not of course that Twain had not always had a sharp eye for human absurdity and pretentiousness, and for the everyday cruelty and violence of human existence. *Huckleberry Finn* (1886) is full of just such an awareness of human folly and callousness, but as early as 1869, in 'A Day at Niagara', Twain was capable of describing the human race as 'this hackful of small reptiles . . . deemed temporarily necessary to fill a crack in the world's unnoted myriads' until such time as they 'shall have gathered themselves to their blood-relations, the other worms, and been mingled with the unremembering dust'. What happens in the later stories is no more than that such a vision is presented with no qualifying relief. In 'The Man That Corrupted Hadleyburg' and 'The Mysterious Stranger', the narrative voice now assents to the negative vision that the stories' actions create. In *Huckleberry Finn* Twain could still envisage the triumph of human feeling and human integrity over the distorted values produced by a 'deformed conscience'. The conscience that teaches Huck he is committing a capital sin by deciding not to betray Jim, the run-away slave who is his friend, is, in Twain's view, wholly the product of the society in which he has been brought up. In 'The Mysterious Stranger' the place of conscience is taken by the similarly socially-determined Moral Sense, the source of that enlightened, prudent, rational, self-interest that ensures that the injustices and cruelties of human life shall remain as they have always been. In the sixth section of the story, Satan offers us a vision of the capitalist economic system at work: the proprietors of the factory are rich and 'very holy'; but their workers are cruelly exploited and degraded. They are slaves, who would be better off dead. The explanation of the employers' readiness to behave in such a manner is not far to seek: 'it is the Moral Sense that teaches the factory proprietors the difference between right and wrong—you perceive the result.'

I want here to divert for a moment from my main line of critical argument. Twain's singling out of the idea of an innate moral sense as the key to the sustaining of an economic, social, and ethical system, however corrupt and inhuman in practice, is an astonishing feat of cultural insight. The notion of the moral sense had been developed by those Scottish common-sense philosophers whose primary concern had been to refute the dangerous and subversive scepticism of David Hume and his followers. Despite its own revolutionary beginnings, American society had embraced the Scottish common-sense school of Scottish philosophy with unparalleled enthusiasm. For most of the nineteenth century, disseminated by every college, university, and seminary, the tenets of that philosophy came to dominate American thinking. In the post-bellum Gilded Age, its inherent conservatism was available to go on providing an apparently adequate philosophical basis for the activities of an unrestrained, ruthless, capitalism. Singling out the Moral Sense as the object of his most devastating satirical attack, Twain was acting much less arbitrarily than might appear.

At the high point of his literary career in the 1880s, Twain had found only one sure defence against the shams and impostures, the selfishness and corruption of human society and human nature, which in these late stories threaten to overwhelm him. That defence was the realism, the truth, enshrined in the vernacular language of America. The vernacular in which Huck Finn narrates his novel challenges the distortions of thought and feeling produced by other, more socially approved, linguistic modes. Huck's vernacular, that is, acquires a kind of moral authority; in a corrupt world, the naturalness of the vernacular is the only surviving source of honesty, integrity, truth. Let me end then by paying tribute to some stories in which the most lasting and memorable of Twain's literary achievements—his transformation of American vernacular speech into a creative and aesthetically satisfying literary medium—is also apparent. In his comic mode, 'Buck Fanshaw's Funeral' from *Roughing It* is a minor triumph of Twain's art: even if the problem of the point of view of the narrative voice as so often remains unresolved. The clash of linguistic modes works marvellously. The Eastern cleric and the Western 'rough' Scotty, find it difficult to communicate:

> The clergyman sank back in his chair perplexed. Scotty leaned his head on his hand and gave himself up to thought. Presently his face came up, sorrowful but confident.
> 'I've got it now, so's you can savvy,' he said. 'What we want is a gospel-sharp. See?'
> 'A what?'
> 'Gospel-sharp. Parson.'
> 'Oh! Why did you not say so before? I am a clergyman—a parson.'
> 'Now you talk! You see my blind and straddle it like a man. Put it there!'—extending a brawny paw, which closed over the minister's small hand and gave it a shake indicative of fraternal sympathy and fervent gratification.
> 'Now we're all right, pard. Let's start fresh. Don't you mind my snuffling a little—becuz we're in a power of trouble. You

see, one of the boys has gone up the flume—'
'Gone where?'
'Up the flume—throwed up the sponge, you understand.'
'Thrown up the sponge?'
'Yes—kicked the bucket—'
'Ah—has departed to that mysterious country from whose bourne no traveler returns.'
'Return! I reckon not. Why, pard, he's *dead!*'

The story ends with Twain's narrative voice re-establishing the normative, taken-for-granted superiority of Eastern gentility and linguistic 'correctness' over the comic vernacular of the Western figure; but the confrontation itself in the body of the story is robust enough to survive such an ending.

Even better and more satisfying, however, is a story which, exceptionally, is entirely without humour. When Twain submitted this piece to William Dean Howells in his capacity as editor of the *Atlantic*, he wrote: 'I enclose also a "True Story" which has no humour in it. You can pay me as lightly as you choose for that, for it is rather out of my line.' 'A True Story' may well be out of Twain's line in its absence of humour, but it is characteristic of his unselfconsciousness as a writer, his uncritical response to his own work, that he does not recognize just how far the story is in his very best line in its wonderful handling of vernacular discourse to create a moment of the highest emotional and imaginative realism. Howells at least was in no doubt about its quality. He found it 'extremely good and touching and with the best and reallest kind of black talk in it'. In a subsequent review of Twain's *Sketches, New and Old* in 1875, he wrote of 'A True Story':

> The rugged truth of the sketch leaves all other stories of slave life infinitely far behind, and reveals a gift in the author for the simple, dramatic report of reality which we have seen equalled in no other American writer.[14]

Howells is no doubt correct in seeing in 'A True Story' Twain's gift 'for the simple, dramatic report of reality'; but the simplicity and drama in question are achieved this time by the defeat of the authorial narrative voice. The tale is told as it were at its author's expense. He is rebuked by his own creation. Here there is therefore no problem over point-of-view. Apart from an opening descriptive paragraph, and a brief exchange between the narrator and Aunt Rachel, the tale's protagonist, the story is sustained by the black woman's narration of how she was separated from her favourite child at a slave auction and how they were reunited twenty-two years later during the Civil War. The story ends with Rachel's last words. For the narrator there is only silence. He had suggested that Rachel had had a life without trouble. The story has answered him.

'A True Story' looks forward to *Huckleberry Finn* in its sustained use of a first person, vernacular narrative voice. (And to a degree in subject-matter as well.) The success of both these works well suggests how crucial for Twain's art both vernacular language and narrative consistency are. All too often Twain's fiction is flawed by what one comes to feel is the uneasy relationship between author and his fictions. Out of this uneasiness flows Twain's flippancy, evasiveness, and cynicism. (No doubt the formal problem is itself a reflection of Twain's ambiguous relationship to that late nineteenth-century American culture which both repelled and sustained him.) The short stories can in no way be seen as differing in this context from the rest of Twain's work; the problem is common to all his writing. But no account of the American short story can ignore the contribution of a writer so representative of the characteristics and contradictions of post-bellum America as Mark Twain.

NOTES

1. Elizabeth McMahan (ed.), *Critical Approaches to Mark Twain's Short Stories* (Port Washington, 1981), p. ix.
2. See Donald Pizer, *Hamlin Garland's Early Work and Career* (Berkeley and Los Angeles, 1960), p. 63.
3. Sherwood Anderson, *A Story Teller's Story* (New York: B. W. Huebsch, Inc., 1924).
4. Quoted by George Feinstein, 'Mark Twain's Idea of Story Structure' in McMahan, op. cit., p. 10.
5. Ibid., p. 10.
6. William Gibson, *The Art of Mark Twain* (New York, 1976), pp. 72–3.
7. Justin Kaplan, *Mr. Clemens and Mark Twain* (London, 1970), p. 275.

8. Ibid., p. 391.
9. 'How to Tell a Story' in Charles Neider, *The Complete Essays of Mark Twain* (Garden City, New York, 1963), p. 156.
10. Ibid., p. 158.
11. Ibid., p. 158.
12. For this story see Kaplan, op. cit., pp. 475–77.
13. Quoted by Charles Neider, in his *Mark Twain* (New York, 1967), pp. 178–79.
14. Quoted by Kaplan, op. cit., p. 277.

6

Stephen Crane:
Interpreting the Interpreter

by HAROLD BEAVER

> 'Well, I wish I could make something out of those signals.
> What do you suppose he means?'
> 'He don't mean anything; he's just playing.'
> —'The Open Boat', Part 4

1

By the late nineteenth century the heroic ideal, though noisily encouraged in romantic fiction and by the popular press, had become harder and harder to sustain. For the myth of heroism was dependent on free will. But what Mendel and Ricardo and Marx and Darwin and Freud and Malthus had seemingly taught was that man was trapped; that he was the unsuspecting victim of genetic and economic and political and evolutionary and psychological forces, including an ever-spiralling population growth. The myth of heroism, moreover, depended on a vision of an integrated society with its own economic and sexual hierarchies, its own natural and supernatural controls. But, by the end of the century, the whole universe, it seemed, had disintegrated into a chaos of competing and anarchic forces, receding ever faster to a state of entropic collapse. No counter-attack, however defiant, could be waged by an individual alone.

'We picture the world', wrote Crane,

as thick with conquering and elate humanity, but here, with the bugles of the tempest pealing, it was hard to imagine a peopled earth. One viewed the existence of man then as a marvel, and conceded a glamor of wonder to these lice, which were caused to cling to a whirling, fire-smote, ice-locked, disease-stricken, space-lost bulb. The conceit of man was explained by this storm to be the very engine of life.[1]

For it was as if a blizzard had struck the old American certainties. The new forces of Hegelian idealism and Darwinian biology and economic determinism—of evolution, class warfare, and heredity—were peculiarly stacked against the old Jeffersonian belief in personal self-control. Romantic individualism quickly soured, in the decades after the Civil War, to a documentary pessimism. Even before 1860 a brilliant minority of American writers, which included Hawthorne and Melville, had opted for pessimism. But now there were mass deserters. By 1900 the cleft between high art and 'pop' art was complete. It was in this generation that the moral certainties of capitalism were first subverted and the summons of 'rags to riches', 'Log Cabin to White House', was thoroughly undermined. The hero of self-improvement, U.S.-style, was shown, for good or ill, to be a mere victim of circumstances and/or illusions.

Like Dante, the young Stephen Crane awoke to find the straight way lost. He aimed to fight his way out of that *selva oscura*, the Darwinian jungle. *The Red Badge of Courage* was to be his report from the jungle. It appeared when Crane was still only 24 years old. His subject was that of the hunters and the hunted, predators and victims, in a savagely destructive world. But his theme was to be neither the romance of heroism, nor the triumph of heroism, nor even the quandary of heroism in an unheroic age, but rather (to use the title of one of his own later stories) the 'Mystery of Heroism'.[2] For the Darwinian metaphor, red in tooth and claw, had been miraculously turned inside out on that battlefield to become a scenario for this reportage-like fiction. Here Crane could study the human condition, in all its turbulence, with the most exacting details of historical research. In this, too, he proved himself to be profoundly American. What Puritan New England had been for Hawthorne, the Virginian landscape of the Civil War was to be for Crane. Instead of meeting-houses and custom-houses, he would present the pine barrens (in mist and gunsmoke) of the South. Instead of a *Scarlet Letter*, he would depict a *Red Badge* of shame. Just as Hawthorne, furthermore, had studied John Mason and William Hubbard and Cotton and Increase Mather (his seventeenth-century sources for the Indian Wars), so Crane pored over the *Battles and Leaders of the Civil War*,[3] Harper's *History*, the drawings of Winslow Homer, and the photographs of Mathew Brady. Their battle scenes became for him a kind of ritual test, a crisis of identity even.

For Crane had missed the war. He belonged to a post-war generation, guiltily hankering for some extreme engagement in a commercial and prosaic age. He studied the plans of the attacks and counter-attacks of the battle of Chancellorsville (2–4 May 1863). He mentally reconstructed that wilderness, ten miles west of Fredericksburg on the Rappahannock River, in which Sedgwick and Hooker were forced back across the river by Lee's bluff, and the brilliant fifteen-mile flanking attack, in which Stonewall Jackson was mortally wounded. The fictional exercise came first. The emotional rehearsals came first. As with many young writers, Crane's career seems curiously inverted, though what began as a purely literary experience eventually took him to Mexico, and to Cuba and Greece to cover the Turkish War as a correspondent. Later, when he came to write 'The Open Boat', his text recreated the context of his own life ('Stephen Crane's Own Story').[4] But when he wrote *The Red Badge of Courage*, his text had to follow another's text. It was from Stendhal's *Le Rouge et le Noir*, from Tolstoy's *Sevastopol Sketches* ad the great Borodino scenes, as viewed by Pierre in *War and Peace*, that Crane learnt to use his single incoherent angle of vision. For the confusion of soldiers and cavalry charges, the roar of guns and crackle of rifles, the whole mad inconsequence of war were for Crane hugely symbolic of all terror, all uncertainty, all ultimate loneliness. Everything is questioned: the battle, the wound, the heroism, the resolution and self-respect reassembled out of doubts and lies. Crane's Chancellorsville is revealed as a cosmic trap, an absurd non-event. In the final chapter, the regiment finds itself winding back to the river it had originally crossed a few days earlier, as if nothing had happened.

For nothing, in a sense, had happened. Nothing ever happens. Everything becomes part of the antics of non-communication, which was to become Crane's final symbol (in 'The Open Boat') for the existential void in which his actors prate and strut and cower and flee; and sometimes survive; and sometimes face death with a steady dignity and calm. 'Well, God reigns, and in his hands we are safe, whatever awaits us', was his father's habitual refrain. Again and again (in 'Maggie', in 'George's Mother', in 'The Blue Hotel', in 'The Bride Comes to Yellow Sky') Stephen Crane seems to confront his father's snug Methodism, while simultaneously questioning the American demand for aggression, the American pride in the predatory toughguy, the Bowery kid with patent-leather shoes 'like weapons',[5] or Westerners with guns on their hips. The attack is two-pronged. All attempts to shape a moral vision are ultimately reduced to madness in an amoral universe. From Crane's desperate vision runs a direct line to Hemingway's nihilist litanies.

H. G. Wells was right when he wrote that Crane's writings suggested not so much Tolstoy, or Conrad's Lord Jim, as Whistler. Wells praised him for his 'impressionism'.[6] Brown, red, yellow, blue, grey, green, are laid on with a pointilliste discretion. Even in his titles: *The Red Badge of Courage*, 'The Black Riders', 'The Blue Hotel', 'The Bride Comes to Yellow Sky'. His snapshot vision has the terrible, often hallucinatory clarity of dream. Man is out of control: that is the burden of Crane's message. Far from reason or courage, it is illusion and impulse, again and again, that twitches and throws us. Long before Wilfred Owen and Siegfried Sassoon, Crane had confronted the chauvinism and imperialism, the patriotic humbug of a bellicose decade, that gloried in the honour and self-sacrifice of war. In modern wars, he taught, it is the victims who are greeted as heroes.

For death, he realized, *exposes* man. It is the final betrayal of lives mercifully protected by shame, concealment, lies. Like the paper-thin torn soles of the shoes on the feet of a fallen soldier: 'it was as if fate had betrayed the soldier. In death it exposed to his enemies that poverty which in life he had perhaps concealed from his friends.'[7] Wounds, however, may strangely glorify a man. As he declared in 'An Episode of War':

> A wound gives strange dignity to him who bears it. Well men shy from his new and terrible majesty. It is as if the wounded man's hand is upon the curtain which hangs before the revelations of all existence—the meaning of ants, potentates, wars, cities, sunshine, snow, a feather dropped from a bird's wing; and the power of it sheds radiance upon a bloody form, and makes the other men understand sometimes that they are little.[8]

Crane himself, throughout his short career, seems a wounded man, a suicidally haunted man, in his far-ranging quest for wars from Cuba to Turkey. All his fiction, whether set in the Bowery or in the Virginian or Western wilds, seems to fashion his own psychological skirmish, in tougher and tougher engagements, with the amoral, aggressive, commercial, bourgeois jungle of the 1890s.

How does one plot a meaningful life? How plot a meaningful life in such a meaningless universe? Man cannot be wholly predetermined, he seems to say. Economic and social and hereditary environment cannot be all. Men *must* be seen as first movers. Men *must* retain the illusion of free will, to operate in spite of their environment. Against the sins of pride and self-delusion, the sycophantic faith in society's codes and the dogmas of God, must be asserted the moral responsibility of self-definition. 'In a story of mine called "An Experiment in Misery" ', he wrote, 'I tried to make plain that the root of Bowery life is a sort of cowardice. Perhaps I meant a lack of ambition or to willingly be knocked flat and accept the licking.'[9] Crane viewed the bums of the Bowery flophouses uncompromisingly. Cowards are those who cannot confront the question of self-definition. Heroes can and do. Cowards are those who fall prey to social delusions, from whom Crane abdicates all responsibility as a writer. Cowards are those who fail to stand up against the 'collaboration of sin', like the Easterner in tacit alliance with the card-sharper (of 'The Blue Hotel') versus an outsider. The iron bars of tradition and of the law in which man travels Crane called 'a moving box'.[10] The problem is that of living without bars, without order, outside dogmas or codes, in a blizzard of whirling and competing forces. The question is one of decomposition with dignity in a decomposing universe. Not only the rôles but the writing must be disintegrated to reassert our inherent worth and dignity as men.

The ultimate question is that of heroism: not the passionate heroism of Crane's pseudo-heroes—rushing to save, to kill, to prop the flag—but the stoic restraint of a Jim Conklin (in *The Red Badge of Courage*) or the correspondent (in 'The Open Boat'). Neither the Swede fuelled on Scully's whisky (in 'The Blue Hotel'), nor black Henry Johnson rushing into a blazing laboratory (in 'The Monster'), nor Fred Collins recklessly crossing no-man's-land for some water (in 'A Mystery of Heroism'), nor Henry Fleming in his final berserker fury, is a hero. All are 'blindly led by quaint emotions'.[11] All, even at best, are masters merely of their own visionary worlds. As Emily Dickinson once put it:

> A coward will remain, Sir,
> Until the fight is done;
> But an *immortal hero*
> Will take his hat, and run![12]

True heroes act with a nervous integrity: 'as deliberate and exact as so many watchmakers', as Crane wrote of the Cuban conflict.[13] In his final writings (in 'The Veteran', 'The Price of the Harness', *Wounds in the Rain*, the Spitzbergen tales) Crane dealt increasingly with such cool deliberation. Theirs is the dignity of self-possession. Heroes are those who can go forward, alone; who accept moral responsibility for themselves and others; who can accept isolation; who remain committed to life; who stand up to the 'collaboration of sin'. Though they too, of course, must die. They too, like Jim Conklin, may at any moment collapse with an animal-like kick of death.

Crane's heroes cradle their wounds in careful self-support, grabbing their left arm with their right, or holding their right wrist tenderly as if it were 'made of very brittle glass'.[14] For Crane saw through the dignity to the fragility and the pathos of self-possession. He was still only 28 years old when he died. It was of tuberculosis that he died. Within a generation his fragile dignity was reduced to a mere code, a moral shorthand for stoic self-definition and self-control. That is often called Hemingway's code.

2

All codes imply a system of signs. But how can we read such whirling signs? How can we recognize such codes beyond codes? How can we plot such meaning beyond meaning in the blizzard? How can the writing itself be disintegrated? That was the ultimate question confronting Crane. For the over-riding task remained, as always, one of composition. This alone, in a decomposing universe, made the writer's rôle potentially heroic.

'The Blue Hotel' (1899) is a key text. For here everything depends on the interpretation of signs and the misinter-pretation of signs. For interpretation, of course, entails the risk of misinterpretation: through anxiety perhaps (like the Swede's); or through a puzzled complacency (like the cow-boy's); or through a sly suppression (like the Easterner's); or even through a deliberate switching or manipulation of signs (like Johnnie Scully's). So clues may be overlooked; the wrong model applied for the sake of a joke, or from shocked horror. Misreadings may stem from both comic and tragic blindness. 'Any room', writes Crane, 'can present a tragic front; any room can be comic.'[15] Like the cowboy, the Swede is a potentially comic figure, though he alone is driven headlong to disaster.

'The entire prelude', Crane emphasizes, 'had in it a tragedy greater than the tragedy of action, and this aspect was accentuated by the long, mellow cry of the blizzard. . . .'[16] In reading 'The Blue Hotel', we are invited to misread ('It's funny, ain't it?') what turns out to be only a partial mis-reading. For the Swede is *both* sharp-eyed *and* crazy; he is *both* tricked *and* murdered. It is the chaotic confusion of codes—or rather, the confused adherence to a single code in the midst of such confusion—that turns out to be tragic. Suppressed outrage is the common denominator uniting the native speakers (whether from the East, West, or Midwest) against the impetuous stranger: Johnnie is presented as 'brutish yet heroic'; his father rejects the cowboy as champion 'with mournful heroism'; even to the gambler is attributed a 'tone of heroic patronage'. Heroic outrage, in fact, is the universal American attribute. As soon as their code is challenged, the Americans are silenced in blank amazement.

It is to this edge of silence, this blank amazement, that Crane relentlessly spins his tale. 'Wonder' (with all its synonyms) is the hallmark of its style. Pat Scully, at the start, performs 'the marvel of catching three men'. Once ensconced in his hotel, they gaze at the Swede 'wondering and in silence'. On his departure upstairs, they fall into 'an astounded silence'. At Scully's deference to him, the 'cowboy and the Easterner exchanged glances of wonder'. By supper 'the cowboy sat in wide-mouthed amazement.' (That expression, we are informed, 'was one of his important mannerisms'.) During Johnnie's fight in the storm, 'Scully was immovable as from supreme amazement.' Until, too late, even the Swede catches this all-American mannerism, when (knifed) he falls 'with a cry of supreme astonishment'.

That cry is not ironic. It merely ends his blustering career. For it is in wonder that meaning disintegrates. It is in wonder that the signs and codes are ultimately silenced. It is in wonder that writing itself is decomposed. Now only the narrator is left to wonder:

> The corpse of the Swede, alone in the saloon, had its eyes fixed upon a dreadful legend that dwelt atop of the cash-machine: 'This registers the amount of your purchase.'[17]

Only the narrator is left to marvel at the juxtaposition of the cash-register and the corpse. His is the irony. Crane's characters can only start at each other's comic, or tragic, reflexes. The narrator is left to marvel at the grossest of all their misreadings: not only of the human body (this so-called 'citadel of virtue, wisdom, power'), but of the planet it inhabits. 'One viewed the existence of man then as a marvel, and conceded a glamor of wonder to these lice', who pictured themselves as a 'conquering and elate humanity'. For even our reading of the universe turns out to be a fiction; and fiction itself can only yield 'a glamor of wonder' to such misreadings. All Crane can offer is a variety of competing codes which falters into silence at the moment of crisis.

The code of 'realism', such as it is, might be called the

Nebraska code. It is the genteel code to which Pat Scully, as proprietor of the Blue Hotel, officially subscribes. It is geared to the myth of capitalist progress. It surveys Fort Romper, even as it is, with pride. But the future alone is really real:

> 'Why, man, we're goin' to have a line of ilictric street cars in this town next spring.'
> ' "A line of electric street cars," ' repeated the Swede, stupidly.
> 'And,' said Scully, 'there's a new railroad goin' to be built down from Broken Arm to here. Not to mintion the four churches and the smashin' big brick schoolhouse. Then there's the big factory, too. Why, in two years Romper'll be a met-tro-*pol*-is.'[18]

The founding fathers of this metropolis are found in Fort Romper's saloon. They consist, on closer inspection, of two prominent local businessmen, the district attorney and a professional gambler. These gentlemen form a surreptitious and homogeneous amalgam; for 'a scrutiny of the group would not have enabled an observer to pick the gambler from the men of more reputable pursuits.' By the Nebraska code, technological progress is linked to business, business to law, and law to gambling in a flawless continuum. *No* outsider, however shrewd, could have observed the transition.

This progressive code, then, is an extension of Fort Romper's fraudulent past, just as its social life is still (largely) sustained by a code of honour. A challenge inevitably initiates a duel:

> 'Did you say I cheated?'
> The Swede showed his teeth. 'Yes.'
> 'Then,' said Johnnie, 'we must fight.'
> 'Yes, fight,' roared the Swede.[19]

It is the very ambiguity of the Nebraska code that traps the stranger. For its ultimate touchstone (which he mistakenly touches) is none other than the exemplary, married, suburban gambler: 'this thieving card-player' who was 'so generous, so just, so moral, that, in a contest, he could have put to flight the consciences of nine-tenths of the citizens of Romper'. (Yet it is he who carries a sneaky switch-blade, not even a gun.)

In apposition to the Nebraska code is the 'western' code of dime novel violence which Johnnie, for one, has clearly read, but from which he keeps his distance. He is his father's son. Fort Romper, purportedly, is far removed from such 'shootin' and stabbin''.

> 'But,' said the cowboy, deeply scandalized, 'this ain't Wyoming, ner none of them places. This is Nebrasker.'
>
> 'Yes,' added Johnnie, 'an' why don't he wait till he gits *out West?*'[20]

For if the Nebraska code is (in aspiration at least) midwestern, this literary code is archetypally western. It has to be explicated by the Easterner and independently confirmed ('he thought this was a tough place') by Scully. Certainly the Swede behaves tough. He recklessly throws his weight around. But he is also no fool. He *saw* Johnnie cheating: that is also confirmed. And he will be stabbed to death. It is only in his mouth that the vocabulary of 'tenderfoot' and 'dude' and the 'gang' seems woefully misplaced. It grates. Its easy assurance is incapable of piercing the ambiguities of the 'real' code.

In addition to the local and literary codes, Crane introduces a purely ludic code: that dictated by the rules (under whatever name or 'alias') of the game of High-Five. Being explicitly a game, it can most openly comment on the formal comings and goings of the others:

> . . . and now the whole company of cards was scattered over the floor, where the boots of the men trampled the fat and painted kings and queens as they gazed with their silly eyes at the war that was waging above them.

Or:

> Some of the scarred and bedabbled cards were caught up from the floor and dashed helplessly against the farther wall. The men lowered their heads and plunged into the tempest as into a sea.

Or:

> The cowboy carried Johnnie through the drift to the door. As they entered, some cards again rose from the floor and beat against the wall.[21]

This is a wholly symbolic code, then, to mirror the social and literary codes and confirm their mysterious commutations.

But, above all, it mirrors the code of fiction. For Crane is playing that 'queer game' too for all its worth. It proves an absorbing game. For he is a most self-conscious master of the fictive or aesthetic code, linking the Palace Hotel, a heron's legs and the shadowed snow by colour, as it were, into a single suit. Thus the strange, emblematic opening:

> The Palace Hotel at Fort Romper was painted a light blue, a shade that is on the legs of a kind of heron, causing the bird to declare its position against any background.

If the Swede himself is never blue exactly, he too declares his position against any background (whether in the hotel or saloon). His too is a 'splendor of isolation' (as he leans against a tree), just as the hotel's 'opulence and splendor' has nothing in common with the grey hush of the prairie or the miscellaneous 'creeds, classes, egotisms, that streamed through Romper on the rails day after day'. Colour, as always in Crane, is a symbolic code, just as the symbolic code (of High-Five) reflects the social code of the narration.

For there are five characters in all who play their collaborative rôles: (1) Bill, the cowboy, crudely whacking his cards on the board and overdoing his repertoire of amazement; (2) Mr. Blanc, the watchful and crafty Easterner; (3) Pat Scully, enacting the capitalist code with an Irish compound of 'strategy', 'ceremonies' and 'seductions'; (4) his son, Johnnie, enacting a farcical *reductio ad absurdum* of his father's code (as liar and cheat); (5) and finally Henry, the gambler. Only the Swede (or Dutchman) is anonymous.

But what floored that anonymous Swede or Dutchman? What killed the ex-tailor from New York, with his maniacal laugh and witless wink, who adopted the cowboy's 'fashion of board-whacking' and ultimately even his astonishment? A blade, of course. Not even the gambler. Mr. Blanc finally delivers himself of a 'theory'. For it is the Easterner who speaks the concluding, mysterious epigraph:

> We are all in it! This poor gambler isn't even a noun. He is kind of an adverb. Every sin is the result of a collaboration. We, five of us, have collaborated in the murder of this Swede. Usually there are from a dozen to forty women really involved in every murder, but in this case it seems to be only five men—you, I,

130

Johnnie, old Scully; and that fool of an unfortunate gambler came merely as a culmination, the apex of a human movement, and gets all the punishment.[22]

The question is: do we read the codes through the characters, or the characters through the codes? This text suggests the latter. Characters are not self-generated, the Easterner suggests: not self-referential, concrete or proper nouns. They are merely the collaborative functions of a code. They are merely the *means* which make action possible. They are all merely 'adverbs' in search of a (verbal) author.

As a moral theme, this lesson was common enough in the years after the Civil War. An old priest, in George Washington Cable's *Madame Delphine* (1881), declares:

> We all participate in one another's sins. There is a community of responsibility attaching to every misdeed. No human since Adam—nay, nor Adam himself—ever sinned entirely to himself. And so I never am called upon to contemplate a crime or a criminal but I feel my conscience pointing at me as one of the accessories.[23]

Both North and South were implicated communally in the blame for the Civil War. But Crane decomposed such collaboration to curious semiotic terms. Thus the final outraged cry by the cowboy: 'Well, I didn't do anythin', did I?'[24] All are actors constrained (adverbially) by their code. All codes collaborate (adverbially) in eliminating the isolated reader. This is the blind fog of semiotic 'theory' against which the cowboy mutinies.

But at least it is a theory. Such characters are all in search of an author, an authority. Here Crane supplies such an authority. The Easterner saw Johnnie cheating. He knew it. He saw it. Yet he flinched from the heroic rôle. He refused to stand up and be counted. He can only play the theoretical, or critical, rôle. Excluded from all codes, as Mr. Blanc, he can stand in for the author. 'The Open Boat' had ended on the same teasing, analytical note:

> When it came night, the white waves paced to and fro in the moonlight, and the wind brought the sound of the great sea's voice to the men on the shore, and they felt that they could then be interpreters.

131

For them the problem of 'those signals' was never to be resolved.[25] Did they mean nothing? Were they all a game? Insistently Crane encouraged us to dissolve and resolve all systems, including those of his fictions. On this 'whirling, fire-smote, ice-locked, disease-stricken, space-lost bulb' it is our existential necessity. It is our heroic responsibility.

NOTES

1. 'The Blue Hotel', Part 8, from *The Monster and Other Stories* (New York, 1899).
2. 'A Mystery of Heroism' appeared in *The Little Regiment* (New York, 1896).
3. *Battles and Leaders of the Civil War; being for the most part contributions by Union and Confederate officers; based upon 'The Century War Series'*, edited by the editorial staff of the *Century Magazine*, 4 vols. (New York, 1884–87).
4. 'Stephen Crane's Own Story', New York *Press* (7 January 1897).
5. *Maggie: A Girl of the Streets* (New York, 1893), Part 5.
6. 'Stephen Crane from an English Standpoint', *North American Review*, 171 (August 1900), 233–42.
7. *The Red Badge of Courage* (New York, 1895), Part 3.
8. 'An Episode of War' in *Last Words* (London, 1902).
9. Crane writing to Catherine Harris on 12 November 1896: *Stephen Crane: Letters*, edited by R. W. Stallman and Lillian Gilkes (New York, 1960), p. 133.
10. *The Red Badge of Courage*, Part 3.
11. 'A Mystery of Heroism'.
12. Written in 1852: *The Poems of Emily Dickinson*, edited by Thomas H. Johnson (Cambridge, Massachusetts, 1955), No. 3.
13. *Wounds in the Rain* was a fictional adaptation of Crane's own adventures with the American forces in Cuba, 1898.
14. 'An Episode of War'.
15. 'The Blue Hotel', Part 5.
16. 'The Blue Hotel', Part 6.
17. 'The Blue Hotel', Part 8.
18. 'The Blue Hotel', Part 3.
19. 'The Blue Hotel', Part 5.
20. 'The Blue Hotel', Part 4.
21. 'The Blue Hotel', Parts 5 and 6.
22. 'The Blue Hotel', Part 9.
23. George Washington Cable, *Madame Delphine* (New York, 1896), Ch. 4.
24. Echoing his earlier cry (in chorus with Johnnie): 'Why, we didn't do nothin' to 'im!'

25. See my opening quotation from *The Open Boat and Other Tales of Adventure* (New York, 1898). The introductory paragraphs of this essay first appeared (in an earlier version) in *Yearbook of English Studies*, Vol. 12 (1982), and are reprinted by permission of the Editors and Publishers (Modern Humanities Research Association).

7

'Our Bedfellow Death': The Short Stories of Ambrose Bierce

by HERBIE BUTTERFIELD

To his friend, Herman Scheffauer, Ambrose Bierce (1842–1914?) once claimed in an uncharacteristically defensive mode: 'Maybe, as you say, my work lacks "soul", but my life does not, as a man's life is the man.'[1] Whether or not that 'soul' is absent from the work, the remark may at any rate serve to make the point that more than seventy years after his disappearance, it is still Bierce's life or legend, rather than his writing, that is generally addressed, so that the representative book on him is less the critical study than the literary biography.[2] Even the fact that we have to refer to his 'disappearance' rather than to his death distinguishes him, vanishing, as he did, at the age of 71 shortly after Christmas 1913, in northern Mexico during a time of revolutionary war. He had written his farewell to his niece, Lora Bierce: 'Civilization be dinged!—it is the mountains and the desert for me . . . I don't know where I shall be next. Guess it doesn't matter much. Adios, Ambrose.'[3] He was seeking, surely, 'the good, good darkness',[4] not quite taking the way of suicide, but at least going stoically to meet the death that had always fascinated, drawn, and fixed him.

The life that almost certainly ended there and then had begun in 1842 in Ohio, whence four years later the large family—Ambrose was the tenth child—moved further west to the adjoining state of Indiana. The living, off a small farm, was pinched and mean; the culture was backwoods Calvinist, but entirely literate, even bookish. Bierce was later to proclaim a broad and vociferous hostility to all religions, though in many of his attitudes the lapsed (or perhaps dis-graced) Calvinist remained prominently visible. As for family ties, for only one of those many brothers and sisters did Bierce retain any sort of affection into adult life, while his parents he once famously described as 'unwashed savages'. Imaginary parents are time and again disposed of in his stories, four of the more wishfully straightforward being grouped under the heading, 'The Parenticide Club'. 'Having murdered my mother under circumstances of singular atrocity', begins 'My Favorite Murder', while 'An Imperfect Conflagration' opens with the confession that 'Early one June morning in 1872 I murdered my father—an act which made a deep impression on me at the time.' More economically, with respect to expenditure of energy, 'The Hypnotist' induces his parents into believing under hypnosis that they are bucking broncos, who thereupon set about kicking one another to death.

However, Bierce's family did at least provide one heroic model from his childhood days, his uncle, the self-styled General Lucius Bierce, who was instrumental in sending his nephew to the Kentucky Military Institute, and from whom doubtless Bierce originally derived his authoritarian values and his admiration for the military virtues. In the Civil War he became an outstanding young officer on the staff of the other soldier-hero of his youth, General William B. Hazen. And just as a whaleship had been Melville's University, so the Union Army was Bierce's; the horror, the pathos, the terror, and the courage of war service were imprinted on his mind and senses more deeply than any other of his experiences, so that almost without exception the best of his imaginative work is set in what was by the time of its writing the long-ago world of the war.

In 1866, a year after the war had ended, he accompanied General Hazen on an expedition through the Far West and thus reached San Francisco, where he settled, still doing battle, though now with pen and tongue rather than with

135

pistol and sword. Here began the journalistic career that led to his becoming, in what was admittedly then a small pool, the biggest, the most ferocious, and the most feared of creatures: 'Bitter Bierce', 'Almighty God Bierce', scourge of all who offended him, in whatever manner and for whatever reason, the lash of railroad millionaire and platform socialist alike and of officious minister and effete poet, performing his vituperative work in a succession of newspapers until in 1887 the young William Randolph Hearst sought him out for his San Francisco *Examiner*. Apart from three years in England in the early 1870s with his recently wedded wife, and a few unfortunate months in 1880, gold-mining in Deadwood, South Dakota, he remained in San Francisco until 1896 when he moved to be Hearst's sharp-shooter in Washington. In his personal life he had by that time come to know discord and disaster. He had separated from his wife in 1888, and not long after his elder son had committed murder and suicide at the age of 16; the younger son was to die of pneumonia, aggravated by alcoholism, in 1901.[5] Death, the ubiquitous presence in his fiction, was also outside and all around him, his intimate and familiar long before he found his own oblivion in Mexico.[6]

The *Collected Works* that Bierce assembled and that were published between 1909 and 1912 by his friend, Walter Neale, ran to twelve volumes, a mix of ephemeral journalism, satirical sketches and verse, social and literary criticism, short stories, still shorter fables, and *The Devil's Dictionary*, his tour de force of sardonic and subversive definition. The stories occupy three volumes: Volume II, *In the Midst of Life*, his *Tales of Soldiers and Civilians*, as they had been originally entitled and published in 1891; Volume III, *Can Such Things Be?* of 1893; and Volume VIII, *Negligible Tales*, most of them aptly so-called. For all his long life, as an imaginative writer Bierce is a figure of only one decade, the 1890s, indeed of less than a decade, of the years 1888 to 1893—a single lustrum, to use the sort of latinism he enjoyed. His output of fiction was small, and the part of it worth preserving and returning to much smaller yet, perhaps twenty-five *short* stories, which is to say, discriminatingly selected, a single volume of fiction.[7] The slightness of this remnant certainly points to a creative deficiency, an imaginative baulking; but it also offers a consistent expression of his aesthetics, which in a manner derived essentially from Poe's critical principles stress brevity, concentration, and singleness of narrative purpose. Hence his dislike of the novel form:

> The novel bears the same relation to literature that the panorama bears to painting. With whatever skill and feeling the panorama is painted, it must lack that basic quality in all art, unity, totality of effect. . . . A novel is a diluted story—a story cumbered with trivialities and nonessentials.[8]

Significantly, by far the longest fiction included in his *Collected Works*, 'The Monk and the Hangman's Daughter', is scarcely his own, being little more than an 'amplified'[9] rewriting by him of Adolphe Danziger's translation from the German of Richard Voss.

It was not only to the 'cumbered' size and 'panoramic' spread of the novel that Bierce objected, but also to its realism and to all those documentary and verisimilar elements which might be taken to differentiate the form from the prose romance. The romance was the tradition with which Bierce aligned himself, naming in particular the *Arabian Nights*, Beckford, Poe, Hawthorne, Scott, whom he found to be 'incomparably greater' than Dickens,[10] and Victor Hugo, who fortunately for the world did not stoop to practise the 'barren art' of the 'mere novel'.[11] 'Realism', decreed his *Devil's Dictionary*, is 'the art of depicting nature as it is seen by toads'. It has 'the charm suffusing a landscape painted by a mole, or a story written by a measuring-worm'.[12] Because of the gruesome descriptive detail of his war stories and their refusal of emotional glorification, Bierce has often been assimilated into programmatic late nineteenth-century realism,[13] but in general, those aspects of the 'tales of soldiers' apart, he is no sort of realist. His stories, supernatural, grotesque, surreal, absurd, look back and forward to quite other kinds.

In addition to his dislike of the novel and of realism, Bierce professed a contempt for 'distinctively American literature'.[14] Despite this prejudice, his comic narrative vein in particular is entirely American. In such stories the highly intelligent, acerbic, and penetrating wit that makes *The Devil's Dictionary* an idiosyncratic masterpiece is nowhere to be found. Instead the humour here is heavy, crude, cruel, physically violent, almost universally misanthropic, but above all misogynous.[15] Its antecedents lie in the tall tale, in the frontier humourists of the old South West, and in a rough world of the hoax and the con-trick, of tarring and feathering, riding on a rail, and running out of town. Poe's penchant for human dismemberment and corporeal disintegration, in such comic stories as 'The Man That Was Used Up' and 'A Predicament', may also come to mind, while, looking forward, we may reckon the progeny of this humour to include the sadistic film cartoon and black comic extravaganzas in various media.

Most of these stories are to be found in the volume, *Negligible Tales*, where the narrator is regularly a hoaxer, a con-man, or a quack, heir to a family tradition in such lines perhaps, dedicated to parting the gullible from their money or the still more gullible from their lives, for sound commercial reasons, of course, on the general principle that you can fool all of the people most of the time and most of the people all of the time. So, John Brenwalter's father, in 'A Bottomless Grave', 'had a patent for an invention for making coffee-berries out of clay', while his wife and son 'in our intervals of leisure . . . decoyed travelers into our house and buried the bodies in a cellar'. The narrator of 'The City of the Gone Away' sets up as a quack doctor, who owns also 'some very profitable marble works' and 'an extensive flower garden'. Having treated his patients definitively, he sells the corpses to a medical college and garners a further tidy fortune out of wreaths and tombstones. On being found out, he makes himself scarce, but, as is typical in Bierce's world where everyone gets their unjust deserts, his unimplicated father is hanged. For Boffer Bings and his wife in 'Oil of Dog' 'the conversion of their neighbors into dog-oil became, in short, the only passion of their lives', until, fulfilling the author's parenticidal fantasies, they engage one another in a murderous fight and die together in a boiling cauldron.

As a misogynist Bierce is a respecter neither of age nor of youth. He starts young with the pathetic orphan of 'A Little Story', pelting her to death with every thing she had ever wished for from heaven raining down upon her, until she is eventually crushed flat as a map, any stray, sentimental reader doubtless flattened too. In 'My Curried Cow' old Aunt Phoebe fares similarly, as she is manoeuvred towards her beloved, but infuriated cow, who 'would kick at anything. . . . Gad! how thinly she spread out that good old lady upon the face of an adjacent stone wall! You could not have done it so evenly with a trowel.' 'A Revolt of the Gods', an allegorized satire upon industrial struggle by one whose loathing of trade unionists was surpassed only by his loathing of anarchists,[16] is a partial exception to the general rule that these comic stories have no purpose other than that of casual and mainly sadistic entertainment. 'My Curried Cow' is, for an example, probably the best of its kind, but the kind is coarse fare, wearisomely repeated, for immature tastes. To laugh appreciatively with Bierce, we must go to *The Devil's Dictionary*.

Rather higher claims can be made for a number of what we may call either the supernatural stories, as they are collected in *Can Such Things Be?*, or the 'tales of civilians', as Bierce himself distinguished them from the war stories in *In the Midst of Life*. Many of these too are very slight, but about a dozen are more substantial and quite effective within their own terms. A rare instance of Bierce crossing into the realm of science fiction and future technology is provided by 'Moxon's Master', in which Moxon is 'mastered' and destroyed, throttled, by the automaton of his own invention, which he has just checkmated at chess, but which he has not programmed to accept defeat. The story offers a fearful, essentially pessimistic view of technology's destructive potential from one not much given to placing hope in the future.

However, Bierce's excursions outside the present usually take him elsewhere, into some post-mortem limbo, as in 'An Inhabitant of Carcosa', or psyche's frozen time, as in 'A Resumed Identity'. The former story, which is more overtly symbolic, or more legend-like, than is Bierce's wont, is prefaced with a brief paragraph on 'the divers sorts of death' by a fictional Oriental sage, Hali,[17] concluding: 'Sometimes, as is veritably attested, [the spirit] dieth with the body, but after a season is raised up again in that place where the body did decay.' So here the narrator, a vagrant being in trance or dream, estranged from familiar experience, wanders through a blasted, ruined landscape, once home perhaps 'of a historic race of men', whose tombs and monuments have gone the way of Ozymandias: 'the years had levelled all.' At length he bends to read an inscription still visible on a solitary tombstone, and finding it to be his own, knows that he walks, 'a spirit raised up again', amongst 'the ruins of the ancient and famous city of Carcosa', his own Carcosa, carcass surely, 'where the body did decay'. 'A Resumed Identity' is more personal, more auto-biographical, indeed the most autobiographical story that Bierce ever wrote, in that the central figure is, as Bierce himself had been, 'a lieutenant, of the staff of General Hazen'. He appears, an old man in civilian clothes in a peaceful countryside, who believes himself to be a 23-year-old Federal soldier amidst the ravages of war. He wanders, bemused as Rip Van Winkle, until he comes upon a memorial to his comrades fallen long ago, catches sight of his own aged face in a pool, and, in the moment of dying or resuming the death that had already been his, knows himself to have been in effect a ghost from the past. Likewise, doubtless, Bierce in old age revisiting the sites of his Civil War battles knew himself also to be such a ghost, who had lived at his most intense and so nearly died—perhaps in some essential respect had died—in that war far off in time, yet his perpetual 'dreamland', as he once described it.[18]

The sudden shock or the protracted fear that must have been the young soldier's frequent or regular experience, Bierce later recreated time and again, not only in the tales of war, but also in those with a civilian setting. Being literally frightened to death is a common event in his fiction, with death often coming as a form of ironic justice, an appropriate correction of a previous cavalier or braggart arrogance, a final humbling of false pride. In 'The Man and the Snake' the wealthy dilettante, Harker Brayton, whom we first see contemplating disdainfully the 'nonsense' that 'the wise and learned' had once believed, eventually dies of fright, of a phobia, mesmerized by the shining shoe-button eyes of a stuffed snake, which, fixated, immo-bilized, he had taken to be alive. 'A Watcher by the Dead' and 'The Suitable Surroundings' are intricately plotted and ironically twisted stories of the testing and collapse of nerve and consequent death from shock, as, in the one story, what has appeared to be a corpse takes on life and, in the other, what is in fact flesh and blood appears to be a ghost returned to haunt.

These two stories, it may be noted, are not precisely supernatural, but stories in which the natural is mistaken for the supernatural, in which terror of the supernatural is the natural cause of death. Many of Bierce's stories, though, are of course properly supernatural, and all of the best of them, which I take to be, roughly in order, 'The Death of Halpin Frayser', 'The Eyes of the Panther', 'The Boarded Window', 'The Moonlit Road', 'The Middle Toe of the Right Foot', and 'The Secret of MacArger's Gulch', have in common as their central feature the violent death of a woman at the hands of a husband or lover. The violence, though sometimes accidental, is always horrifying—indeed the most horrifying, that in 'The Boarded Window', is entirely accidental[19]—and the woman is always innocent, tragically misjudged, for instance, in 'The Moonlit Road'. If we remember that these stories were all written in the years immediately following Bierce's separation from his wife, whom he too had by any standard misjudged, we may surely see, on the one hand, in all this violence a self-indulgence on Bierce's part but, on the other, in all this murdered innocence a recognition of his own wife's innocence, a confession of his own guilt or at least fault, and thus a self-punishment.

Most of these stories of ghostly manifestation, metempsychosis, or midnight horror are quite short and simple, but the longest, 'The Death of Halpin Frayser', is psychologically complex, narratively elusive, and metaphysically tantalizing. In a nightmare world, literally blood-bedewed, where 'blood dripped like dew from [the] foliage', a tale is unfolded of lost, exchanged, or transferred identities, of incestuous affinity between mother and son, and of post-mortem evil. Here death releases not a spirit disembodied, but a body devoid of spirit; and here, most terrifyingly irrational of all 'some spirits which in life were benign become by death evil altogether', so that Halpin Frayser in his nightmare journey comes upon his mother's dead body 'regarding him with the mindless malevolence of a wild brute', which 'then thrust its hands forward and sprang upon him with appalling ferocity'! It is the climactic moment in Bierce's festival of terrors; and, it must be, the primary source of those terrors, the alpha and omega of all such: the 'soulless' mother, inaccessible to humanity (though—

because?—erotically imaginable), tearing her own child to pieces.

For all the dreadful power of such a story, it is nevertheless in the 'tales of soldiers' that Bierce comes fully into his own, and literally into his own, in so far as he produced there a small body of work, with a quite distinct, even unique mark. The best of his supernatural stories might deserve their place in an anthology of such tales; but the war stories have, as the supernatural do not, an originality and, as a group, an integrity that must surely derive from their being less exercises in a genre of short fiction by a versatile writer than compulsory expressions of a man's most intense experience, a long-pent-up force released. Bierce's 'tales of civilians' can be lost amongst other such spine-chillers and blood-curdlers; his 'tales of soldiers', in their concentrated enactment of scenes and evocation of moments from the American Civil War, are like no other.

They are first highly pictorial stories,[20] their physical settings regularly depicted for us with startling clarity and detailed precision, visualized with the trained eye, for instance, of the 'topographical engineer' who tells the story of 'killed at Resaca', with the recollecting trained eye, that is of course, of Lieutenant Bierce. Says the narrator in 'George Thurston':

> Our frequent engagements with the Confederate outposts, patrols, and scouting parties had, incidentally, the same educating value; they fixed in my memory a vivid and apparently imperishable picture of the locality.

So in the beginning we *see*, see a picture. And the picture is pre-cinematic, not a moving picture, nor for that matter a talking picture. Of course, there is often movement, and of course there is often sound, but what adheres is the silent image, the still life, the statue, the tableau. Thus in 'A Horseman in the Sky':

> On a colossal pedestal, the cliff—motionless at the extreme edge of the capping rock and sharply outlined against the sky—was an equestrian statue of impressive dignity. The figure of the man sat the figure of the horse, straight and soldierly.

Thus in 'An Occurrence at Owl Creek Bridge':

> Excepting the group of four at the center of the bridge, not a man moved. The company faced the bridge, staring stonily,

motionless. The sentinels, facing the banks of the stream, might have been statues to adorn the bridge. The captain stood with folded arms, silent, observing the work of his subordinates.

Thus, concisely, in 'One Kind of Officer': 'Captain Ransome sat motionless and silent on horseback.'

It is an eerie atmosphere that Bierce conveys, this 'silence and fixity', this vivid stillness. It is clear and sharp in quality, yet remote, estranged, alien from usual, daily perception, dream-like. Indeed in two especially memorable instances we do pass over for much of the length of each story into the unusually and silently perceived world of the deaf-mute ('Chickamauga') and into the unusually and silently perceived world of the dying man's last-moment dream of desire ('An Occurrence at Owl Creek Bridge'). Both pellucid and disturbing, these visual effects find their closest analogies outside writing in the exotic paintings of le Douanier Rousseau and in the metaphysical paintings of de Chirico.[21]

In these pictorially arranged settings, the figures seem to move, or stand, essentially in isolation one from another. There is scant human interaction; men (and women) merely impose or intrude upon others to bring about the bitter, ironic end that for Bierce signifies about all there is of universal purpose.[22] Lethal orders are given (for instance, in 'The Affair at Coulter's Notch'); fatal entrances are made (for instance, in 'The Coup de Grâce'). The rest is solitary business, and often silent: the sentry in lonely bondage to his human target; trapped or doomed men facing their death; men locked within their own terror, shuffling the cards of cowardice, bravado and courage; the deaf-mute child alone first with his grotesque misunderstanding and then with his terrible comprehension. In consequence, they are for the most part stories with little or no dialogue, in which often what conversation there is merely unleashes in conclusion the full, overwhelming force of irony. The chief exception, 'Parker Adderson, Philosopher', which consists largely of a discussion between a simple soldier and a witty sophisticate about how to go to one's death, effectively proves the rule that, as Edmund Wilson has put it, 'Death may perhaps be said to be Bierce's only real character.'[23] And to be precise, of the sixteen war stories, eleven end with the

143

death of the principal or only actor, two with him having to expect death, and the remaining three with him causing or witnessing the death of his dearest relative.

A war story by Bierce, then, characteristically possesses a vividly depicted situation, in which a man either physically or morally alone faces a supreme challenge, of conscience or nerve. This protagonist is less a complex idiosyncratic individual than a particular, uniformed type (the soldier at war) or a general human representative seen in a single, particular aspect (at a time of intense conflict between duty and affection, in an extremity of fear, under ultimate stress). In the background, briefly sketched in or scarcely more than hinted at, may be a web of tangled lives and emotions, but within the story itself a relatively simple series of events will lead, often by means of the obtrusive device of coincidence,[24] to a surprising or at least shocking end in which the ironic point is made, sometimes grimly, blackly comic (as in 'One Kind of Officer'), sometimes pitiful, pathetic (as in 'Chickamauga'), sometimes reaching in sparse outline towards the dimension of tragedy (as in 'A Horseman in the Sky'). Thus, in both their formal and psychological structure, are Bierce's tales of war signed by an unmistakable hand, sealed and delivered, closed, always closed in death, in a death that is finite.

Leading up to these conclusive deaths, two themes predominate in the stories, two kinds of thematic study: of conscience; and of terror. Explicitly entitled is 'The Story of a Conscience', Captain Hartroy's conscience, which obliges him, first, to condemn to death as a deserter and spy the man who had previously saved his life at immense risk to himself; and which obliges him, secondly, having ordered the execution, to take his own life, as a matter of honour. 'A Horseman in the Sky' and 'The Affair at Coulter's Notch' are woven of the tragic stuff of all civil war, the division of loyalties within a family, and the clash of military necessity and personal tie. As Carter Druse takes leave of his family home in Virginia border country to join a Union regiment, his Confederate father, type of the courteous patrician, bids farewell with the instruction, 'whatever may occur', to 'do what you conceive to be your duty'. An age later, albeit only months, as a Union soldier he knows his duty to be to kill his father whom he spots looking out, a horse-back sentinel for the Confederate forces, from a cliff-top, a figure of 'heroic' and 'noble' quality. Firing at the horse, the son makes of his father as he plunges, still mounted, to his death in the valley below, a 'Horseman in the Sky', a horseman of 'some new Apocalypse'. In 'The Affair at Coulter's Notch', Captain Coulter, a Southern planter fighting on the Union side, mounts an artillery attack, in reluctant obedience to military imperative, on his family home, in which his wife, 'a red-hot Secessionist', and child are killed. But more than civil war's tragic irony is in play here, for outright, murderous evil is present in the shape of the Union general who has ordered the attack. It makes for that general an exquisite revenge upon Coulter's wife, who a little previously had rejected his advances and lodged a complaint about his conduct.

The studies of momentary terror or constant fear take various forms. There is the fear of fear itself, the fear of cowardice that leads to the bravado of 'George Thurston' and of Herman Brayle in 'Killed at Resaca', taunted into fool-hardiness by his girl-friend from the distant safety of her comfortable home in San Francisco. There is the terror of battle so great that rather than face its horrors Captain Graffenreid chooses suicide, during an abortive engagement in which only one other man dies. The battalion thus suffers the loss not of two brave, upstanding soldiers respecting them-selves as men, but, as the title of the story discriminates, of 'One Officer, One Man'. There is the terror, as in the civilian 'A Watcher by the Dead', of the dead body that Lieutenant Byring hacks to shreds before taking his own life in 'A Tough Tussle'. There is the terror of the man in a deadly trap, the terror that leads to the emotional disintegration of the perfect soldier, Jerome Searing in 'One of the Missing', who for all his 'extraordinary daring', regular pulse, and steady nerve eventually, as ironic circumstance succeeds ironic misappre-hension, dies of fright. And there is the apparently even-tempered, jaunty stoicism of 'Parker Adderson, Philosopher' exposed as so much unrooted verbiage, when he learns he is to die not then, tomorrow, but now, tonight, and the whole of his vaunted philosophy shatters into pieces of wild panic.

Evidently the author of such stories was no stranger to terrors; but he was also a man with clear, unambiguous opinions about the military obligation to control those fears. His sympathies go to the dutiful soldier, frightened, yet disciplined and courageous; and though there are instances of vicious or evil-hearted men in uniform (the general in 'The Affair at Coulter's Notch', Creede Halcrow in 'The Coup de Grâce'), it is notably civilians who bear his contempt, intervening as they do in the stories chiefly to send soldiers to their deaths (the Governor in 'An Affair of Outposts', Marian Mendenhall in 'Killed at Resaca'). War bequeathed Bierce horrors to plague his nights and paint corners of his fiction in lurid colours; but it also bequeathed him a respect for the profession of arms greater than the little respect he felt for the majority of callings, a preference later in his life for the company of soldiers over that of most of his other fellow-beings, and a positive regard for traditional military values in so far as these were stoic and essentially aristocratic. The most admirable figures in these few stories are of course soldiers, but significantly they are also Southerners, like General Clavering in 'Parker Adderson, Philosopher', or, still more significantly, Southerners fighting out of conscience and principle for the Union, like Carter Druse, Captain Coulter, and Captain Armisted of 'An Affair of Outposts'. Thus does Bierce allow himself to be loyal to the Union side for which he fought, whilst being true to the liking he established for Southerners during and immediately after the war and true to the aristocratic slant of his values which Southern myth encouraged more than did the rhetorically democratic, progressive North. Peyton Farquhar, the protagonist of 'An Occurrence at Owl Creek Bridge', as 'a planter of an old and highly respected Alabama family' also fits this mould. Although he has remained a civilian, he has risked his life for the cause, so that we meet him only at the moment of his execution and of his imagination's last wondrous, mysterious flight by which this remarkable story is lifted and sustained aloft.[25]

To a friend's daughter, possessed of literary ambitions but also keen to set the world aright, Bierce once gave this advice: 'The best service you can perform by writing is to write well with no care for anything but that.'[26] It is this explicit concern with the craft of the thing, with visual sincerity and clarity, with precise setting and description, with efficient, vigorous, if occasionally self-consciously over-dressed syntax, and with shapeliness of structure, that makes Bierce in the best of his stories a precursor of some of the modernist masters in their similar concerns. In an unfavourable light that craftsmanship can look like mere formulaic know-how, mechanical expertise, a neat, repetitive way with irony. But when grounded in those memories of the Civil War, when thus freighted, and fraught, with ethical and emotional substance, when inspired by the moral difficulty of 'A Horseman in the Sky', or by the pity of 'Chickamauga', or by the blazing, imaginative yearning of 'An Occurrence at Owl Creek Bridge', or by the nervous extremity of 'One of the Missing', or by malignity's ambush of mercy in 'The Coup de Grâce', Bierce himself becomes a master, of form *and* content, of the craft of the short story. On such occasions at least—to return to those words of his with which we began—his work does have 'soul', perhaps best expressed by Edmund Wilson as 'bitter nobility'.[27] It is a limited achievement in fiction, decidedly; it consists, not to complicate matters, of a few short stories drawn, torn, from a single and highly particular kind of experience—fighting in the American Civil War. But it is his own achievement, his mark, not to be erased.

NOTES

1. Quoted in Carey McWilliams, *Ambrose Bierce: A Biography* (Hamden, Connecticut: Archon Books, 1967), p. 186.
2. For example, Carey McWilliams, op. cit. (first edition, New York: A. C. Boni, 1929); Paul Fatout, *Ambrose Bierce, the Devil's Lexicographer* (Norman: University of Oklahoma Press, 1951); Richard O'Connor, *Ambrose Bierce: A Biography* (Boston: Little, Brown, 1967). M. E. Grenander, *Ambrose Bierce* (New York: Twayne, 1971), follows the Twayne series format in being both critical and biographical, while there is one book-length study devoted largely to his imaginative work, namely, Stuart C. Woodruff, *The Short Stories of Ambrose Bierce: A Study in Polarity* (Pittsburgh: University of Pittsburgh Press, 1964).
3. Letters of 1 October and 6 November 1913, in Bertha Clark Pope (ed.),

The Letters of Ambrose Bierce (San Francisco: Book Club of California, 1922), pp. 196 and 198.

4. Letters to Josephine McCrackin, 13 September 1913. Ibid., p. 196.
5. However, his daughter, Helen, lived on to talk extensively and affectionately of her father to Carey McWilliams when he was researching for his biography.
6. It may seem that he had indeed the fatal touch. His two closest disciples, Herman Scheffauer and George Sterling, were both to die by their own hands.
7. Such a volume, for instance, as Marcus Cunliffe put together for Signet in 1961.
8. From 'The Novel' of 1897, included in *The Collected Works of Ambrose Bierce*, Vol. X, *The Opinionator* (New York and Washington: Neale Publishing Company, 1909), pp. 18–19.
9. 'In reading it I was struck by what seemed to me certain possibilities of amplification, and I agreed to do the work if given a free hand by both author and translator.' Quoted in Richard O'Connor, op. cit., p. 202.
10. Quoted in Paul Fatout, op. cit., p. 158.
11. *Collected Works*, Vol. X, op. cit., p. 24.
12. *The Enlarged Devil's Dictionary* (London: Victor Gollancz, 1967), p. 237.
13. See, for instance, Howard W. Bahr, 'Ambrose Bierce and Realism', *Southern Quarterly*, July 1963, Vol. I, pp. 309–31, where the author concludes tentatively: 'Bierce's realism, if we can call it that, has its origin in his artistic purpose of presenting man and human nature as they appear to him, to tell the truth about what he has observed.'
14. 'The "distinctively American literature" has not materialized, excepting in the works of Americans distinctively illiterate.' *Collected Works*, Vol. X, op. cit., p. 42.
15. Like many other misanthropes, Bierce felt an extraordinary affinity for birds and animals, apart from dogs, after all 'man's best friend', which he loathed and now and again shot. Birds, however, would readily take food from him and perch upon him.
16. 'I draw the line at anarchists, and would put them all to death if I lawfully could.' Letter to Lora Bierce of 19 February 1911. *Letters*, op. cit., p. 171.
17. Bierce also prefaced 'The Death of Halpin Frayser' with a quotation from Hali. The Indian Islamic poet, known as Hali, was roughly contemporary with Bierce, but as far as I know Bierce was unaware of him, and the name Hali thus a coincidence.
18. In a letter to George Sterling of 12 September 1903. *Letters*, op. cit., p. 75.
19. In fact, the events of 'The Boarded Window', alone of this group of stories, are not supernatural.
20. David R. Weimer, 'Ambrose Bierce and the Art of War', in Rudolph Kirk and C. F. Main (eds.), *Essays in Literary History* (New York: Russell and Russell, 1965), pp. 229–38, is excellent on this aspect of the stories. Other useful discussions, more or less extensive, are to be found in M. E. Grenander, op. cit., Stuart C. Woodruff, op. cit., Robert A. Wiggins,

Ambrose Bierce (Minneapolis: University of Minnesota Press, 1964), and John R. Brazil, 'Behind the Bitterness: Ambrose Bierce in Text and Context', *American Literary Realism, 1870–1910*, Vol. XIII, 1980, pp. 225–37.

21. Or that at least is how they seem, appear, to me. Valerie Shaw, *The Short Story: A Critical Introduction* (London: Longman, 1983), discusses at length the short story's affinity as a form with painting. This affinity is especially pronounced in Bierce's work.

22. Bierce sometimes subscribes to the sort of fatalism his almost exact contemporary, Thomas Hardy, expresses in a poem like 'The Convergence of the Twain'. For instance, in 'One of the Missing', he writes that 'It was decreed from the beginning of time that Private Searing was not to murder anyone that bright summer morning', and that 'For countless ages events had been so matching themselves together.' If Hardy has been nicely described as 'a churchy atheist', Bierce may perhaps be described similarly, though less neatly, as 'a Revivalist camp-meeting atheist'.

23. Edmund Wilson, *Patriotic Gore: Studies in the Literature of the American Civil War* (New York: Oxford University Press, Galaxy Book, 1966), p. 622.

24. Under coincidence is to be included the failure of coincidence, the failure to coincide, i.e. the rescuer arriving not in the nick of time but a moment too late.

25. F. J. Logan, 'The Wry Seriousness of "Owl Creek Bridge"', *American Literary Realism 1870–1910*, Vol. X, 1977, pp. 101–13 has argued at length that Farquhar is in fact presented by Bierce, subtly, deceptively, as ignoble and unheroic, 'part villain, part fool'. His argument is ingenious and provocative but based, it seems to me, on highly selective verbal evidence from within the story and not finally convincing.

26. Letter to Blanche Partington of 31 July 1892. *Letters*, op. cit., p. 4.

27. Edmund Wilson, op. cit., p. 633.

8

Kate Chopin: Short Fiction and the Arts of Subversion

by JUDIE NEWMAN

From the early nineteenth century onwards, when America first established its decisive claims to possession of a national literature, the short story has been one of its most distinctive features. The first 'practical' manual we have in short story writing, published in 1894, was American,[1] and it was in 1901, in *The Philosophy of the Short Story*, that the American critic and editor Brander Matthews actually launched the term 'Short-story' as a literary *genre* to be regarded on its own discrete terms.[2] He could look back to a line of American short story writers which includes, among others, Irving, Poe, Hawthorne, Melville and Twain, whose experiments in the 'tale' and fable in his own time had led on to still subsequent major figures like Stephen Crane and Henry James.

The emergence of the short story as a form in nineteenth-century America is perhaps not altogether surprising. It has been noted, especially by Frank O'Connor,[3] that the short story flourishes in 'marginal' cultures and areas and that it deals very often with submerged population groups and with figures who find themselves situated within 'frontier' or 'outsider' conditions. O'Connor was able to illustrate his contention with examples from outside American literature— the officials in Gogol's stories, the prostitutes in Maupassant and the dreamers in Chekhov. It is a form, too, readily found in emerging colonial societies, whether Ireland, India or

Africa. O'Connor's case is also supported by the dominance, in nineteenth-century American short fiction, of 'local colour' writing. Local colour, while catering to an emergent sense of nationhood after the Civil War, which stimulated interest in the far-flung corners of the Union, tended to treat isolated communities, separated from their readers by creed, origins or language, groups which were marginalized by geography and the dominant culture.

One such submerged or 'outsider' group, especially in the nineteenth century, was that of women, who, if they wrote at all, tended to operate in the local colour field. Yet who now reads 'regional', local colour story-telling like Grace King's *Balcony Stories* (1893), or Ruth McEnery Stuart's *A Golden Wedding and Other Tales* (1893), both set in Louisiana? Or Tennessee local colour fiction like that of Mary Noailles Murphree, especially *In The Tennessee Mountains* (1884)? Even the fine New England stories of Sarah Orne Jewett—work like *A White Heron* (1886), *The King of Folly Island* (1888), *A Native of Winby* (1893), *The Life of Nancy* (1895) and above all *The Country of the Pointed Firs* (1896)—receive insufficient critical attention.[4]

An exception to this critical neglect has been Kate Chopin (1851–1904), whose career among other things illustrates the changes in critical fashion from the 1890s to the present. In the '90s Chopin enjoyed success essentially as a local colourist, despite her abhorrence of the term, publishing two collections, *Bayou Folk* (1894) and *A Night in Acadie* (1897), which take for their subject-matter the life of the Acadians in Louisiana. With the appearance, however, of her novel *The Awakening* (1899), a frank account of a woman's sexual and spiritual awakening, adultery and suicide, late nineteenth- and early twentieth-century interest in her took a different direction. Guardians of taste proclaimed themselves at once shocked and deeply offended, especially at such explicitness in a woman. The novel was publicly condemned and duly banned from libraries, and Chopin erased from the literary scene. In 1923, the critic Fred Pattee praised Chopin but he, too, saw her erasure as final: 'She must be rated as a genius, taut, vibrant, intense of soul, yet a genius in eclipse, one, it is to be feared, that is destined to be total.'[5] Only one story continued to attract attention, 'Désirée's Baby', usually anthologized for its treatment of miscegenation. Chopin's re-emergence was to be based essentially upon her novel; Edmund Wilson devoted a chapter of *Patriotic Gore* (1962)[6] to Chopin, and in 1969 Per Seyersted produced both a major critical biography and the standard edition of Chopin's complete works.[7] This renewed attention was largely the result of the interest in Chopin's sexual frankness and different depictions of women. As Kenneth Eble has commented, on *The Awakening*: 'Quite frankly, the book is about sex. Not only is it about sex, but the very texture of the writing is sensuous, if not sensual, from the first to the last.'[8] But with the increasing sophistication of feminist criticism the interest in sex has broadened to an interest in gender, with spirited discussions of Chopin's attitudes to motherhood, marriage and male possession. It has also led on to the founding of the *Kate Chopin Newsletter*[9] and various republications, both of *The Awakening* and of her stories.[10]

The direction and measure of Chopin's own feminism have been hotly debated. Historical fact indicates that Chopin took no part in emancipatory movements, that she was happily married and devoted to her six children. The evidence of her stories is various. While 'The Storm' suggests that adultery is good for you, or while 'The Story of an Hour' portrays a wife who dies of grief when her husband is NOT killed in a railroad accident, or while in her first published story, 'Wiser than a God', the heroine chooses a career instead of a husband, other tales are less readily to be construed in 'propagandist' terms. Athénaïse, in the story of that title, vigorously condemns the institution of marriage: 'It's jus' being married that I detes' an' despise. I hate being Mrs. Cazeau, an' would want to be Athénaïse Miché again.'[11] Yet when Athénaïse discovers her pregnancy all is forgiven in an orgy of baby-clothes buying and a return to her husband's arms, ending quite literally in an erotic clinch. 'Regret' takes as its theme the regret of a betrousered old maid for the children she has never had. Many stories end conventionally in matrimony ('Miss Witherwell's Mistake', 'Aunt Lympy's Interference', 'A Family Affair').

Where the heroine is initially portrayed as suffering within the institution of marriage she frequently reaffirms its value after a brief excursus (for example in 'A Visit to Avoyelles', 'Madame Célestin's Divorce', 'A Lady of Bayou St. John'). To some extent this conventionality may be explained by cultural gate-keeping on the part of male editors and publishers. Certainly more explicit stories tended to be rejected: 'The Storm', for instance, remained unpublished until 1969. But Chopin's own distaste for idealized or cut-and-dried solutions and her attraction to transient states and the contingent individual, makes her position difficult to define. Without an awareness of the subtleties of Chopin's craft, the issue of her feminism is unlikely to be either fully understood or resolved. While the direction of interest in her fiction has shifted of late, from exotic 'Cajun' customs, to race, sex and gender, much criticism nonetheless remains thematic. As Patricia Hopkins Lattin aptly remarks: 'Kate Chopin criticism has been slow to mature from discussions of the author's unusual, sometimes revolutionary themes to analysis of the craft behind these themes.'[12]

It is the function of the present essay to examine how theme and technique interact in Chopin's stories, using as a departure-point 'Charlie', a miniature *Bildungsroman* which foregrounds the issue of a woman's place in society as it charts the development of Charlotte Laborde from adolescence to womanhood. Ostensibly the story records the taming of an independent spirit, Charlotte's feminization and acculturation to patriarchal norms. Charlie enters the story rebelliously, bounding off her horse and into the schoolroom, a sweating, grubby figure in 'trouserlets' and the strongest possible contrast to her six demure sisters. Her name and apparel are masculinized, her father sees her as 'that ideal son he had always hoped for' (p. 644; p. 187) and the local people remember her as the heroine who saved the levee in her father's absence. Charlie has a pistol and is a good shot, but when she inadvertently wounds Firman Walton, a visiting stranger, in the arm she is disgraced. Sent to school in New Orleans to be 'sivilized', Charlie enthusiastically takes to fashion and accomplishments, a process assisted by her infatuation with Walton. When her father in his turn loses an arm in an accident, and Walton marries her sister, Julia, Charlie takes over the running of the plantation as her father's helpmeet, and accepts an eventual marriage to the inarticulate Mr. Gus. On a psychological level her development thus appears to be recessive. Charlie is also a writer, though from the examples given her poetry does not promise over much. She has used her gift to prevent her father's remarriage, by means of a 'touching petition' (p. 643; p. 187), and she ends up as her father's scribe, writing letters at his dictation. Indeed, the Oedipal/Electral content of the story seems wincingly apparent in the excursions Charlie makes with Mr. Laborde, especially the emphasis on his youth and good looks, and on the heroine's final assumpion of the maternal rôle as mistress of the plantation and surrogate mother to the twins. Chopin's fiction thus appears to be coercive, supporting rather than subverting the norms of her society.

Yet such a bare outline belies the psychology behind the tale which is carefully structured to subvert the rôles constructed by and for the heroine, and to argue that Charlie finally transcends the script offered by her culture. Chopin establishes the subversive meaning of the story by drawing on a complex of images associated with the hand. Two incidents set the plot in motion, each involving the wounded arm of a male figure, while Charlie's development involves her written hand, hands given in marriage, her father's 'hands' (employees) and such apparently minor props as hand-cream, handkerchiefs, gloves and rings. In the first movement of the story Charlie is established as inhabiting a narcissistic fantasy world. Taking refuge with the Bichou family, Charlie regales them with news and stories 'colored by her own lively imagination' (p. 645; p. 188), informing Xenophore that she is going to the woods to write poetry, slay panthers and shoot tigers and bears. She sees herself as protected by her diamond ring: 'all I have to do is to turn the ring three times, repeat a Latin verse, and presto! I disappear like smoke' (p. 646; p. 189). Significantly, from a psychological point of view, the ring is her mother's engagement ring, which Charlie has invested with magical protective powers. Once in the wood, which is really only a 'shady grove' (p. 647; p. 190), Charlie tears up her writing-pad for target practice and in her shooting wounds Firman Walton. As a result she is doubly disarmed. Her father makes her 'stand and deliver her firearm' (p. 650; p. 193) and in an effort to attract

Walton she abandons her male dress.

The episode suggests that Charlie is more a Tom Sawyer than a Huck Finn, and that the masculinized 'derring-do' rôle which she has assumed is counter-productive. Importantly her play-acting injures both men and women. Her father suffers from wounded feelings and Walton is actually hurt. In addition two women suffer at Charlie's hands, a mother and a bride. Expelled from the schoolroom Charlie procures writing materials to offer a highly coloured account of the 'adventures' (p. 640; p. 183) which occasioned her delay. In fact she has been supervising the delivery of a new bicycle. Chopin hints mysteriously here at a preceding accident. Charlie has earlier given her old bicycle to Ruben's bride, who has not been seen in public since its presentation. Charlie warns Zenophore darkly not to tamper with the bicycle: 'I reckon you heard about Ruben's bride' (p. 646; p. 189). Charlie's unwillingness to specify what did happen hints at an indelicate accident. When her efforts at writing prose fail to win Charlie's readmittance to the female group in the schoolroom, she turns to poetry with no better results. Interrupted by Aunt Maryllis scolding her son, Charlie launches a missile at her with the words: 'If there are going to be any bones broken around here, I'll take a hand in it' (p. 641; p. 184). Though the missile catches Maryllis on the side, the text emphasizes her hand rubbing the bruise (p. 642, p. 643; p. 185, p. 186). Maryllis's threat to inform Mr. Laborde also draws attention to hands: 'Marse Laborde ain' gwine let you keep on cripplin' his han's scand'lous like you docs' (p. 642; p. 185).

Chopin ironizes Charlie's writing succinctly here. The would-be poet is particularly irritated at the interruption 'as she was vainly striving after a suitable rhyme for "persecution" ' (p. 642; p. 185). Charlie's self-absorbed writing, as the earlier petition to her father implies, is coercive, potentially dangerous and a threat to sexual development, whether her own or others'. Far from applauding Charlie as independent creator, Chopin underlines the fact that the products of her creative imagination are linked to a narcissistic desire to maintain the emotional status quo. As the engagement ring suggests, Charlie would like to remain at the Oedipal stage, an ideal son and a loving daughter. Her fantasies injure maternal and paternal figures, the lover and the bride. Writing will not gain her access to the female world, and is a weapon turned as much against herself as against men.

Banished to New Orleans, however, Charlie acts from a different prepared script, much enjoying a fortnight with her Aunt Clementine who 'provided entertainment such as Charlie had not yet encountered outside of novels of high life' (p. 657; p. 200). Plunging into the rôle of society lady, Charlie takes to the delights of jewellery and dress. Her attitude to the engagement ring changes: 'Hitherto she had worn it for the tender associations which made her love the bauble. Now she began to look upon it as an adornment' (p. 656; p. 199). Charlie applies cream to whiten her hands, sleeping at night in a pair of her father's old gloves. Ostensibly Charlie has merely exchanged the rôle of ideal son for that of ideal daughter. When her father consigns her to the seminary he 'kissed her fervently' (p. 654; p. 197). When he visits her he comes alone, and carries her off with him for a day at the lake.

> He did not tell her how hungry he was for her, but he showed it in a hundred ways. He was like a schoolboy on holiday; it was like a conspiracy; there was a flavor of secrecy about it too. (p. 661; p. 204)

Despite the erotic language, however, the fixation is on the father's not the daughter's side. Mr. Laborde's misreading of the situation is indicated by reference to Charlie's hands. When Walton is about to impose his company on the pair, Laborde assumes that Charlie does not like him because 'She gave her whole attention to her gloves' (p. 661; p. 204). When Charlie draws off a glove and offers a hand for her father's inspection, his eyes are drawn only to the ring: 'No stones missing, are there?' (p. 662; p. 205). Charlie's interest, however, has transferred itself to Walton. She asks her father to admire the whiteness of the hand: 'do you think it's as white as—Julia's, for instance? (p. 662; p. 205). Julia, Charlie's rival, is noted for her hands which are described in the opening of the tale as 'as white as lilies' (p. 638; p. 185). Mr. Laborde is blind to these implications: 'He held the hand fondly in both of his, but she withdrew it, holding it at arm's length' (p. 662; p. 205).

Just in case the reader were in any doubt as to Charlie's major focus of erotic interest, the scene is preceded by a description of Charlie writing lines of poetry, inspired by Walton, which she secretes in a locket. Chopin's description implies the limitations Charlie must now assume: 'Charlie wrote some lines of poetry in the smallest possible cramped hand' (p. 658; p. 201). In bedecking herself for Walton Charlie has written herself into a rôle which is as cramping as the preceding one, a point clarified in a scene at the seminary. Charlie's other poetic opus, an address in honour of the seminary's foundress, procures her some attention from the other young ladies who retire to her room to consume her saccharine works, together with a box of chocolate creams. 'One by one the poems were read, with fictitious fire, with melting pathos as the occasion called for, while silently the chocolates were passed around and around' (p. 659; p. 202). While she has now gained admission to the female circle, Charlie has simply swopped the rôle of adventurous male for that of the milk and water miss, all creamy sweetness—and her writing reflects the fact.

Ironically the sickly idyll in New Orleans is abruptly terminated by an accident at the sugar mill on the plantation. Chopin's indirection here again serves a subtle purpose. The reader is encouraged to see Charlie as returning to her father's arms. Charlie, fearing her father's death, dwells upon the fact that he will not be there at the station 'with outstretched arms' (p. 663; p. 206), that he will never again be as he was at the lake 'clasping her with loving arms' (p. 663; p. 206). Events prove the premonition all too true. Mr. Laborde has actually lost his right arm, though the reader gleans this information only near the close of the story when he embraces Charlie with 'the arm that was left to him' (p. 668; p. 211). Instead of her father's embrace, Charlie is met by Gus who 'took her hand' (p. 664; p. 207). The text emphasizes in its imagery that Charlie does not simply return to her father as a socialized young lady. On her return the house is pervaded by 'a sweet, sickening odor . . . more penetrating than the scent of the rain-washed flowers' (p. 664; p. 207), but this is the odour of anaesthetic, administered while the mangled arm is being amputated, a scent which undermines the associations of sweetness with young girls in flower. When Aunt Clementine outlines her plans to take the girls out into the world, she employs the conventional image: 'She had plans for separating these blossoms so that they might disseminate their sweetness' (p. 665; p. 208). Charlie, however, interrupts her aunt, rejecting her plans, and with them the image of woman as sweetness and light.

Nor is this decision merely governed by the desire to remain with her father. After the announcement of Julia's engagement, Charlie's speech to her father looks like a return to an earlier self: 'from now on I'm going to be—to be your right hand—your poor right hand' (p. 668; p. 211). But several points suggest that Charlie has now evolved a more mature relation to her father, and that her return marks an expansion of possibilities for her, rather than a limiting rôle. Firstly, Charlie burns the cramped lines of poetry. Secondly, she removes the ring and sends it to Julia, an action which indicates that she is now free from the desire to replace her mother. Thirdly, the reader's attention is drawn to the discrepancy between Charlie's real feelings and her family's image of them. Both her sisters and the servants misread Charlie's fury at the engagement as the result of a dislike for Walton. Irene says that 'She can't bear him' (p. 666; p. 209). Blossom reiterates that 'Miss Charlie f'or hate dat man like pizen' (p. 666; p. 209). Earlier in the story Irene had watched Gus and Charlie in conversation and had assumed that she was rejecting a proposal of marriage. (In fact the two parties were discussing a remedy for horse-gall.) Now, however, Charlie no longer inhabits the fictions of others. Her acceptance of Gus marks her entry into a world distinct from her own and others' fantasies. Significantly Gus, an active practical man, is described as having no connection with the 'fevered' (p. 654; p. 197) modern day. Unlike Walton, who is seen in a fever (p. 651; p. 194) he will not treat Charlie like a hothouse flower. Near the close of the story Aunt Maryllis reappears:

> 'Miss Charlie,' she called out, 'heah dis heah grease you mix' up fo' yo' han's; w'at I gwine do wid it?'
> 'Throw it away, Aunt Maryllis,' cried Charlie over her shoulder. (p. 668; p. 211)

The inherent silliness of the whitening cream is underlined when the black woman takes it to apply to her own hands. Far from retreating into the embrace of a patriarchal culture, Charlie has avoided the worst extremes of young ladyhood or of unproductive rebellion. At the close she has integrated the rôles of active male and mature woman, taking power into her own hands. The story takes the reader through three alternatives—the aggressive female-as-male, the milk and water miss who conforms, the Oedipal fantasy—to a more workable position. At the end of the story Charlie's femininity is emphasized: 'Now, with all the dignity and grace which the term implied, she was mistress of Les Palmiers' (p. 669; p. 212). But Charlie's accommodation to the rôle is an active one. The fantasies to which she contributed and which others orchestrated around her have been transcended.

'Charlie' offers a useful instance of Chopin's strengths and preoccupations, especially the contrast between a fantasy world of romance and the world of reality which recurs as a key focus. Chopin repeatedly places romantic dreams of escape in an ironic context, and turns 'convention' against itself.[13] In 'Athénaïse', the heroine's husband may have yielded to fiction when he envisages married life as 'w'at the story-books promise after the wedding' (p. 435; p. 112). But when Athénaïse rebels, she merely takes on a different rôle in another man's scenario. Her brother, Montéclin, engineers her escape as if it were an elopement, complicating the arrangements unnecessarily to cater to his spirit of adventure:

> the clandestine nature of the affair gave it a savor of adventure which was highly pleasing to him. Eloping with his sister was only a little less engaging than eloping with some one else's sister. (p. 441; p. 118)

Alone in New Orleans Athénaïse is seen looking at pictures in a magazine, her eyes drawn particularly to one which reminds her of Montéclin: 'It was one of Remington's Cowboys' (p. 446; p. 123). When she decides to return, it is Montéclin who comments that 'the affair had taken a very disappointing, an ordinary, a most commonplace turn, after all' (p. 454; p. 131). The reader is distanced from any similar judgement by the preceding irony at his expense. Heroines who appear to conform often, in fact, escape from the images prepared for them by others to generate their own scripts.

In 'Miss Witherwell's Mistake', for instance, Francis Witherwell is parodied as a female littérateur who combines local colour stories with journalism of the household hints variety. When she is not penning treatises on 'Security Against the Moth' or 'The Wintering of Canaries' Miss Witherwell excels in tales of passion 'acted beneath those blue and southern skies traditionally supposed to foster the growth of soft desire' (p. 59; p. 10). Miss Witherwell's contributions are assured their place in the Boredomville *Battery* by her own financial backing and investment in the paper. When her niece, Mildred, is sent to visit her, to help her forget an unsuitable (because impoverished) lover, Miss Witherwell is somewhat taken aback, despite her tales of passion, since for her 'two such divergent cupids, as love in real life, and love in fiction, held themselves at widely distant points of view' (p. 60; p. 11). The lovers are reunited, however, by Miss Witherwell—firstly when she sends Mildred to correct the errors in her proofs, and secondly when Mildred fictionalizes their story to her aunt and asks for advice on an ending. She asks whether the lovers should marry. Miss Witherwell's response is telling: 'The poison of the realist school has certainly tainted and withered your fancy in the bud, my dear, if you hesitate a moment. Marry them, most certainly, or let them die' (p. 65; p. 16). The happy ending in life is therefore a result of the correction of errors in fiction, as Mildred uses the conventions against her aunt.

Another Mildred, in 'A Shameful Affair', has gone to the country 'to follow exalted lines of thought' (p. 133; p. 20), but when she finds that the farm does not conform to its image in 'humorous fiction' (p. 131; p. 18), she becomes bored, throws her book aside, and walks by the river where she is promptly kissed by Fred Evelyn. When, however, Fred presents himself in the conventional rôle of 'the most consummate hound that walks the earth' (p. 136; p. 23), Mildred does not act the part of outraged virtue, but admits her own desire for him, leaving the hero all ablush.[14] In 'A Family Affair' Bosé arrives with the full paraphernalia of the young lady, bustles about in house-wifely fashion, acts the 'ministering angel' (p. 583; p. 164) to her aunt and captures the heart of the young doctor. The rôle of housewife and nurse is only assumed, however. Bosé departs with her mother's share of the family inheritance, her aim from the start. In other stories fictional conventions and conventional fictions are similarly exploded. 'The Storm' ends: 'So the storm passed and everyone was happy' (p. 596; p. 180), offering a happy ending which runs counter to the reader's expectations of a tale of adultery.[15] In 'Ma'ame Pélagie'. the dismantling of the plantation legend brings happiness to Pauline, while in 'The Story of an Hour' the correction of an erroneous newspaper report has less fortunate consequences.

Other Chopin stories highlight the tragic implications of being bound to a fictionalized rôle or image. In 'La Belle Zoraïde' the slave Zoraïde prefers, in her insanity, a pretend-child (a bundle of rags) to her real infant, whom her mistress has removed. Zoraïde's story is narrated to Madame Delisle, who completely ignores its tragic content, considering it simply as a comfortable fiction to lull her to sleep. The story foreshadows 'A Lady of Bayou St. John' in which Madame Delisle figures as a wife whose remembrance of her husband, absent in the Civil War, has grown faint, and who is tempted to take a lover. When the husband dies, however, Madame Delisle erects a shrine to his memory, preferring, as Zoraïde does, a fictional image to reality.[16] More shockingly, in 'Fedora', the heroine constructs a false self-image with disastrous consequences. Although Fedora is only 30, she cultivates a severe expression and affects superior years and wisdom. When she falls in love with Young Malthers she is unable to escape the fixed image, and instead implants a passionate kiss upon Malthers's sister, who is his image in features and expression. The Sapphic overtones to the tale are less important than its analysis of damaging narcissism.

Chopin's concern is not simply with what women do to themselves, but also with what society does to them. Several of her stories hinge upon the juxtaposition of opposed images of women. 'Two Portraits' contrasts two women, each named Alberta, each described in an identical opening paragraph, one 'The Wanton', the other 'The Nun'. The story implies that the contrast between these two socially learned rôles is not so very great. The tale ends with the nun quivering and swooning in sensual ecstasy before the image of Christ. In 'Lilacs' two rôles are internalized in one woman, Adrienne Farival, who returns each year at lilac time to her convent school to assume an innocence which, in reality, she has long left behind. Carefully costumed in drab brown, bearing gifts for the chapel, Adrienne paints herself as a respectable woman. Sister Agathe commends her to 'your household duties . . . and your music, to which, you say, you continue to devote yourself' (p. 359; p. 89). In fact Adrienne is a Parisian chanteuse and dancer, of suspect virtue. (The reader notes the swift replacement of a Monsieur Henri by Monsieur Paul.) When Adrienne returns a year later to the convent she is denied admission, her gifts are returned and the actress confronts a hostile house: 'she saw only the polished windows looking down at her like so many cold and glittering and reproachful eyes' (p. 365; p. 95). The irony of the story is primarily directed at the harsh behaviour of the Mother Superior, who is herself not free from Adrienne's evident weakness for the male. Adrienne notes that the nun has replaced the image of Saint Catherine with the Sacré Coeur, embellished the statue of Saint Joseph, but allowed that of the Virgin to grow shabby. Though Chopin is arguing for an integration of rôles in Adrienne, her most biting censure is reserved for a woman like the Mother Superior who bolsters the social standard by excluding what Adrienne herself has become.

While contemporary readers must beware of imposing an anachronistic feminist image on Kate Chopin, it is nonetheless clear that her stories go beyond the conventions of both the fiction and the society of her day. Chopin's analysis of the way in which women perceive themselves, or allow others to perceive them, is subtle and wide-ranging in its implications. Her touch is light, unprescriptive and often humorous. The 'techniques' of her stories serve—subvertingly and with striking artfulness—to render the whole complex problematic of fitting self to image. While she is no polemicist, her stories suggest that women are amply capable of enlarging the rôles available to them, and that active accommodation transcends empty conformity or withdrawal into one or another pre-ordained fantasy.

Kate Chopin: Short Fiction and the Arts of Subversion

NOTES

1. A. Sherwin Cody, *How to Write Fiction, Especially the Art of Short Story Writing: A Practical Course of Instruction after the French Method of Maupassant* (New York: Dillingham, 1894).
2. Brander Matthews, *The Philosophy of the Short-story* (New York: Longmans Green, 1901).
3. Frank O'Connor, *The Lonely Voice: A Study of the Short Story* (London: Macmillan, 1963).
4. For a perceptive exception see Valerie Shaw, *The Short Story: A Critical Introduction* (London: Longman, 1983), pp. 167–81.
5. Fred Lewis Pattee, *The Development of the American Short Story* (New York: Harper and Bros., 1923), p. 325.
6. Edmund Wilson, *Patriotic Gore: Studies in the Literature of the American Civil War* (New York: Oxford University Press, 1962).
7. Per Seyersted (ed.), *The Complete Works of Kate Chopin* (Baton Rouge: Louisiana State University Press, 1969) and Per Seyersted, *Kate Chopin: A Critical Biography* (Oslo: Universitetsforlaget, and Baton Rouge: Louisiana State University Press, 1969). The latter completely updates the only preceding biography: Daniel S. Rankin, *Kate Chopin and her Creole Stories* (Philadelphia: University of Pennsylvania Press, 1932).
8. Kenneth Eble, 'A Forgotten Novel: Kate Chopin's *The Awakening*', *Western Humanities Review*, X (Summer 1956), 263.
9. The *Kate Chopin Newsletter* (now retitled *Regionalism and the Female Imagination*) was first published in 1975 by Pennsylvania State University.
10. For example, Kate Chopin, *The Awakening* (London: Women's Press, 1978) and Kate Chopin, *Portraits* (London: Women's Press, 1982). Both have useful introductions by Helen Taylor.
11. Seyersted, *Complete Works*, p. 431; *Portraits*, p. 108. Subsequent page references will follow quotations in parentheses, the reference to the *Complete Works* preceding that to *Portraits*.
12. Patricia Hopkins Lattin, 'Kate Chopin's Repeating Characters', *Mississippi Quarterly*, 33 (1980), 19.
13. See Emily Toth, 'Kate Chopin and Literary Convention: "Désirée's Baby"', *Southern Studies: An Interdisciplinary Journal of the South*, 20, 2 (Summer 1981), 201–8.
14. A point remarked upon by Per Seyersted in *Kate Chopin: A Critical Biography* (op. cit).
15. See Robert D. Arner, 'Kate Chopin's Realism: "At the 'Cadian Ball' and 'The Storm'"', *Markham Review*, II, 2 (February 1970), 4.
16. See Lattin, pp. 29–31.

9

'The Infected Air' and 'The Guilt of Interference': Henry James's Short Stories

by ERIC MOTTRAM

1

In his Notebooks Henry James told himself that he had learned from his recent disasters in the theatre that his strength lay in the 'mastery of fundamental statement', a concision in which there would be 'almost no room at all for my people to talk'. In planning 'The Spoils of Poynton'—in 1895, the year the audience at *Guy Domville* booed him—he writes: 'To *be* heroic, to achieve beauty and poetry, [Fleda Vetch] must conceal from [Owen Gereth] what she feels.' Her sacrificial renunciation lies in the gap of silence. The trap of her enclosure is sprung from internal and external coercions, so that her 'sacrificial exaltation' and 'free spirit' is 'successful' as well as 'sterile'.[1] James remembered his father's advice on how to be released from such 'debt', inherent in the false American success system: 'we were . . . to *be* something . . . free and uncommitted.'[2] Otherwise the sterility of 'too late in life altogether . . . the wasting of life' which is 'the implication of death'[3] encloses creative potentiality—the plot of 'The Beast in the Jungle' (1903)—a deathliness only the 60-year-old writer could fully face.

These two stories contain James's steady materials: entrapment, sterility and the morbid possibility of incorporating the 'Dead Self' into 'the sympathy, the fidelity (the relation of some kind) of another'. He had recognized in Poe an antecedent obsession with the 'sterilizing habit' and the possibility that in recognizing this condition a man or woman woul be 'overwhelmed'. So the plots tend towards 'great negative adventure'[4] and towards madness. In 'The Beast in the Jungle' Marcher speaks of his 'lunacy' as that of 'the most harmless of maniacs', a sterility he has elevated to 'one's law'. Psyche is transferred to fate and living reduced to 'the state of suspense' in a 'void' or 'desert', which elsewhere in the James map becomes 'The Bench of Desolation' (1909), 'the old house at Marr' ('The Third Person', 1900), or Cocker's in 'In The Cage' (1898). Terms such as 'heroic' and 'courage' slide mockingly off Marcher's claim on May Bartram: 'You help me pass for a man like another'. Such figures have lost 'the ability to function'. Undernourished, they slope towards suicide.[5]

The necessity in the Marcher plot has become a dictate, 'the law that had ruled him . . . the true voice of the law', within which he is devoured by the leaping beast of realization. James had experienced the slavery in *Uncle Tom's Cabin* as a child,[6] and years later, in an essay on Turgenev, he wrote that

> life is, in fact, a battle . . . Evil is insolent and strong; beauty enchanting but rare; goodness apt to be weak; folly very apt to be defiant; wickedness to carry the day; imbeciles to be in great places, people of sense in small, and mankind, generally, unhappy.

From this programme, the writer can rely on a steady plot basis:

> Only make the reader's general vision of evil intense enough . . . and his own experience, his own imagination, his own sympathy . . . and horror . . . will supply him quite sufficiently with all the particulars. Make him *think* the evil, make him think it for himself, and you are released from weak specifications.[7]

James's Malthusian world of scarce nourishment resists Isabel Archer's fatuous confidence, in *The Portrait of a Lady*, that 'the world lay before her—she could do whatever she chose.' In James's scene 'the uncleanness of the air' barely conceals that energy behind 'immediate and apparent life' which is 'deeper and darker and unapparent, in which things *really* happen to us', and which may learn under the 'hygiene' of this understanding to stay in its place. Let it get out of its place and it swamps the scene.'[8] A letter to Edith Wharton characterizes in 1908 'the thing hideously behind'—a phrase in *The Golden Bowl* of 1904. It is a familiar inheritance from the nineteenth century and the fears in Frazer's volcanic barbarians, Carlyle's final fears of the masses, Darwin's predatory survivors, Freud's return of the repressed in history. James's version in the *Notebooks* is the 'overwhelming self-defeating chaos or cataclysm toward which the whole thing is drifting', or, in the vein of Jack London's Darwinian 'call of the wild', 'the natural inheritance of everyone who is capable of spiritual life, is an unsubdued forest where the wolf howls and the obscene bird of night chatters'. James's stories of caged energy barely enclose the creature that may well leap from the 'deep well of unconscious cerebration'[9] that nourishes monsters.

Unlike Marx, James embeds his dramatizations of radical insecurities, conditions of restlessness and needs for security and minimal stability in nostalgia rather than a metaphysical future—a nostalgia for a future which could not exist either in his lifetime or—given his philosophy—at any time. His 'documentary' of a 1904 return to the United States hunts out things that have *not* changed in a quarter of a century. The owner of 'The Jolly Corner' (1908) gives his investment in a tall building as a compromise with morality; the author of *The American Scene* (1907) shuns exhausting cities for 'the Umbrian note' to be found in vestiges of 'the time of settled possession'.[10] In spite of his fascination with cars, trains and city bridges, and his endless enclosures in shops, houses and other non-agrarian locations (country houses are hardly agrarian), New York resisted his urges to form—as he suspected it would in his 1879 Hawthorne monograph. His distinction between 'real' and 'romantic' in the preface to *The American* is neither a separation of urban and country, nor between art and life. It is more of a dialectic between 'things we cannot possibly *not* know, sooner or later' and 'things that . . . we *can* never directly know' and which are perceived through 'circuit and subterfuge of our thought and our desire'. The 'deep well' is located virtually anywhere.

James's stories employ both *real* and *romantic* tactics; that is their narrative strength, across the slow probing of similar situations between 1879 and 1910. Reaching between direct-ness and subterfuge in 'The Turn of the Screw' (1898) produces a text, the preface says, 'inviting [the imagination] to act on a perfectly clear field'. The field is both visible and the location of imagination, socially and psychologically that 'darkest abyss' the preface to *The American* refers to. His criticism of *Arthur Gordon Pym*, in the preface to 'The Altar of the Dead' and *The Golden Bowl*, assumes that Poe's reader does not examine the narrative as both 'real' and 'romantic'. In fact Poe's novel is a fantastic structure employing both repeatedly.[11] The political implications of James's usage of this movement of procedures is contained in what the sons called 'Father's Ideas'—Henry James senior's polarities within 'Socialism and Civilization': 'the idea of a perfect fellowship or society among men' and 'the present political constitution of nations', the possibility of a perfect life on earth, or 'the insubjection of man both by nature and society'. Henry James learned at an early age, therefore, that 'social tyranny' is the state in which 'scarcely one in a million believes that he has any individuality or sacredness apart from his natural and social ties.' Within this 'slavery' Art 'feeds into fawning sycophancy', the work of 'perfectly docile genius'. Socialism offers 'to lift man out of harassing bondage' and 'our limited property in men and things'. In 'The Social Significance of our Institutions' (4 July 1861), James senior bases 'the intensely artificial structure of society' on 'acute and stifling . . . class-distinctions, and . . . the consequent awkwardness and *brusquerie* of its upper classes, and the consequent abject snobbery or inbred and ineradicable servility of its lower classes'.[12] This part of 'Father's Ideas' reads like the programme for 'In the Cage', 'The Birthplace' (1903) and 'The Bench of Desolation', while the passages from 'Socialism and Civilization' are bases for 'The Pupil' (1892), 'The Author of Beltraffio' (1884) and 'The Turn of the Screw' (1898).

In the mid-1880s, the English upper middle class seemed to James 'very much the same rotten and *collapsible* one as that of the French aristocracy before the revolution' or 'the heavy, congested and depraved Roman world upon which the barbarians came down. In England the Huns and Vandals will have to come *up*.' But his gaze remained that of the perceptive tourist 'oppressed and darkened by England's problems', 'deadly weary of the whole "international" state of mind', wishing to remain 'an outsider' indistinguishable as 'an American writing about England or an Englishman writing about America'. Such a politics of writing could only be maintained by an expatriation in which his 'notions' of England grew 'distincter' as America 'faded from him'. F. O. Matthiessen concludes that although 'his father had dwelt always on the promise of a new society that was about to come to birth. . . . Henry James's thought was never dynamic.' He remained 'the recorder of a society that he knew to be waning'. But his sense of the drama of that diminution is the plot of his stories. In a letter to his brother William on the occasion of the Spanish-American War, he wrote: 'I see nothing but the madness, the passion, the hideous clumsiness of rage, of mechanical reverberation . . . the foul criminality of the screeching newspapers.' The press, he wrote to his brother a few years later,

> is the organ and promulgator of [a] state of mind which means . . . a new 'dark' age that may last more centuries than the first one . . . a new phenomenon in history—involving every kind of diseased sensationalism and insincerity in the collective mind.[13]

The 'more or less mad panorama' is in fact the scene of both his own entrapped women in the competitive cage, and that of the women in the Naturalist plots of Crane's *Maggie: A Girl of the Streets* (1893) and Dreiser's *Sister Carrie* (1900). In James's words, 'there is such a thing, in the United States . . . as the freedom to grow to be blighted, and it may be the only freedom in store for the smaller fry of future generations.'[14] James's politics emerge through his fiction and nonfiction 'documentary'—his own term—of that world which broke in 1914, 'black and hideous'. 'I'm sick beyond cure to have lived to see it', he wrote to Henry Adams; now the 'act of life' had to be continued as 'alert reaction' to even this 'tragedy'.

James's stories concentrate that alertness as versions of

enclosure under gaze at the intersection of social, political and psychological inevitabilities. They concentrate on detailed nuances within a limited realism.[15] When the terms shift towards allegory in 'The Author of Beltraffio'—with terms such as 'Paul Overt', 'Summercroft' and 'St. George'—condensing or what James calls 'a nucleus for aggregation' may become arch and obvious. And here, too, the masking manner of not exposing what will not profitably yield for the plot becomes an irritable withholding, a set of gaps and silences which are also obvious. What St. George's 'success' actually consists of, is concealed. But this is the crux of Overt's taste. All we are offered is that 'passion' must go into aesthetics. Elements of money, family, sex, literary production with quality, and the 'corruption' of quality through family, women and the market produce basic treachery. Nine years later, in 'Greville Fane' (1893), condensing produces these materials through an increased use of images and of sardonic innuendo, as James hunts down the 'vulgar'. The form of extended obituary probes Mrs. Stormer's trapped life with an irony as ferocious as some of Jane Austen's opening paragraphs, but it limits James's insights into the 'deep well'.

'Greville Fane' explores success as vulgarity, productivity as exploitation, and the 'sacrifice' entailed. Competition, passion and money enclose social and sexual life and writing into a grim zoo. Journeys to wealthy houses mobilize the sacrificial. The fate of the creative under market conditions is James's criticism of society; what a writer does for a life while he is writing is a perpetual obsession with James. 'Live all you can' may be a trap, but otherwise there is nothing. Your life may become your money and nothing more. As James writes of the Monarchs in 'The Real Thing' (1893), 'Their good looks had been their capital.' A mindless parasitism awaits the exploited and unaware. For such probes, James cannot use psycho-mythical short cuts and alibis from pseudo-authenticities culled from Freud and Jung. But he employs a recurrent and augmenting vocabulary-set arising from his concentration of the material field and his limiting perception. The reduction of resources to first person narrative frequently including the author himself pretending to a limited gaze, usually controls in a singularly telling way. James needs no Vereker 'figure', nor does any major writer, since the Vereker type ('The Figure in the Carpet', 1896) cheaply plays a game of detection for readers prone to hunting out 'the real thing'. James has no time for such pretence.

One of James's intentions is clear in the *Notebooks* for November 1882: 'I must do a *short* thing, in such measure as I need, which will leave me intervals for dramatic work. . . . If only I can concentrate myself: this is the great lesson of life.' One result is a series of designs which have a fine absence of both detection and discussion. Another is that the 'intermediate intelligence', which R. P. Blackmur believes enables James not to give the reader 'direct contact' with his subject, is really not there at all, but replaced, as it were, by James's vocabulary of enclosure and survival, and sometimes by James's ironic insistence on 'our friend' and other invitations to the reader to be an accomplice to the narrative. His dense loquacities barely conceal crucial ignorances of information which verbal sets and elaborate images scarcely fill. The 'measurable state' cannot necessarily be found, let alone verbalized.[16] James does not totalize. 'The muddle of fate' must not, he wrote, be cleared by 'clever' characters—or, we might add, by a 'clever' author. The picture-anecdote—to fuse his terms at the end of the preface to 'The Spoils of Poynton'— is a limited representation against 'the constant force that makes for muddlement'. 'Total effect' includes 'the restrictive truth', the 'irresistibly prescribed', as against 'improvisation, the running on and on of invention'. James's interest in the Vereker effect is only a demand that the reader be able to discover 'the intended sense of things . . . a spirit and a form, a bias, of his own'. The reader's 'test' enters the author's concentrate:

> I undertook the brevity . . . [and] arrived at it by the innumerable repeated chemical reductions and condensations that tended to make of the very short story, as I risk again noting, one of the costliest, even if, like the hard shining sonnet, one of the most indestructible, forms of composition in general use.[17]

This method and its risks enables James to enter 'Father's Ideas' in his own way. He confronts the fact that the ruling classes betrayed the social contract. Disloyalty is, as it is in

Conrad, a major immoral centre; that 'unsafe nature' in 'The Two Faces' (1903) haunts him. Hawthorne's Unpardonable Sin is rampant still, and James certainly knew its dangers:

> a want of love and reverence for the Human Soul; in consequence of which the investigator pried into its dark depths, not with a hope or a purpose of making it better, but from a cold philosophical curiosity . . . only desiring to study it out.[18]

Such 'diabolizing', as Hawthorne called it, is the evil at the core of 'The Turn of the Screw'. Eliot noticed both Hawthorne's and James's probes into 'the deeper psychology'. They both use their perception 'by antennae'[19] to penetrate the desire for control, security, erotic exploitive pleasure and sacrifice, the agent's desire for a manacled victim. As William S. Burroughs puts it, the face of evil is the face of total need. Eliot read correctly: 'the real hero, in any of James's stories, is a social entity of which men and women are constituents', 'a quicksand', into the narrative of which the reader is gripped 'uneasily [as] the victim of a merciless clairvoyance'.[20] James's clairvoyant gaze uses the gaze which the heroine of 'In the Cage' exchanges with her customers, the gaze of the governess in 'The Turn of the Screw' as she encounters the gazes of the two children and the two ghosts, the 'glare' that Spencer Brydon receives from his *alter ego* in 'The Jolly Corner', and the smuggler's presence in 'The Third Person'—and, in society, of both the eyes of Clare Vawdrey in 'The Private Life' (1893) and 'the public' on Lady Gwyther in 'The Two Faces'. James's method reaches deeply into the arena of power:

> an encompassment that is stifling . . . and, at the same time, draining. . . . The ego then plunges into a pursuit of identifications that could repair narcissism—identifications that the subject will experience as in-significant, 'empty', 'nul', 'devitalized', 'puppet-like'. An empty castle, haunted by unappealing ghosts—'powerless' outside, 'impossible' inside.[21]

James's penetrations into the nature of Control—one reason why Eliot believed him to be 'the most intelligent man of his generation'[22]—bear comparison with Jean-Paul Sartre's study of slavery as 'reciprocal and moving relations', those conflicts in 'Being-for-others', which shape as masochism and sadism.[23] The Jamesian drama occurs in *Being and Nothingness*:

171

But now I suddenly raise my head. Somebody was there and
has seen me. . . . the Other has not only revealed to me what I
was; he has established me in a new type of being which can
support new qualifications. . . . he is the one for whom I am not
subject but object. . . . the abstract moment of self-identity is
given in the knowledge of the Other. . . . the appearance among
the objects of *my* universe of an element of disintegration in that
universe is what I mean by the appearance of a man in my
universe. . . . the look (*le regard*) will be given just as well on
occasion when there is a rustling of branches, or the sound of a
footstep followed by silence, or the slight opening of a shutter,
or a light movement of a curtain. . . . It is that I am vulnerable,
that I have a body which can be hurt, that I occupy a place and
that I cannot in any case escape from the place in which I am
without defence—in short, *I am seen.* . . . with the Other's look a
new organization comes to superimpose itself on the first. . . . I
am no longer master of the situation.[24]

So Daisy Miller is regarded, in the fullest sense, by
Americans and an Italian, until she becomes an object. She is
caged by Mr. Giovanelli's 'idiom', his 'clever' English.
Winterbourne's gaze is impotence arising from training and
emotional restriction, his 'fear' of women. Daisy's death occurs
at the intersection of social and personal causes which James's
preface calls 'practical terms', and they resemble the structure
of Caroline Spencer's disintegration in 'Four Meetings'
(1879). What James calls his 'little exhibition' converts a
social blunder into a Hawthornian trap and a sacrificial game
located suitably in the Colosseum. The American is enclosed
in European locations of power—St. Peter's, the Palace of the
Caesars and the arena. Daisy catches her death precisely at
the base of the Cross at the centre of the Colosseum. Winterbourne is left 'staring at raw protuberance among the April
daisies'—Daisy's grave (1879). In her struggle for freedom,
she is desocialized by intersecting gazes, suspended between
pathetic mother, absent money-making father, and amusing
but helpless brother—the useless family of many of James's
dramas of indiscriminate judgement. The centre of his 'drama
of discrimination' (preface to *The Ambassadors*) is a particular
loss, given in a letter: 'The port from which I set out was . . .
that of the essential loneliness of my life, and it seems to be the
port also, in sooth, to which my course again finally directs

itself. This loneliness (is) deeper than my "genius", deeper than my "discipline", deeper, above all, than the deep counterminings of art.'

2

The sacrifice of the precocious boy in 'The Pupil' (1892) to his family is told also as the sacrifice of his tutor, Pemberton, caught between money and loving responsibility. Morgan's 'cleverness' extends to giving his life as a 'gift' to his tutor, but at least with more resistance than Dolcino, destroyed by his parents' exploitation in 'The Author of Beltraffio'. The American narrator gazes in impotence. The young are as dislocated as the women in 'In the Cage', 'The Third Person', 'The Real Thing' and 'The Altar of the Dead'. 'Need' moves into 'sacrifice', and the summary story is 'The Turn of the Screw', whose double detection structure involves the governess narrator and the reader trying to possess a gapped field of fact and inference as it possesses them. They have to detect just how the gaze of the Other—the ghosts of Quint and Jessel—defines the living subjects. The governess, in Section 4, repeats Quint's gaze into the room. She remembers the gothic romance of Udolpho and 'an insane, an unmentionable relative kept in unsuspected confinement' in *Jane Eyre*. Such intertextuality enters her 'state of mind' in Section 6, into 'a joy in the extraordinary flight of heroism the occasion demanded of me', 'greatness' in 'service', the possessiveness of 'I—well, I lead *them*' masked as 'united in danger' overlapping 'affection', and the 'screen' of 'disguised tension' which could become 'something like madness' which enables her to read interpretations as 'horrible proofs'. These terms appear in a single paragraph. The gaps in the governess's report to Douglas show morbidity masked as confession. Between the end of Section 6 and the beginning of Section 7, she leaps from facing the Jessel face to her gaze on Flora 'playing very hard' to 'they know, they know' only inferred from 'I saw with my eyes: saw she was perfectly aware.' The opening 'delicious' Christmas tale of 'terror'—a young woman's narrative of 'a visitation' on two children—is transferred to Douglas's record of 'uncanny ugliness and horror and pain', the tale of a governess 'in love'. Like the telegram clerk in 'In the Cage', she is infatuated with the class above her—her employer as 'gallant and splendid', 'rich . . . fearfully extravagant . . . in a glow of high fashion, of good looks, of expensive habits, of charming ways with women'—and left with two orphan relatives he does not wish to see. The author infers that she 'succumbed' to his 'seduction'—based on seeing him only twice. The screw's turn is both the visitation on the children and the governess's two visits to their uncle. She is further trapped by her romance of children's needs—'a trap . . . to my imagination, to my delicacy, perhaps to my vanity; to whatever in me was most excitable'.

As usual in James, the cage contains the beast and its victim: 'something gathers or crouches. The change [is] actually the spring of the beast' (Eliot rightly absorbed this as 'the horror of it'). Quint's presence for the governess is 'the image that had been in my mind'. His erotic, existential gaze 'fixes' her, breaks the 'romance' of the children, doubles the 'master' in the master's clothes as the figure of control, figures as 'strange passages and perils, secret disorders, vices more than suspected'. She infers that he did 'what wished' with Miss Jessel because 'it must have been also what *she* wished.' Her need to 'possess' the children is the binding term of her narrative—she becomes a variant of Quint and Jessel, the characteristic subject in James: self-destruction within desire to control and be free beyond the exigencies of submissive survival. The vicar's daughter plays out her need for 'victory' (Section 24) as the children's salvation. Once she plants corruption into them, they become 'immensely more interesting'. What she takes to be her own 'lucidity' is the Vereker mania of reading everything as a signifier of some 'figure in the carpet'. James's terminology is complete. The surface is 'game', 'policy' or 'fraud' perpetrated by 'babies' (which they are not) who persist in 'simply leading a life of their own'. 'They're not mine', the narrator complains. Everything must be 'traceable', for 'possession', 'story', 'art', 'obsession', 'dreadful passages of intercourse', under the gaze of 'a jailor with an eye to possible surprises and escapes' and enthralled to 'horrors gathered behind'. She virtually murders her charges as 'collapse engulfed us all'. She has converted Bly into 'a prison' under her 'decree' of 'salvation' against 'demons'. The beast emerges from herself: ' "What does [Quint] matter now, my own?—What will he *ever* matter? *I* have you", I launched at the beast, "but he has lost you for ever!" ' She 'grasps' Miles, but his heart has stopped, 'dispossessed'. James's story is a psychic romance of 'possessive individualism' in which the self and the other have become 'prisoners of dominant significations, every signifying desire referred back to dominated subjects'.[25]

The plot of 'The Private Life' (1893), in elucidating what generates or prevents form, what lies behind 'performance', can substitute social for literary production because James is secure in his knowledge of literature as a product of social situation—a set of controls in which matter is being shaped. He challenges society's desire to reduce art to entertainment, propaganda and pornography. Both here and in 'The Birthplace' (1903) the schizophrenia of public and private life, 'exhibition' and 'imagination', the socialite and the writer, set the plots going. The owners of the Great Writer's birthplace enclose a genteel couple in this genteel 'prison', a 'temple', a 'cage', 'the Mecca of the English-speaking race'. The Gedges believe that their absence of 'the vulgar' qualifies them as 'priests': 'the more we do the more we shall love Him.' So James draws control-religion into the vortex of class and employment, the whirl of His 'worshippers' and the owners, '*Them* . . . the powers above'. Morris Gedge hopes to gain 'some secret' from Him to develop another self, like Brydon in search of the 'spirit' of the Jolly Corner and Miss Amy in search of 'risk' at Marr. In private, he prowls 'the Holy of Holies'; in public he puts on 'the Show' as 'a good parrot' about the 'works', the 'relics' and 'the idol': 'he was splitting in halves, unmistakably', hoping to be unified through 'the salvation of the showman'. But the cage of performance for money closes. The gaze of realization again comes from a class above the victim, a young American couple, the Hayes, possessed of

> the high luxury of freedom . . . not simply because they had money . . . but because they could in some supreme degree think and feel and say what they liked. They had a nature and a culture, a tradition, a facility of some sort—and all producing in

175

them an effect of positive beauty—that gave a light to their
liberty and an ease to their tone.

It is one of James's few full statements of his ideal confidence,
a freedom which combines tradition, wealth and love into an
aesthetics. The Hayes are not seduced by 'Europe' (1900) as
Daisy Miller and Caroline Spencer are. They interrupt 'the
showman's song' by their 'transcendent freedom', expose His
ghost and challenge the 'blasphemer' of 'the sacred doll' (as in
'a Spanish church') to reveal his honesty, however hidden for
money. The altar of the Dead is accurately estimated by an
American:

> He escapes us like a thief in the night, carrying off—well,
> carrying off everything. And people pretend to catch Him like a
> flown canary, over whom you can close your hand, and put him
> back in the cage. . . . [But] He won't come back. He's not such
> a fool! It makes Him the happiest of all great men.

The real show is the works: ' "The play's the thing." Let the
author alone.' But He is 'killed everyday' in the ownership of
his Body. Gedge decides, on Hayes's advice, to 'keep up' his
sacrificial rite by satisfying public demand for 'false facts',
urged on by his wife Isabel, and to 'strangle' his 'critical sense
. . . in the dark . . . there must be blood. Which, indeed, on the
altar of sacrifice, is all right. But the place is for ever
spattered.' And James rubs it in: 'The axe was in the air—yes;
but in a world gorged to satiety there were no revolutions.'
Gedge becomes a star performer with a 'strained grin'. 'The
receipts speak' under the control of the 'best-tamer in a cage,
all tights and spangles and circus attitudes'—the very image
used for the audience of *Guy Domville*, in a letter to his brother
(1 January 1895): 'a cage of beasts at some infernal zoo'. It is
the qualifying scene for what he would call the political field in
1914: 'the plunge of civilization into this abyss of blood and
darkness by the wanton feat of those two infamous aristocrats'.

The country-house performance in which Lady Valda
Gwyther is to be sacrificed ('The Two Faces') is 'the Roman
mob at circus' awaiting 'the next Christian maiden brought out
to the tigers' and 'decked for sacrifice'. Valda's face gains the
'pathos' of experience, while her betrayer becomes 'perfection
resplendent', a beauty invaded by the eyes of 'something else'.

3

The periphrastic manner of 'The Death of the Lion' (1894) produces the scene as a quicksand effect of suction into surfaces, insidious movements continuing into conversations. The 'desire' for 'success', the public's desire for 'an immediate exposure of everything', the editor of *The Empire*'s desire to confirm his 'professional flair'—'he had smelt the coming glory as an animal smells his distant prey', and the 'clever' journalist's desire to be involved in a major writer's abilities become a process of demolition, an exposure of market parasitism. Paraday, the writer, is 'anointed and crowned' by *The Empire*, placed on 'the dais and the throne', given 'national glory' in 'a temple vast and bare' which replaces the small 'customary altar'. *The Empire* world is Henry James senior's 'upper classes', an enclosure that sterilizes the creative. But 'security'—a key word in James—is also invaded by illness and insufficient married leisure, and by the 'adoration' of 'the faithful' turned into market values and the Press. The narrator of 'The Next Time' (1895) 'cyphers up' the life of Ray Limbert and produces a rich Jamesian language-set: 'artistic', 'sell', 'heroic eminence', 'market', 'success', 'vulgar', 'money', 'reputation', 'glory', 'respect', 'the age of trash triumphant' and 'the hard doom of popularity'. The public is a dog wagging its tail for more. For 'gentility' the author must relate to 'earls' and such, as well as having both 'babies' and 'books'. The result is 'an altar of sacrifice', 'the luxury of dropped discrimination' and 'journalism' against 'success in the line of idiosyncracy'. The vocabulary stiffens as Limbert shifts to 'prostitution', the 'supply' of 'public want' and 'the common'. The criterion is 'an unscrupulous, an unsparing, a shameless masterpiece'. There is no alternative to this conflict and 'The Figure in the Carpet' is an episode in perpetual battle. The assumed secret of a career attracts the uncreative predator and his mass market employers, those who need to control the creative spring. Once Vereker owns to a Pateresque 'flame of art', 'the particular thing', 'an idea', a 'little trick' and 'an exquisite scheme' critical Grub Street moves in on his 'organ of life'. To George Corvick Vereker's 'primal plan' and 'complex figure in a Persian carpet' are simply ways in to his art and life as 'all one thing'. Then Drayton Deane claims he has the 'secret' and the 'buried treasure' from Vereker himself. Once again the James narrates possession and the possessed, the vampiric urge within social Darwinism, how 'fate sometimes deals with man's avidity.' The narrator ends in his self-created 'dungeon': 'I was shut up in my obsession for ever—my gaolers had gone off with the key.' His narrative 'revenge' still leaves him in 'unappeased desire', a well-established definition of Hell.

The country houses which the couple frequent in 'Broken Wings' (1900) are 'great gilded cages' of 'fundamental facility', 'general exemption', 'a universal blandness' and the perpetual 'show' of the theatricality of 'success' versus 'failure', 'popularity' versus neglect. Straith and Mrs. Harvey have to discover the 'courage' 'not to keep up'. Their decision obviates shelves of academic Jamesian criticism:

> Everything costs that one does for the rich. It's not our poor relations who make us pay . . . We can't afford the opulent. But it isn't only the money they take. It's the imagination . . . As they have none themselves—it's an article we have to supply? We've certainly to use a lot to protect ourselves.

They decide to be 'beaten together' and move out toward love and work like some Chekhovian pair—not to a puritan or success ethic, nor a Thoreauvian establishment of 'a lone isle in a tepid sea', but their own 'separate peace'.

By 1903, James condenses his inferential word-sets into a few pieces in a ruled space, with wordless spaces for the unsaid and unsayable. 'The Story in It' opens with 'vicious rain', a 'violence of watered green' and 'troubled light', and then places within this scene 'silence' and 'a consistent air of selection and suppression'. The 'inmates' exist in a 'tension' about to be 'snapped', moving between 'impulses', 'calculations' and 'reserve'—a vocabulary of wary inference preparing, once again, for 'the real thing' which Maud Blessingbourne hopes to obtain from her French novel—'to get more life for my money'. Knowing and saying are separated in the cage. The surface of terms is a system of strategies eliciting relationship and motive. James calls it 'inquiry'—which includes three silent connections—Mrs. Dyott and Colonel Vogt hold hands,

Maud touches 'the region of her heart', and a kiss. It is the one story for which Eliot's observation on James's Flaubertian mind seems right: 'so fine no idea could violate it'—provided the emphasis is on 'violate' and not 'idea'. But sacrifice, altar and cage are still the triad of power, and the complex workings between art and life.

A will may come to imprison anyone. In Lacan's terms, relationship may turn into:

> the aggressivity that becomes the beam of the balance on which will be centred the decomposition of the equilibrium of counterpart to counterpart in the Master-Slave relationship, a relationship that is pregnant with all the cunning tricks (*ruses*) by which reason sets its impersonal reign in motion.[26]

Value in 'The Madonna of the Future' (1873) is 'invent, create, achieve', threatened by tension between 'profane desires' and 'pure masters', the 'strong' and the 'innocent'. The word-set for value reflects James's *fin de siècle* aesthetics at this date: 'divine mood', 'spotless image', 'miracle', 'the flame', the 'law' of 'beauty', 'force' and 'purity', 'genius' and 'perfection'. Worse than poverty may result from such idealism: isolation and decay within stasis, a terrible 'silence' which predicts the ensuing sacrifice of talent, and death itself. Mark Ambient's 'masterpiece' produces both social status and the deterioration of marriage, together with the death of a son with that 'particular infant charm that's as good as a death-warrant'. The wife who takes the crucial step towards virtual infanticide turns 'frantic' and dies. Such may be the results of 'the gospel of art', in James's chosen 'melodramatic romance' method.[27]

The writer here, in 'The Author of Beltraffio', and generally in the pre-1900 stories, sacrifices the more as he edges towards the gentleman—a prime issue in 'The Lesson of the Master' (1888). A gentleman does not condense and create; he is committed to 'general diffusion' and 'no particular set of ideas'. Paul Overt discovers that his idol is in turn locked into

> the idols of the market; money and luxury and 'the world'; placing one's children and dressing one's wife; everything that drives one to the short and easy way. . . . One has no business to have any children. . . . if one wants to do anything good . . . an incentive to damnation, artistically speaking.

So St. George lives 'a kind of Hell', without 'honour' or 'the real thing'—but his boys are at Harrow, Oxford and Sandhurst. Marriage and society trap him to 'miss everything', 'the concentration, the finish, the independence'. He can finally marry Miss Fancourt *because* 'it's too late.' Nine years later, James can be sardonic about Greville Fane whose scene of writing is 'passion in high life', 'exalted circles', that 'aristocracy' that 'constituted for her the romance of the world'. Making money, 'she never recognized "the torment of form" '— she parodies Hawthorne's 'fairy precinct' with her aristocratic fairyland: 'the fairies love you and *they* never change.' She slaves for her two children to enter the fairy world, and since she has saved nothing, she is enslaved for life. When her 'vogue', collapses, she composes 'form' for the vulgarities of her son Leolin, who 'forages' among the fairies. As James writes of the decayed gentlefolk in 'The Real Thing', they were 'the real thing, but always the same thing'.

Paradoxes of 'the real' obsess James. Gazing at the sea, Dencombe ('The Middle Years', 1893) construes it as 'the abyss of human illusion that was the real, the tideless deep'. He temporarily forgets his novel, absorbed in 'the sense of ebbing time, of shrinking opportunity'. His career 'had taken too much of his life'. If that sacrifice is to be valid he must have 'a better chance', if his reputation is not to 'stand on the unfinished', having ripened 'too late'. When the opportunity to be revived by young doctor Hugh occurs, he is sick with 'the guilt of interference'. James writes Dencombe's response to Hugh's offer of self-sacrifice with a condensed complexity, modifying his sea and tide figures, preparing for Dencombe's death, and offering his own statement on creative and existential life:

> A response so absolute, such a glimpse of a definite result and such a sense of credit, worked together in his mind and, producing a strange commotion, slowly altered and transfigured his despair. The sense of cold submersion left him—he seemed to float without an effort. . . . 'A second chance—that's the delusion. There never was to be but one. We work in the dark—we do what we can—we give what we have. Our doubt is in our passion—and our passion is our task. The rest is the madness of art.'

180

In 'The Middle Years' existence for art and for others, through care for writing and medical care, fuse into another definition of 'the real thing'. And for once the central relationship resists the slavery of circus performance.

But between 1895 and 1898 James composed situations in which offering the self to another under the other's gaze veers towards the suicidal. Dr. Hugh could not be repeated. The sense of lost opportunity haunts the stories from 1903 to 1909. Stransom is 'ruled by a pale ghost', the 'sovereign presence' of his potential wife whose death day in December is fixed into 'his nerves'. At 55 he sacrifices himself to 'The Altar of the Dead' (1895). He collects her and his other ghosts into life as a 'simplified, intensified essence', a condensed 'purgatory', a 'great charity' fed with 'the ample resources of his soul'. These neurotic possessions are transformed into the art of multiple candles in an altared shrine, the public enclosure of the private obsession. Stransom settles back into the 'cost'. The missing ghost and candle is that of Acton Hague, 'the only man with whom he had ever been intimate' and 'almost adored' in his 'university years'. In fact Stransom's energy is absorbed in erotic and ecstatic draining. The shrine 'takes possession of him', an 'esoteric' transference, 'a masterpiece of splendour and a mountain of fire', an 'enjoyment', 'a new necessity', into which he will himself be finally enclosed in his totalizing fantasy. His candle is to be placed by the woman Hague had forsaken. Between their 'haunting' of the shrine and listening to Beethoven and Schumann at St. James's Hall, a strange love emerges (the *Notebooks* show how carefully James chose his names). The woman is another of James's 'tragically sacrificed' women, fallen socially into a slum existence eked out from 'her little remunerative art', her pseudonymous magazine-writing. The affair has its characteristic James set: 'quite intimate', 'relation', 'friendship', 'confidence', 'safety', 'certitude', a 'fine way' around the 'central hollow' of Stransom's life, with the woman as 'priestess of his altar'—as Gedge is to the birthplace. Under 'the dreadful clockface of time' love becomes mutual 'haunting' in a 'chamber of remembrance and homage', and behind it haunts Hague who has enslaved both of them. James guides the narrative towards sterility with intimacy 'diminished', love 'coldly sacrificed'

181

into 'shining coldness': 'they both missed the rich future.' The set is grim: 'renouncement', 'privation' (twice), 'going down', 'melancholy', 'failed' health, the shrine 'a great dark cavern' and the church a 'void'—and then James's characteristic image of the unpenetrated edge of the desired or once-desired: 'a group of sea-lights on the edge of the ocean of life'. Life is relegated to a desire for harmony and symmetry; form—the altar—becomes the enclosure of both narcissism and suicide, and the couple unite in a psychopathology of their candle art for the dead. The woman is left with Stransom's corpse and 'a great dread . . . of what might still happen'.

But the sacrificial enclosures of 'In the Cage' are more brutal. A declined gentlewoman's fantasies out of romance fiction focus on a male customer from whom she receives telegram forms in her performance as assistant in Crocker's store. May's erotic foreplay, prior to her offer of sacrificial servitude, is the snobbish product of a victimizing class system. Behind her wire cage, a literal class barrier, 'bringing their heads together . . . as far as it was possible', May carries on with Captain Everard. Obscene suggestions of touch without touching reinforce her imaginings of 'high reality', 'expensive feelings'—that 'magnificent security' of the Hayes couple—a world where women were 'after men' who spent more on tulips and telegrams than 'would have held the stricken household of her frightened childhood . . . together for a lifetime'. Interpreting the scene as romantic, May is 'thrilled' by the imagined blackmail she could operate. Her alternative enclosure is marriage to Mr. Mudge, a tradesman who dreams of manipulating the upper classes that use him for his own 'advantage of trade'. He is in fact, as James intervenes to state, 'made out of his betters'. Everard is his 'symbol of success', as he is May's opportunity for female 'sacrifice for love' in her proto Mills and Boone fantasies—'it beat every novel in the shop.' James gloats sardonically, without entering the complex scope of satire. May watches Lady Bradeen's 'eyes and lips that so often have been so near his own', and 'thrills'. In a brief park meeting, she tells Everard 'I'd do anything for you', after wallowing in her imaginings: 'your extravagance, your selfishness, your immorality, your crimes . . . I like them, as I tell you—I revel in them.' No wonder Everard is reduced to a typical 'I *say!*'

Edwardian society produces consumers and their needs. Reality becomes simulation and simulation reality, 'the desert of the real itself'.[28] 'In the Cage' condenses the meanings of seduction in class society. James penetrates to 'the thing hideously behind' the need to earn money and to fantasize about those who apparently do not, the sterilizing law within 'The Bench of Desolation'. The state control system concerns him in its immediate instances. Here, Kate Cookham's 'action for "breach"' against Herbert Dodd brings law to ensure security of income, revenge against betrayal through broken promise and the wreckage of confidence, and a regaining of passionate intimacy—themes from 'The Altar of the Dead'. The language-set is brutal: Dodd's 'pluck or confidence' destroyed, female vulnerability—the constant theme of the English novel from Defoe onwards—is 'grossness', 'indelicacy', 'excess of will', 'destitution of scruple', 'ignoble threat', 'a master hand' and 'entanglement'—all in the *third* paragraph. 'The squalor of the court' invades private life and naïve ideas of love. The exploitive woman is 'devilish'. The scene is 'morbid', the once 'drawn blind' is up, the 'vulgar' is loosed by a 'terrorist'.

Dodd's condition between education and trade—the Pemberton and Gedge tension—parallels Kate's position as governess and teacher—as in 'The Turn of the Screw'. He 'holds' his 'educated customers'; she holds him in 'the cheapest of traps'. Dodd recovers from 'scared sobs' in his bookshop cage through 'righteous resentment', teaching himself '*how* to suffer, and how almost to like it'. The *petit bourgeois* snob feels his 'gentleman type' ought not to suffer 'coarse usage'. May and Dodd are twins. Love again turns into the 'annexing' of another person, the 'price' of 'having to pay'. But the schizophrenic plot of debt here moves to the existential at 'Land's End' and the bench of desolation on which Dodd and his second woman, Nan Drury, sit 'together when time and freedom served, one of the very last, the far western benches of the interminable sea-front', where Kate 'had made the straightest and most unabashed love to *him*'. Again intimacy has to combat the enclosure of the real: Dodd demands that love should be 'absolutely unreserved and abandoned, absolutely reckless and romantic . . . a refuge from poisonous reality'. Public court, bankruptcy and prison must be avoided at the cost of private anguish, humiliation and poverty. James's vocabulary inside spreading, virulent sentences sets up a darkening web, a generative enclosure incorporating its victims. Females 'wreck the infinite'. The 'vulgarity' of the law reduces gentility to criminality. The sexuality of power, the power of sexuality, penetrate to the point of abjection. In Kristeva's terms the 'socialized' and degraded woman turns dangerous:

> The unbridling is then changed into crafty reckoning, hysterical spells turn to murderous plots, extreme masochistic poverty becomes a commercial triumph. While hysterical woman is merely a carnival puppet, under a law she perversely attempts to get around, the paranoid woman becomes successful, by making herself the expression of a murderous sociality.[29]

James's cage in 'The Bench of Desolation' is so apparently timeless that he cannot open or demolish it. Kate becomes an archetypal destructive female force, mythological even: she is 'gorged with [Dodd's] unholy tribute . . . as soon as he had begun regularly to bleed'. Dodd's 'morbid bravery' remains a gaze from Narcissus; his return to the bench is 'the power of ritual', a parody of 'order, rectitude, law'. James cannot break through law, the limits of the gaze, into 'extreme freedom'.[30] Dodd's set remains: 'grim', 'dingy', 'evil, unsociable, possibly engaged on working out the idea of a crime', 'the worship of some absolutely unpractical remorse'. He sinks to abjection by the open sea, waiting for the third woman, 'passive' to whatever she might do 'in possession of him'. 'The grey desert of his consciousness . . . suddenly opened and flamed' but he is invaded by the 'lady-like' with 'some ulterior view', and 'authoritative' woman whose 'outrageous vulgarity' is a 'prime assault' and an 'atrocity' against 'the refinement of his art'.

The issue of debt is equally familiar, with puns on 'pay', plus 'obligation', 'owe', 'pay up that balance', and Kate's moves towards 'repayment with interest'. But Kate claims the puritan price of 'suffering' for 'good': 'it was *for* you.' Desolation is to be an opening in the closure of 'my poor agonized old money—my blood'. To which she counters: 'It's *my* blood too, you must know now.' The sterile futility of mutual blood sacrifice—blood money spattered on the bench of debt—is a final twist of the Unpardonable Sin, 'using you yourself'. And the interest is to be 'five-fold'. Recoiling from the law's 'vulgarity', Dodd has lost. He takes Kate's blood money, and the narrative moves from 'bewildered consciousness' and 'the length of his leash' to the curtailing of speech itself, a grim silence, with Kate's arm around him, on the desolate bench. And James uses his title for the ninth and last occasion. It is part of his final sense of *impasse*: fictions whose self-destructiveness dramatizes his sense of a 'black and hideous' world. He knows more than his characters and pushes them to sterilities under severe moral language-sets. He knows more than his readers, who are given fragments and silences inside a prose continuity which is in fact spaced-out clues. The gaze closes in on itself. James is haunted by misplaced alternatives and locations of unused potentiality—themes there from the beginning in 'Four Meetings', 'Europe', 'The Pupil' and 'Broken Wings'.

'The Beast in the Jungle' offers the man who sacrifices potentiality in terms both economic and passionate: 'sold it, bartered it, exchanged it for something very different and interior, but mercenary and worldly', while his Dead Self lives in a woman's feelings.[31] 'Passions that might have been': and the preface also speaks of how 'each item of his experience' is sterilized by 'the failure to find it good enough and thence appropriate it'. The gaze of May Bartram exists in 'the chill of his egotism and the light of her use'—that cold shine from 'The Altar of the Dead'. Marcher expects an overwhelming but unsharable experience—the analogue of falling in love or orgasm or death—taken as 'abominably' lonely and

> possibly destroying all further consciousness, possibly annihilating me; possibly, on the other hand, only altering everything, striking at the root of all my world and leaving me to the consequences, however they shape themselves.

So he awaits 'the real truth'—with James's quotation marks—his privilege with 'the real thing'. It is in fact his 'lunacy'. Ignoring May's gaze, he establishes narcissism as law, as a form of 'the gods', and although this set includes 'heroic' and 'courage' the bias is towards 'exposed and impotent' and the fear that the imminent catastrophe will not be '*the* catastrophe'. In Part 4, May appears as the ghost-goddess to the 'haunted' man: 'almost as white as wax', 'impenetrable sphinx', 'artificial lily', a figure on 'some island of rest that she had already reached'. She says he has had his experience—'It's past. It's behind.' It is the key phrase in James's fiction, layered with meaning his stories continually probe. The Beast has in fact 'stolen away' leaving Marcher's 'unidentified past . . . his fortune impenetrably muffled and masked', one of James's sacrificed children: 'the lost stuff of consciousness became thus for him as a strayed or stolen child to an unappeasable father.' May's names on her tomb, the sacrificial altar, remain her gaze, 'a pair of eyes that didn't know him'. As he travels to Asia 'he was the dust . . . [he] had wandered . . . from the circumference to the centre of the desert', under the narcissistic gaze, the 'raw glare of his grief'.

Spencer Brydon at least survives with a career and a woman, money and property. The glare of the ghost of his unlived but potential past in New York is the 'power' he might have had rather than his search for 'pleasure' under the 'tension', 'stalking', 'the joy of the instant, the supreme suspense' and its 'strain'. Now he stimulates himself by the 'terror of apparitions', forcing his ghost to terror and being terrorized by him, his 'blighted' self, the 'bud' never 'full-blown', the 'form' Europe and the non-American prevented. Brydon is a Jamesian artist-type, becoming aware that the producing of form in life and art, so that life *is* art, is a design necessity for the creative fulfilment of energy, resisting the sterile, the warped and the perverse. Brydon risks awakening 'possibilities' into 'such measure of ghostly life as they might still enjoy', into 'the Form he so yearned to make them take'. He 'hunts' the Form of his '*alter ego*', forcing it to 'walk' as a ghost in the New York family house. The childless man who does not 'care for anything but himself' opens his Narcissus enclosure to a 'visitation' from the Other, whatever the 'small tight bud' may have grown into. Alice Staverton, the story's third figure, is, like many other James women, the 'risk' not taken—and James twice in two pages brings his writer's presence into the narrative in order to enter Brydon's privacies. The ghost of the author haunts his own locations in complicity, like a form of Freud's *Unheimliche*:[32] 'familiar and congenial' or 'concealed and kept out of sight' by 'processes at work, concealed beneath ordinary appearance'. Control by gaze may arise from 'the soil of unbounded self-love, from primary narcissism', and the ghost, or 'double', experience from that part of the ego which acts as a censor leading to 'delusions of being watched' and the end of 'the illusion of Free Will'.

The 56-year-old man's return to New York prompts a 'dormant' and 'unpenetrated capacity for business and a sense of construction', the alternative—associated with Alice Staverton—to his 'freedom of a wanderer, overlaid by pleasure, by infidelity, by passages of life that were strange and dim to her, just by "Europe" in short'. The former might, Alice believes, have 'anticipated the inventor of the sky-scraper', a belief that makes a 'small silver ring' over 'the queerest and deepest of his own lately most disguised and most muffled vibrations'. *Das Unheimliche* comes to haunt the house he preserves from city developers, 'a reason of dollars' that he might have simulated. Following 'strange paths' and 'strange gods' has in fact made him 'an attractively capable man', but he still needs 'a preposterous secret thrill', a 'surrender to his obsession', to 'project himself . . . into the other, the real, the waiting life'. So Spencer Brydon relates to 'The Turn of the Screw' and 'In the Cage'. The 'jolly corner' becomes, not a cage or a desert or a prison, but a 'great glass bowl, all precious concave crystal, set delicately humming by the play of a moist finger round its edge', the location of possibilities beyond the edge. 'Stalking' the *alter ego* here is more pleasurable than hunting 'any beast of the forest'. His 'thrill', unlike Marcher's beast sterilities, is to produce his own 'dead', his own uncanny, his own form. Narcissus turns hunter-builder in his own house-jungle, a 'monstrous stealthy cat' confronting the Other and its 'large shining yellow eyes' with the pleasurable terror of the creative act. And Brydon, too, like many other James figures places his thrill in 'an age of greater romance'. This is 'the form of success his imagination had most cherished'.

The ghost is a 'grizzled' haired man in formal dress and the accessories of wealthy gentility, face covered with hands one of which has 'lost two fingers, which were reduced to stumps, as if accidentally shot away' (Freud draws attention to the relationship of maimed limbs, castration and the *lex talionis* in uncanny scenes). The uncovered face gazes with a horror James reserves for his late probes into the cage:

> the bared identity was too hideous as *his*, and his glare was the passion of his protest. . . . the presence before him was a presence, the horror within him a horror, but the waste of his nights had only been grotesque and the success of his adventure only an irony.

The ghost does not 'fit' Brydon's identity; romance form is reduced to a 'fantastic image projected by the magic lantern of childhood'. He faints under the assault of 'the roused passion of a life larger than his own' ('I can only have died'). That life is James's sense of the American city, 'the unmitigated "businessman" face' in *The American Scene*, 'the hideous clumsiness of rage' in official policy, the 'black and hideous' material world (the ghost is 'a black stranger'), everything James meant by 'vulgar'. Brydon's 'vastation', to use Henry James senior's term, causes a simulated death, beyond which he can accept Alice's part of him she '*could* have liked' had he stayed—'ruined sight', 'lost fingers', and all. Their concluding silence parallels the end of 'Broken Wings' five years earlier: two rare second chances in James's work. The interrogative situation, as in the world of *Being and Nothingness*, may yield a freedom. It rarely can. More often, for James, the self is self-enclosed, possessed or possessing, vampiric or enslaved.

James's long enquiry almost habitually represents a cage, an exploitation, a market of sado-masochistic reciprocities, infinite interrogations in a sisyphean drama. Creativity is threatened by sexual and market desires to exploit or be exploited. Children necessarily live within the parental enforcement, the social they are born into, 'Father's Ideas'. What Sartre calls '*la caresse*' is absent or tentative, except in 'Broken Wings', 'The Jolly Corner' and 'The Story in It' (we can recall here Isabel Archer's refusal of the cage of Caspar Goodwood's mouth). '*La caresse*', writes Sartre, 'causes the Other to be born as flesh for me and for himself'. It breaks repressions as 'touch' moves towards 'adhesiveness' in

Whitman's poetry. But property and debt relationships remain the governing model against which love and mutual respect must converge. James's stories challenge that set of beliefs which preach eternal individual freedom while disregarding actual social controls against life. His strength lies in a refusal of 'idealistic mystification', to use another phrase in Sartre's 'materialism and Existentialism'.[33] His stories do not project conditions for change but concentrate on recognition of fear, tyranny, resignation, frustration, and the nature of combat in the encounters they enforce.

NOTES

1. F. O. Matthiessen and K. B. Murdoch (eds.), *The Notebooks of Henry James* (New York: Oxford University Press, 1947), pp. 208, 217, 248–49; preface to *The Spoils of Poynton*, in R. P. Blackmur, *Henry James: The Art of the Novel* (New York: Scribner's, n.d.).
2. Frederick W. Dupee (ed.), *Henry James: Autobiographies* (London: W. H. Allen, 1956), p. 268.
3. *Notebooks*, pp. 182–83.
4. Blackmur, preface to Vol. XVII of the New York edition of James's fiction.
5. Edmund Wilson (ed.), *F. Scott Fitzgerald: The Crack-Up* (New York: New Directions, 1956), p. 69.
6. *Autobiographies*, 'Notes of a Son and Brother', Chapters 12 and 18.
7. Blackmur, preface to *The Turn of the Screw*.
8. *Notebooks*, p. 77.
9. Blackmur, preface to *The American*.
10. Henry James, *The American Scene* (London: Chapman and Hall, 1907), pp. 33, 43, 221.
11. Eric Mottram, 'Poe's Pym, and the American Social Imagination', R. J. Mott and S. E. Marowitz (eds.), *Artful Thunder* (Ohio: Kent State University Press, 1975), pp. 25–53.
12. Henry James senior, 'Socialism and Civilization' and 'The Social Significance of our Institutions', F. O. Matthiessen (ed.), *The James Family* (New York: Knopf, 1947), pp. 49–58, pp. 59–66.
13. Matthiessen, pp. 297, 508, 647.
14. *The American Scene*, pp. 653, 655.
15. Herbert Marcuse, *Counter-Revolution and Revolt* (London: Allen Lane, 1972), p. 98.
16. Blackmur, preface to *The American*.
17. Blackmur, pp. 149, 158, 168, 171–72, 241.
18. Nathaniel Hawthorne, *The American Notebooks*, Malcolm Cowley (ed.),

The Portable Hawthorne (New York: Viking Press, 1948), pp. 562, 567.
19. T. S. Eliot, 'On Henry James', F. W. Dupee (ed.), *The Question of Henry James* (London: Allan Wingate, 1942), pp. 129–30.
20. Eliot, p. 125.
21. Julia Kristeva, *Powers of Horror: An Essay in Abjection* (New York: Columbia University Press, 1982), p. 49.
22. Eliot, p. 125.
23. Mary Warnock, *The Philosophy of Sartre* (London: Hutchinson, 1965), pp. 83–4.
24. Jean-Paul Sartre, *Being and Nothingness* (New York: Citadel Press, 1964), pp. 197–98, 204, 216, 231, 235, 241.
25. C. B. Macpherson, *The Political Theory of Possessive Individualism* (London: Oxford, 1964), pp. 263–64; Gilles Deleuze and Félix Guattari, *On the Line* (New York: Semiotext (e), 1983), p. 52.
26. Jacques Lacan, *Ecrits* (London: Tavistock Publications, 1977), p. 308.
27. Richard Chase, *The American Novel and its Tradition* (New York: Doubleday, 1957), p. ix.
28. Jean Baudrillard, *For a Critique of the Political Economy of the Sign* (Missouri: Telos Press, 1981), p. 136.
29. Kristeva, p. 168.
30. Maurice Blanchot, *The Gaze of Orpheus* (New York: Station Hill Press, 1981), pp. 99–104.
31. *Notebooks*, p. 183.
32. Sigmund Freud, 'The Uncanny', *On Creativity and the Unconscious* (New York: Harper, 1958), pp. 122–61.
33. Herbert Marcuse, *From Luther to Popper*, London: Verso, 1983), pp. 164–82.

Notes on Contributors

HAROLD BEAVER is Professor of American Literature at the University of Amsterdam. He has contributed five editions of Melville and Poe to the Penguin English Library. He has recently completed a book, based on past essays and articles, *The Great American Masquerade*, which is to be published in the Critical Studies Series.

HERBIE BUTTERFIELD is Reader in Literature at the University of Essex. He is author of a book on Hart Crane, a monograph on Robinson Jeffers, and miscellaneous shorter pieces on, among others, Poe, Hawthorne, Longfellow, Henry James, Willa Cather, Hemingway and Melville. He is also the editor of *Twentieth Century American Poetry* (1984) in the Critical Studies Series.

HOWELL DANIELS is Academic Secretary to the Institute of United States Studies, London and a Senior Lecturer in the University of London. He has written about the 'international theme' of America and Europe and Henry James especially.

ANDREW HOOK is Bradley Professor of English Literature at Glasgow University. His American interests are reflected by his books, *Scotland and America 1750–1835* (1975) and *American Literature in Context, 1865–1900* (1982) as well as by articles on Anglo-American relations.

A. ROBERT LEE is Lecturer in American Literature at the University of Kent at Canterbury. He is editor of the Everyman *Moby-Dick* (1975) and five previous collections in the Critical Studies series—on Afro-American Fiction, Hawthorne, Hemingway, Melville and Nineteenth-Century American Poetry. His other publications include a B.A.A.S. pamphlet *Black American Fiction Since Richard Wright* (1983) and recent essays on Chester Himes, Richard Wright, Emily Dickinson, Stephen Crane, Mark Twain and Robert Penn Warren.

ERIC MOTTRAM is Professor of English and American Literature in the University of London, at King's College. He has published books on Kenneth Rexroth, Paul Bowles, Allen Ginsberg and others, and with Malcolm Bradbury, edited and contributed to the *Penguin Companion to American Literature* (1971). He has written widely on nineteenth-century and twentieth-century America. His last three books of poems were *Elegies, A Book of Herne* and *Interrogation Rooms*.

JUDIE NEWMAN is Lecturer in English Literature at the University of Newcastle upon Tyne. She has contributed essays on English and American novelists to a range of literary journals. Her *Saul Bellow and History* was published in 1984.

DAVID TIMMS is Lecturer in American Literature at the University of Manchester. He is the author of *Philip Larkin* (1973) and has written articles on contemporary British poetry, Conrad, Hawthorne and James.

MICHAEL WOOD is Professor of English at the University of Exeter. He is the author of *Stendhal* (1971) and *America at the Movies* (1975) and a regular contributor to the *New York Review of Books, New Society* and the *Sunday Times*.

Index

Adams, Henry, 168
American Long Poem, The, 7
Anderson, Sherwood: *Winesburg, Ohio*, 9, 107
Arabian Nights, The, 137
Atlantic Monthly, 7, 117
Austen, Jane, 169

Barthes, Roland, 63, 98; *S/Z*, 63
Battles and Leaders of the Civil War, 122
Baudelaire, Charles, 13, 23, 31, 32; *Les Fleurs du Mal*, 35
Becker, Samuel, 10
Beckford, William, 137
Bierce, Ambrose, 7, 10, 11, 35, 134–49; Collections: *Can Such Things Be?*, 136; *Collected Works*, 136, 137; *In the Midst of Life*, 136, 139; *Negligible Tales*, 136, 138; *Tales of Soldiers and Civilians*, 136; *The Devil's Dictionary*, 136, 137, 139; Stories: 'A Bottomless Grave', 138; 'A Horseman in the Sky', 142, 144, 145, 147; 'A Little Story', 138; 'A Resumed Identity', 139; 'A Revolt of the Gods', 139; 'A Tough Tussle', 145; 'A Watcher by the Dead', 145; 'An Affair of Outposts', 146; 'An Inhabitant of Carcosa', 139; 'An Occurrence at Owl Creek Bridge', 142–43, 143, 146, 147; 'Chickamauga', 143, 144, 147; 'George Thurston', 142, 145; 'Killed at Resaca', 145, 146; 'Moxon's Master', 139; 'My Curried Cow', 138; 'Oil of Dog', 138; 'One Kind of Officer', 143, 144; 'One of the Missing', 145, 147; 'One Officer, One Man', 145; 'Parker Adderson, Philosopher', 143, 145; 'The Affair at Coulter's Notch', 143, 144, 145, 146; 'The Boarded Window', 141; 'The City of the Gone Away', 138; 'The Coup de Grâce', 143, 146, 147; 'The Death of Halpin Frayser', 141, 141–42; 'The Eyes of the Panther', 141; 'The Man and the Snake', 140; 'The Middle Toe of the Right Foot', 141; 'The Monk and the Hangman's Daughter', 137; 'The Moonlit Road', 141; 'The Secret of MacArger's

Gulch', 141; 'The Story of a Conscience', 144; 'The Suitable Surroundings', 140
Blackmur, R. P., 170
Blackwood's Magazine, 104
Bloom, Harold, 13, 22, 32
Borges, Jorge Luis, 10, 36
Brady, Mathew, 122
Brontë, Charlotte: *Jane Eyre*, 173
Burroughs, William, 171

Cable, George Washington: *Madame Delphine*, 131
Carlyle, Thomas, 166
Chekhov, Anton, 150
Chopin, Kate, 7, 9, 10, 11, 150–63; Books: *A Night in Acadie*, 151; *Bayou Folk*, 151; *The Awakening*, 151, 152; Stories: 'A Family Affair', 152, 160–61; 'A Lady of Bayou St. John', 153, 161; 'A Shameful Affair', 160; 'A Visit to Avoyelles', 153; 'Athénaïse', 152, 159–60; 'Aunt Limpy's Interference', 152; 'Charlie', 153–59; 'Desirée's Baby', 151–52; 'Fedora', 161; 'La Belle Zoraïde', 161; 'Lilacs', 162; 'Ma'ame Pélagre', 161; 'Madame Célestin's Divorce', 153; 'Miss Witherwell's Mistake', 152, 160; 'The Storm', 152, 153; 'The Story of an Hour', 152, 161; 'Two Portraits', 161–62; 'Wiser Than A God', 152
Coolidge, Calvin, 8
Conrad, Joseph, 8, 123; *Lord Jim*, 123
Cooper, James Fenimore, 50, 104
Crane, Stephen, 7, 11, 65, 120–33, 150; Books: *The Red Badge of Courage*, 9, 10, 121, 122, 123, 125; Stories: 'A Mystery of Heroism', 121, 125; 'An Episode of War', 124; 'George's Mother', 123; 'Maggie', 123, 168; 'The Black Riders', 123; 'The Blue Hotel', 123, 125, 126–32; 'The Bride Comes to Yellow Sky', 123; 'The Monster', 125; 'The Price of the Harness', 125; 'The Veteran', 125
Crèvecoeur, M. G. J. de, 8

193

Index

Dante, 121
Darwin, Charles, 86, 120, 166; *The Origin of Species*, 86
Democratic Review, 7
Dickens, Charles, 109
Dickinson, Emily, 7, 125
Dreiser, Theodore: *Sister Carrie*, 168
Duyckinck, Evert, 58, 98
Dwight, Timothy: *Travels in New England and New York*, 97

Eliot, T. S., 13, 29, 171
Emerson, Ralph Waldo, 7, 96; *Nature*, 98; 'The American Scholar', 98
Endicott, John, 67–9

Faulkner, William, 7, 107
Fitzgerald, Scott, 7; *The Great Gatsby*, 8
Foucault, Michel, 71
Frazer, James, 166
Freud, Sigmund, 27, 120, 169, 188

Garland, Hamlin: *Main-Travelled Roads*, 107
Gogol, Nikolai, 15
Graham's Magazine, 10

Harper's New Monthly Magazine, 7, 77, 80, 82
Harte, Bret, 9
Hawthorne, Nathaniel, 7, 9, 10, 35, 57–75, 77, 96–9, 104, 105, 106, 121, 122, 137, 150, 171, 172; Books: *French and Italian Notebooks*, 72; *Mosses from an Old Manse*, 57, 72, 96–9; *The Marble Faun*, 72; *The Snow Image*, 57, 72; *Twice Told Tales*, 10, 57, 61, 62; Stories and Sketches: 'A Select Party', 98; 'Alice Doane's Appeal', 60–1; 'David Swan', 63; 'Egotism; or the Bosom Serpent', 61; 'Endicott and the Red Cross', 67–8; 'Ethan Brand', 61, 72; 'Fancy's Show Box', 63; 'Little Annie's Ramble', 62–3; 'Time's Portraiture', 62; 'Rappaccini's Daughter', 61; 'The Birthmark', 66; 'The Bosom Serpent', 63; 'The Christmas Banquet', 61, 63; 'The Devil in Manuscript', 58–9; 'The Grey Champion', 67; 'The Intelligence Office', 98; 'The Man of Adamant', 67; 'The Maypole of Merry Mount', 68–70; 'The Old Manse', 61, 72; 'The Snow Image', 66; 'Young Goodman Brown', 64–6, 98
Hazlitt, William, 98; *The Spirit of the Age*, 49
Hearst, William Randolph, 136
Holmes, Sherlock, 29, 36

Homer, Winslow, 122
Howells, William Dean, 117
Hubbard, William, 122
Hurston, Zora Neale, 9
Hume, David, 115

Irving, Washington, 7, 9, 35, 40–56, 105, 150; Books: *A Chronicle of the Conquest of Granada*, 55; *A History of the Life and Voyages of Christopher Columbus*, 55; *Bracebridge Hall*, 40, 42, 50, 51, 53; *Gleanings in Europe: England*, 50; *Tales of a Traveller*, 40, 43, 48, 52, 54; *The Alhambra*, 40; *The History of New York*, 47; *The Sketch Book of Geoffrey Crayon, Gent.*, 40, 41, 42, 44, 46, 50, 53, 105; *Wolfert's Roost and Other Papers*, 40–1

Jackson, Andrew, 113
Jackson, Stonewall, 122
James, Henry, 7, 8, 11, 14, 23, 49, 78, 104, 105, 106, 150, 164–90; Books, Plays, Notebooks: *Guy Domville*, 164, 176; *Notebooks*, 166, 170, 181; *The Ambassadors*, 172; *The American*, 166, 167; *The American Scene*, 166, 188; *The Golden Bowl*, 166, 167; *The Portrait of a Lady*, 165; *What Maisie Knew*, 9; Stories: 'Broken Wings', 178, 185, 188; 'Daisy Miller', 9, 172; 'Europe', 176, 185; 'Four Meetings', 172, 185; 'Greville Fane', 169, 180; 'In the Cage', 165, 167, 171, 173, 174, 182–83; 'The Altar of the Dead', 173, 181–82, 183, 185; 'The Author of Beltraffio', 167, 169, 173, 179; 'The Beast in the Jungle', 164, 165, 185–86; 'The Bench of Desolation', 165, 167, 184–85; 'The Birthplace', 167; 'The Death of the Lion', 177; 'The Figure in the Carpet', 170; 'The Jolly Corner', 82, 166, 171, 175, 186–88, 188; 'The Lesson of the Master', 179; 'The Madonna of the Future', 179; 'The Middle Years', 180–81; 'The Next Time', 177; 'The Private Life', 171, 175; 'The Pupil', 167; 'The Real Thing', 169, 173, 180; 'The Spoils of Poynton', 164, 170; 'The Story in It', 178–79, 188; 'The Turn of the Screw', 167, 171, 173, 183; 'The Two Faces', 171, 176
James, Henry, Sr., 164, 167, 177, 188; 'Socialism and Civilization', 167; 'The Social Significance of our Institutions', 167
James, William, 168, 176
Jewett, Sarah Orne: *A Native of Winby*, 151; *A White Heron*, 151; *The Country of the Pointed Firs*, 151; *The King of Folly Island*, 151; *The Life of Nancy*, 151

194

Index

Joyce, James, 8; *Ulysses*, 15
Jung, Carl, 169

King, Grace: *Balcony Stories*, 151

Lacan, Jacques, 14, 16, 179
Lamb, Charles, 98
Lee, Robert E., 122
Lévi-Strauss, Claude, 16
Literary World, 77, 96, 98
London, Jack, 9, 166

Malamud, Bernard, 9
Mallarmé, Stéphane, 17
Malthus, Rev. T. R., 120, 165
Marx, Karl, 120, 166
Mason, John, 122
Mather, Cotton, 122
Mather, Increase, 122
Matthews, Brander: *The Philosophy of the Short Story*, 150
Matthiessen, F. O., 168
Maupassant, Guy de, 150
McCullers, Carson, 9
McLuhan, Marshall, 71
McPherson, James Alan, 9
Melville, Elizabeth, 79
Melville, Herman, 7, 35, 57, 76–102, 104, 105, 121, 135, 150; Books: *Billy Budd, Sailor*, 9, 78, 96; *Israel Potter*, 9, 96; *Mardi*, 78; *Omoo*, 78; *Piazza Tales*, 9, 11, 76, 77; *Pierre*, 78; *Redburn*, 78; *The Confidence Man*, 78, 82, 92; *White-Jacket*, 78; Stories and Other Prose: 'Agatha' Letters, 89, 90, 96; 'Bartleby', 79, 80, 82–5; 'Benito Cereno', 79, 80, 93–6; 'Cock-a-Doodle-Doo', 91; 'Daniel Orme', 96; 'Fragments from a Writing Desk', 96; 'Hawthorne and his Mosses', 57–8, 77, 96–9; 'I and my Chimney', 90–1; 'Jimmy Rose', 91–2; 'John Marr', 96; 'Poor Man's Pudding and Rich Man's Crumbs', 92; 'The Apple-Tree Table', 90, 91; 'The Bell Tower', 93; 'The Encantadas', 79, 80, 86–90; 'The Fiddler', 91; 'The Gees', 96; 'The Happy Failure', 91; 'The Lightning-Rod Man', 90, 91; 'The Marquis of Grandvin', 96; 'The Paradise of Bachelors and the Tartarus of Maids', 92–3, 99; 'The Piazza', 76–7; 'The Town Ho's Story', 80–2; 'The Two Temples', 92; 'Three "Jack Gentian Sketches" ', 96
Mendel, Gregor, 120
Murphree, Mary Noailles: *In the Tennessee Mountains*, 151

Nabokov, Vladimir, 15; *The Event*, 37
Naipaul, V. S., 8
Nasby, Petroleum V, 109

O'Connor, Flannery, 9
O'Connor, Frank, 150, 151
Owen, Wilfred, 123

Paine, Albert Bigelow, 114
Paulding, James Kirke: *The Diverting History of John Bull and Brother Jonathan*, 52
Poe, Edgar Allan, 7, 10, 13–39, 62, 104, 105, 106, 137, 150, 165; Books: *Prose Romances of Edgar A. Poe*, 36; *Tales of Grotesque and Arabesque*, 35, 36; *The Narrative of Arthur Gordon Pym*, 167; Poetry: 'The Sleeper', 10; Stories: 'A Descent into the Maelstrom', 28; 'A Predicament', 138; 'Eleanora', 24; 'Four Beasts in One—The Homo-Cameleopard', 15; 'How To Write a Blackwood Article', 15; 'King Pest', 20; 'Ligeia', 15, 21, 22, 23, 24, 28; 'Loss of Breath', 20, 32; 'Metzengerstein', 19; 'Morella', 21, 22, 23; 'Mystification', 37; 'Silence—A Fable', 15; 'The Black Cat', 19, 30, 32, 33, 34; 'The Facts in the Case of M. Valdemar', 15–16, 17–19, 21; 'The Fall of the House of Usher', 15, 25–6; 'The Gold-Bug', 27; 'The Imp of the Perverse', 32; 'The Man of the Crowd', 21, 26; 'The Man that was Used Up', 20, 36, 138; 'The Masque of the Red Death', 36; 'The Murders in the Rue Morgue', 27, 28, 32, 36; 'The Mystery of the Marie Rôget', 28, 29; 'The Pit and the Pendulum', 20; 'The Premature Burial', 20; 'The Purloined Letter', 28; 'The System of Dr. Tarr and Professor Fether', 34; 'Why the Little Frenchman Wears his Hand in a Sling', 15
Porter, Katherine Anne, 9
Proust, Marcel, 23
Putnam's Monthly Magazine, 7, 77, 82

Ricardo, David, 120

Salinger, J. D., 9
Sartre, Jean-Paul, 188, 189; *Being and Nothingness*, 171, 188
Sassoon, Siegfried, 123
Scheffaner, Herman, 134
Scott, Sir Walter, 51, 52–5, 137; *Peveril of the Peak*, 51
Shakespeare, William, 96, 97; *Cymbeline*, 77; *Hamlet*, 54; *Lear*, 98

Index

Southern Literary Messenger, 7
Spenser, Edmund, 77, 86
Stafford, Jean, 9
Stendhal: *Le Rouge et Le Noir*, 122
Stevens, Wallace: 'Anecdote of the Jar', 106
Stowe, Harriet Beecher, 9; *Uncle Tom's Cabin*, 165
Stuart, Ruth McEnery: *A Golden Wedding and Other Tales*, 151

Tate, Allen, 13, 14
Thoreau, Henry David, 7, 85; *Walden*, 7
Tolstoy, Count: *Sevastopol Sketches*, 122; *War and Peace*, 122
Transcendentalism, 96
Trollope, Anthony, 71, 104; *Barchester Towers*, 71
Twain, Mark, 7, 9, 35, 79, 103–19, 150; Books: *A Tramp Abroad*, 114; *Following the Equator*, 114; *Huckleberry Finn*, 79, 115, 118; *Life on the Mississippi*, 114; *Pudd'nhead Wilson*, 79; *Roughing It*, 114, 116; *Sketches, New and Old*, 117; Essays: 'How to Tell a Story', 10, 103, 109, 110; 'Report to the Buffalo Female Academy', 110, 112; Stories: 'A Double-Barreled Detective Story', 113; 'A Fake', 113; 'A Medieval Romance', 110; 'A True Story', 117–18; 'The Golden Arm', 109–10; 'The Man that Corrupted Hadleyburg', 113, 114; 'The Mysterious Stranger', 113, 114–15; 'The Notorious Jumping Frog of Calaveras County', 110, 113; 'The £1,000,000 Bank Note', 113; 'The Story of the Old Ram', 110; 'The $30,000 Bequest', 113; 'Tom Quartz', 110; 'What Stumped the Bluejays', 110

Valéry, Paul, 13, 27

Walker, Alice, 9
Ward, Artemus, 109
Webster, Daniel, 113
Wells, H. G., 123
Wharton, Edith, 166
Whistler, James, 123
Whitman, Walt, 35, 105, 189; *Leaves of Grass*, 7
Williams, Roger, 68–9
Wilson, Edmund, 147; *Patriotic Gore*, 152
Winters, Yvor, 32
Wittgenstein, Ludwig, 37
Wright, Richard: *Uncle Tom's Children*, 9; *Eight Men*, 9

Zola, Emile, 73; 'The Experimental Novel', 73